THE PERELANDRA GARDEN WORKBOOK

A Complete Guide to Gardening With Nature Intelligences

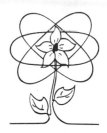

PERELANDRA

GARDEN WORKBOOK

A COMPLETE GUIDE TO GARDENING WITH NATURE INTELLIGENCES

MACHAELLE SMALL WRIGHT

PERELANDRA, LTD.
JEFFERSONTON, VIRGINIA
1987

This book is manufactured in the United States of America.
Designed by James F. Brisson, Williamsville, VT 05362.
Cover design by James F. Brisson.
Edited by the nature intelligences, David, John, Caroline Myss and Machaelle Wright.
Copyedited by Tish Ellerbeck, Clarence N. Wright, Jr., Teantros and Machaelle Wright.
Legwork, pasteup, computer technician, support and meals by Clarence N. Wright, Jr.
Formatting, typesetting and computer wizardry by Machaelle Small Wright.
This book was formatted, laid out and produced using the Xerox Ventura Publisher software along with the Kyocera F-1010 laser printer.
Published by Perelandra, Ltd., Box 136, Jeffersonton, VA 22724.

Library of Congress Card Catalog Number: 87-090410
Wright, Machaelle Small
The Perelandra Garden Workbook:
A Complete Guide to Gardening with Nature Intelligences

First hardcover printing: March 1987
ISBN 0-9617713-1-3
2 4 6 8 9 7 5 3

First softcover printing: May 1988
ISBN 0-9617713-2-1
2 4 6 8 9 7 5 3 1

To all the
devas and nature spirits
who have come together to
teach me, show me, and work with me,
so that I could begin to understand
how their slice of reality
fits into the larger
whole.

My appreciation
and love for them is
beyond words.

TABLE OF CONTENTS

INTRODUCTION

In the spring of 1985, I received the insight that I was to write a second book and that it would impart everything I had learned these past ten years of working with nature intelligences in the Perelandra garden. I was to cover every lesson, process, scheduling, chart and handy tip I had learned and practiced over the years. I had reached a point in my development where I could describe all that goes into the Perelandra garden in practical and precise ways. To emphasize the moment, I was given a full outline of what was to be covered.

To be honest, I did not receive the news of tackling a second book with joyous enthusiasm. But I sure felt its timing. And God knows, I believe in what is happening here at Perelandra and am eager to share this with you. I am also eager to introduce my "influential friends" to you—the nature intelligences who have diligently, dramatically and patiently taught me a different way of relating to and working with nature.

In *Behaving As If the God In All Life Mattered,* I described how I came to meet these influential friends and their impact on my life. In this second book, I not only get to share all that I have learned from them, but also I get to share them directly with you. And this is what made facing a second book not only palatable but downright exciting.

As I moved through the garden's annual cycle in this book, giving as many details as I possibly could about how and why I do what I do, I was joined by the individual devas and nature spirits involved, and they added their insight and information. In essence, I said to them, "If you had a chance to say something right now on this subject, what would you say?" For each session, I have identified the deva or nature spirit so that you'll be able to keep the players straight and also so that you may begin to sense the differences between them. The word "you" in these sessions refers to you, the reader. I have functioned as merely the translator between you and nature. There are a few sessions included that were given to me over the past couple of years. I have indicated them by giving the date they were translated in the paragraph just prior to the session. In these, the word "you" is referring to me, for I functioned in the duel role as translator and recipient.

One last thing: I have included a glossary. If you are anything like me, you won't notice this until you finish reading the book and wonder what's on all those remaining pages. But in case you have difficulty with some of the terminology, be it horticultural or esoteric, I thought it might help to warn you up front that a glossary exists.

Perelandra
December 1986

THE PERELANDRA GARDEN WORKBOOK

A Complete Guide to Gardening With Nature Intelligences

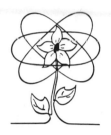

1

WHY BOTHER? A MATTER OF SPIRITUAL INTEGRITY, A MATTER OF THE HEART

Why bother going through the effort it will take to incorporate an entirely different approach to your gardening? Especially in light of the fact that there are a number of approaches out there that are proven, established and successful enough.

I'm very aware that this is a valid issue. I've raised the question myself. I'm especially prone to raising it when crouched over in the garden working on the third day to do something that takes regular gardeners less than an hour to do. I've been known to stand my weary bones upright, look toward the sky, and give serious thought to the state of my sanity. But each year as I watch my garden flourish under adverse conditions and the other gardens around me struggle, even die under the same conditions, I find I raise the question less and less. I also have grown to realize that my garden does not flourish because I'm a good gardener. I'm surrounded by good gardeners who have been at it a lot longer than I. And to be quite frank, in the world of gardening, there are many who are more technically advanced than I.

WHY BOTHER? A MATTER OF SPIRITUAL INTEGRITY, A MATTER OF THE HEART

The Perelandra garden thrives because of the approach I have been taught and the underlying consciousness and reality that motivates the approach. What I'm going to describe to you in this book does not fit comfortably in the recognized notions of tradition, logic or even sanity. In fact, it tends to thumb its nose at all three, especially sanity. Be that as it may, it works. And that's what drives traditional-gardening thinkers a little nuts. It's also what will drive you a little nuts. Everything you know which has gone into establishing your sense of order, stability and balance, in other words, logic, both in the garden and in your life away from it, will be constantly challenged. For you see, this gardening is, in fact, a metaphor for the whole of life. As you change how you approach the garden, you will, in turn, change the very fabric of how you approach your life.

It takes a lot of effort and struggle to change our way of thinking. It takes many times more effort to change our thinking and then turn around and change how we actually do something. All the tools, information, expectations, manuals, and charts are geared toward the established ways. It takes effort to take what is already available to us and change it to accommodate the new. Or invent what we need. I've been taught that everything on Earth is changing and that includes how mankind responds to and works with nature—and how he gardens. Old traditions and proven practices must be updated in order for them to respond fully to our changing times. I've also been taught that because of the differences in environments between one spot on Earth and another—and here I refer to ecological impact as much as anything else—no one method can be used in two different gardens with the exact same results. So it would be useless to tell you step by step how to duplicate the Perelandra garden. In fact, *I* can't even duplicate it from one year to the next. Conditions change. There is constant ecological shifting which I have to adjust to for each year. All I can do is share what I've been taught, how I get my information, and the processes I've developed as a result.

OVERLIGHTING DEVA OF PERELANDRA

I would like to address the issue of change as well. Specifically, the change the planet Earth is experiencing at the present time. Understand that the change we speak of regarding the movement from one era to the next—in your terminology, "Piscean" to "Aquarian"—is universal and Earth is a part of this massive shift. Try to keep in mind that Earth is not experiencing some isolated process, but is actively and intimately linked with an overall process. I say this to you, and will most likely repeat it from time to time, in order to keep things in perspective for you. We on the devic level find that you on the human level have the habit of disconnecting yourselves from the larger picture. This is a self-imposed isolation.

Now, regarding nature and this change. It only stands to reason that if the whole universe is experiencing a major shift, that shift would have to be fully demonstrated in form on Earth. Mankind has the idea that he is participating in a change, but he has not on the whole looked beyond himself and recognized that everything around him is also participating in the same change.

Those souls and intelligences who have been a part of Earth's evolution for the past two thousand years have diligently focused on establishing all functions of life in such a way that they fully demonstrated the energy dynamic of the Piscean era. All that existed on Earth, in whatever form, had to respond to the Piscean environment prevalent within the universe. To do otherwise would have been to place the planet in a position of disharmony within its own universe.

Earth is not of the Aquarian Age yet. It is in a transition period that is moving toward the Aquarian Age. This very same can be said about the universe as well. The law of the universe dictates that there be transition between points of change. To go directly from point A to point B would place an unacceptable strain on all life forms, either on this planet or within the universe. There would be spasm. Instead, there is transition. During the transition all that existed during the Piscean Age begins its movement toward the Aquarian Age. Form, structure, action, intent, attitude—all of this begins to shift.

Earth is now fully participating in the transition. The chaos which you are experiencing and observing around you is in part a response to the transition. I say "in part" because, although a sense of chaos on some level is inherent in change, the degree of chaos and how it is manifested in action is up to mankind and however much he wishes to fight the transition.

We turn our focus to gardening, for it is an excellent example of what we have been talking about. Those who were drawn to agriculture and gardening during these past two thousand years worked very hard to develop understanding, knowledge, tools, and frameworks for action which successfully meshed themselves with the nature with which they were working in light of the Piscean environment in which they were living. What they developed, by and large, responded to the Piscean dynamic. It had to if this aspect of reality on Earth was to be in harmony with the universe. Their struggles, growth and development were within this larger harmony. We on the devic level recognize their heart connection with the nature around them. Because of the present fragile

WHY BOTHER? A MATTER OF SPIRITUAL INTEGRITY, A MATTER OF THE HEART

WHY BOTHER? A MATTER OF SPIRITUAL INTEGRITY, A MATTER OF THE HEART

state of the planet's natural environment, it is easy for mankind today to turn to these people and point a finger of blame. Accuse them of wrongful action. Even look to them as being stupid.

What they accomplished was not wrongful or stupid. It was Piscean and for the most part worked well within that era. But then the planet began to make its movement in response to the transition. In Earth time, that would be approximately fifty years ago. And those things that worked so well within the Piscean era began to not work quite so well. The demands of the planet began to change and the old forms could not respond in balance to the new demands. The clashing of the old forms with the new demands for change, along with mankind's reluctance to let go of the old, have created a mess.

What was developed in the area of agriculture and gardening during the Piscean era is not to be discarded, but rather used as the foundation upon which to build. Remember, you are in the transition, not the New Age itself. Therefore, allow for growth and change, not destruction. For the sake of order and harmony, look to what has been and what worked well and allow that to be your starting point for the transition.

The reason why the garden at Perelandra is so successful is because Machaelle has opened herself to us—what she refers to as "nature intelligences"—in a co-creative partnership and allowed us to direct her through this period of change. Her description to you of standing up in the garden from time to time and questioning her sanity is her way of expressing the chaos of change which I have referred to. As you see, because she is willing to move with the currents of the times, her response to the inherent chaos is not one of destructive revolution, but rather gentle recognition.

The changes that have been instituted in the Perelandra garden work because they have the power of the existing dynamic of the universe behind them. If she were to hold onto those practices which worked so well in the Piscean era, she would then be acting contrary to the universal flow—and the Perelandra garden would reflect this. In short, to add our answer to the question "Why bother?," we feel that to do otherwise, to buck universal flow, would be akin to attempting to stop a tidal wave with your hand.

I would like to add one more insight. Just as you humans are working to adjust to the changing times, so, too, is nature. In the areas where man comes into active partnership with nature—forestry, conservation, gardening, farming, landscaping, etc.—he has the opportunity to help facilitate nature's response to the transition. In these areas we not only need mankind's cooperation, we need his active partnership. Notice that the areas I have singled out would not exist if it were not for man's desire to interface with nature. Therefore it is essential to our evolution in these areas that mankind open the door to us and consciously link with us in a new level of partnership so that we may work together to bring into form the necessary changes.

Let me give you a brief background on how Perelandra and I got started in this partnership.

We moved from the city to the country in 1973. While city dwelling, I began to open myself to the area of ecology and its corresponding responsible life styles. By the time Clarence and I moved to the country, the idea of putting in a vegetable garden on our new land was as practical and logical as putting a house on the land. I didn't give much thought to the matter. I just put it in. To do otherwise would have seemed odd to me. I had not had any gardening experience prior to this, so I spent the first couple of years educating myself in the ins and outs of "good" gardening. I also listened to the advice of my neighbors, some of whom have fifty, sixty and seventy years of gardening under their belts. These are legitimate farmers who depend on the produce from their gardens for their main food supply. As a result, my first couple of years were quite successful. We had more food than we knew what to do with. However, the high amount of produce was directly related to the fact that I was using the insecticide Sevin. Being told on the back of the bag that I should not eat vegetables within twenty-four hours after spraying made me think. Using Sevin pretty much assured me of successful production. But what was I doing to my body once I ate the food? And did spraying this stuff do anything to an already fragile environment? I didn't even raise the question of killing all those bugs—I still considered them pests who stood between me and a successful garden. But the questions I did manage to raise led me to organic gardening.

Organic gardening certainly addressed my concerns over our health and the environment. Its focus on overall balance, especially in the soil, as being the key to better quality food made all the sense in the world to me. It still does. I consider organic gardening to be the foundation upon which *co-creative energy gardening* (the term I use to describe the Perelandra gardening process) is built. But anyone who practices organic gardening knows that it is made up of a huge volume of hints, tips, ideas and practices—some of which, when tried, work for you and some of which don't, despite the fact that the organic gardener just down the road did exactly the same thing and got incredible results. Reading the volumes of organic gardening material in the effort to find the magical combination of practices that would give me the kind of garden one always sees photographed on the cover of that material made me feel that not only would I not reach a respectable level of gardening until age eighty-five, but that I had no right to expect it before eighty-five. I had to put in my time like everyone else. I was just thirty-one years old, and the road to eighty-five seemed awfully long.

By this time, it was 1976 and that's when Clarence handed me the Findhorn garden books. They introduced me to the idea that there was an intelligence in nature and if one applied oneself just a bit, one could communicate with these intelligences and "be told" what to do, especially in the area of gardening. To say the least, I found the notion appealing and worth a try.

This is when I met and began working with devas and nature spirits. That meeting and my early education is described in *Behaving As If the God In All Life Mattered.*

I think I better define for you what I mean when I use the names "deva" and "nature spirit."

"Deva" is a sanskrit word meaning body of light. This has little correlation with what I experience when I am open to the devic level, but I accept the word. The devic level is the architectural dynamic within nature. It is the force that formulates every individual aspect of form on Earth. It is the creative force which determines the size, color, shape, weight, texture, taste, life cycle, and requirements of all form, all of nature. Each form has inherent in it its own deva. There is, for example, the Deva of Soil, the Deva of the Shasta Daisy, the Oak Tree Deva, the Carrot Deva. Each deva holds, as in a computer bank, all the specific information relative to its form. It also holds the information pertaining to how its individual natural form fits into the grand scheme of things both on Earth and within the universe. If there are to be any physical changes made—for example, changing carrots from the color orange to pink—they must be made within the devic level in order to maintain natural balance. Change made through the pure will and desire of us humans disregarding the devic dynamic is called "manipulation" and results in a weakening imbalance and becomes part of the ecological disaster we are experiencing.

OVERLIGHTING DEVA OF PERELANDRA

Machaelle's understanding of what she calls the "devic dynamic" is quite accurate, as it should be since she has been directly working with this level for more than ten years now. Over that period of time, her understanding has broadened and grown due to her continuous experience with us, as with a friendship which has gone on for years. We point this

WHY BOTHER? A MATTER OF SPIRITUAL INTEGRITY, A MATTER OF THE HEART

out so that you'll understand that your working relationship with us may be small in scope in the beginning when compared with what Machaelle has presented to you now. Don't be discouraged with this. As you consciously open to our level, allow our friendship to touch you and then slowly and organically grow. She does not consciously remember, but ten years ago Machaelle saw the devic level as little more than a giant phone bank in the sky. We considered her imagery creative and most workable. From this clear but limited scope of reality, our friendship has developed and along with this so, too, has our understanding of one another.

At this point, we might add one additional thought to Machaelle's description of our level. It is generally believed that form, that is nature or what you call "physical reality," is indigenous to Earth only. This is only part of the picture and we feel that in order for you to relate in a fuller, more balanced manner toward nature and the form around you, we must expand the understanding of the devic level.

All that exists on Earth exists in one dynamic or another in every dimension of reality beyond Earth. Form is but one expression of what you see around you. That expression shifts and changes in countless ways that directly relate to the many realities which exist on all levels. There is not one thing on Earth that does not exist on all other levels of reality. The devic level, in its role as creator and architect, is the bonding dynamic between all that is physical on Earth and its corresponding levels of existence elsewhere. To relate and respond to, for example, the Carrot Deva is to relate and respond to all existing levels of reality on Earth and beyond through the specific dynamic of the carrot. In basic language, it may be said that one simple carrot is the key to the universe.

We find in our attempts to reach out to mankind on Earth that the biggest stumbling block we presently face is his limiting and demeaning attitude toward form—nature. His allocating relative spiritual worth on a sliding scale with physical form invariably being placed at the bottom of the scale we find impossible to work with and it is certainly the root of the massive ecological imbalance which now faces him.

Here is my understanding of nature spirits.

In *Behaving....* I referred to nature spirits as the blue collar workers within the realm of nature intelligence. I still hold to this imagery today but feel it is simplistic. My work with the nature spirits has convinced me that they are truly masters of understanding and working with the concept of bringing spirit into matter, energy into form. They tend to the shifting of an energy reality which has been formulated on the devic level and assist the translation of that reality from a dynamic of energy to form. In short, they constantly work with the principle of manifestation on Earth. They also function in a custodial capacity with all that is of form on the planet. That is, when not interfered with by us humans, they tend to the care and needs of all physical reality, assuring perfection within form. The catch phrase in this is "when not interfered with by us humans." One of my major learning areas at Perelandra has been to understand the relationship between nature spirits and form and learn how to *cooperate* with it. Even become an equal partner in it.

When I am in the design and layout period of the garden planning early on in the season, I am primarily working hand in hand with the devic realm. Specifically, the Deva of the Perelandra Garden. It is from this deva that I receive what is to go into the garden and where it is to be placed. This is all part of the creative process. Once I have the information, I shift my attention to the nature spirit level, for it is here that I receive insight and assistance on process. That is, the best way to bring this garden into form. My day-to-day work in the garden is a co-creative process with the nature spirits. My focus is on bringing that which is of spirit in to form and facilitating the perfection of that process. This is the nature spirit role as I understand it, and it is to them that I turn for my insights and lessons concerning how I am to participate.

In terms of how I relate to nature spirits, let me assure you that I do not have a phalanx of little elves and gnomes wielding pitch forks and shovels in my garden. I experience nature spirits as individuated energy presences, but not in specific forms. In relating to humans, nature spirits have occasionally taken on specific form, but since my personal sensitivity is to energy, it is this level through which we connect. Their daily operations here at Perelandra are unseen by the naked eye. The results of their work, however, are very noticeable and the energy that surrounds the quality of their work is easily felt.

There is another distinguishing feature about nature spirits that will help you understand them and the differences between them and devas. Nature spirits are regional. Although I do not have a phalanx of little people visible in the garden, I do have my group of nature spirits who are connected to this land and what is happening here. Your connection will be with your own group. They are an intelligent reality that is individuated enough to be connected with specific geographic areas on Earth. Devas, on the other hand, are universal in dynamic. When I contact the Carrot Deva, I touch into the very same intelligent reality someone in China would touch into when making the same contact.

WHY BOTHER?
A MATTER
OF SPIRITUAL INTEGRITY,
A MATTER OF THE HEART

To my knowledge, there is only one exception to this regional dynamic within the nature spirit level. This is Pan. As you probably know, there is a huge volume of traditional literature around nature spirits and Pan. Usually nature spirits are portrayed as cute and Pan is portrayed as powerful and demonic. I've experienced many individual character traits with nature spirits, but *never cute.* I experience enormous power when connected with Pan, but I have never felt anything that can even remotely be characterized as demonic from him. Only his power, which is equally balanced by love and care for me, Perelandra, and all of Earth.

My working understanding of Pan is that he is "in charge" of the nature spirit level. He is devic in his presence. Pan is everywhere and available to us all. Whenever I wish to be connected to the nature spirit level in a general manner for whatever reason, I connect with Pan. If I have a question regarding an issue around spirit and form and I don't know which specific nature spirit to contact for help, I go to Pan. From him I get whatever insight or answer I need and direction as to which nature spirit I'll be working with regarding this specific issue. It is my understanding that Pan oversees which nature spirits are where and doing what jobs. In essence, he is that level's organizing force.

In light of his special position within the nature spirit level, I'll open to Pan for further clarification.

PAN

Mankind's immediate relationship to Earth is through his contact and work with the nature spirit level. For, as Machaelle has pointed out, it is here that he learns the practical lessons concerning the fusing of soul power into form. This is why man has come into the Earth plane. To learn these lessons of relationship between the individual soul and physical reality. If one were to look at the dismal state of the natural environment on Earth, it would be easy to see that on the whole, man has barely begun to recognize the purpose of his existence on Earth, let alone explore ways to facilitate the fusion of soul energy into form for the perfect functioning of that energy through form. This same dynamic of purpose exists within all nature form on Earth and it is here man has the opportunity to learn these lessons and demonstrate them outside himself within the arena of nature. From this experience, he may draw what he needs in order to seat his own fully functioning soul dynamic into a fully functioning body reflection.

All within the nature spirit level not only understand precisely what I am communicating to you here but are especially adept, due to the nature of our work, at practically grounding universal and soul energy into form. So rather than relegating us to entertaining and charming you through your arts, I suggest that you seriously consider looking to us as your teachers. This is the contact with you that we eagerly desire. All you need do is open your heart and your intent toward us and you will be most surprised at how quickly we will work to communicate what we know and what you need.

It has been over ten years since I began gardening under the tutelage of these nature intelligences and the result has been a garden in which all inhabitants, be they animal, mineral or vegetable are truly compatible with one another. Each member of the garden enhances the health and well-being of all the others. And this includes the bugs. This garden is inclusive, not exclusive. I do nothing for the purpose of repelling. The focus is to create a balanced, wholistic environment in which all within that environment are enhanced. The results are not only more food than I know what to do with, but also food that has contained within it a very high level of life energy—light.

This brings me to why I bother. Recently I have been asked by several people what the Perelandra garden means to me. I can hardly believe the question is being asked and I have barely been able to articulate even a sentence in response. I keep wanting to say, "Isn't it obvious!" My friends say I am naive to believe that it is. So I will try to answer.

The Perelandra garden is my life, my heart and my very breath. It is my friend, my healer, my nurturer, and teacher—about myself, my planet and my universe. It is my key to the universe. It is my access to spiritual truth and universal natural law contained within the universal flow. It is the demonstration of these truths and laws played out before my very eyes. It is my proof that what is spiritual truth and universal law courses through all reality—and this includes a garden. It shows me that what I see and experience in that garden is beyond all structures, all forms, and well beyond the notion of worship.

It is my university of life. I draw from it my questions, answers, approach and direction. How I live springs from what I've learned and experienced in the garden.

It has been my spiritual teacher in the deepest sense. On a daily basis, within the mundane framework of the garden, I experience and consciously work with truth and natural law. This little garden links me to the greater whole and allows me to experience reality beyond space and time—the fact that it sits on land on this planet is purely coincidental.

WHY BOTHER?
A MATTER
OF SPIRITUAL INTEGRITY,
A MATTER OF THE HEART

And it has taught me that we are a vibrant, active planet fully participating in a larger, loving whole.

It has taught me about power—my own and that which is contained in all life around me. About equality. About balance. About teamwork on a peer level. I have experienced an environment where the focus is maintained on the welfare of the individual parts as well as the health, balance and well-being of the whole. And I have experienced the extraordinary results from that focus. It has taught me that life is truly beyond form and that form is the essence of truth and life itself. Through it, I have dramatically changed my thoughts, my thought process, my knowings, actions, and reality.

This garden is a way of life which touches into the core of my soul and through which my soul sings. It reconnects my conscious reality to the truths held within both my heart and soul, and from this I am reconnected back into the universal life force itself.

This is what the Perelandra garden means to me and this is why I bother.

When I was about to begin *The Perelandra Garden Workbook,* I felt that I was to draw one card from the Aquarian tarot and that this card would clarify the direction of the book. I drew "The Knower" which says in part:

> The Knower holds an egg to his heart and the egg sprouts a root with two leaves. The fruit of this plant is the winged and shafted Sun above his head. The Knower shall plant this egg in the earth and a new kingdom shall be grounded on Earth.

I took an egg into the center of the garden, planted it, and returned to my desk to begin this book.

2

CRACKING THE COMMUNICATION CODE

The backbone of the Perelandra garden is communication. I depend on the devas and nature spirits to inform me of my direction and the step-by-step process I need to take. Without that information, I would be guessing along with everyone else.

Communication also happens to be the biggest stumbling block people face when they consider gardening in conscious partnership with nature. Now, I think it's fair to say that some people use the communication issue as a convenient excuse. They can support, even admire this kind of gardening but because they aren't one of the "gifted ones" and feel they can't get this kind of information, they don't have to practice it.

Well, I happen to be someone who feels deeply that this communication is possible for everyone. We are talking about a natural partnership between humans and nature and it is not meant to be exclusive. It only stands to reason that there be simple ways for us and nature to communicate with one another. There have to be language frameworks that are just waiting to be developed.

I see the communication problem as being similar to the problem that arises when you are faced with someone from another country who speaks a language that is completely foreign to your ear. There isn't one sound they are making that strikes a familiar note. We can back off the situation and say, "This is impossible." Or we can tackle the situation together with the other person, begin to learn each other's language, and devise additional techniques for communication.

This is what I've done with nature. I've worked to develop techniques which we can use for the purpose of sending and receiving information. And it's not difficult. In fact, it's embarrassingly simple. But that's as it should be.

TEANTROS

I have asked to share with you some of our views on the issue of communication. My name is Teantros. I am one of a large group of nature spirits who are working at Perelandra. My specialty, if I may say, is communication. This may seem strange to you. A nature spirit working in the area of communication. Traditionally, you see us as having our attention on the various forms within the nature kingdoms—the trees, the rocks, grasses, animals, clouds. But this is just one area of our focus and involves only some of us who are working within the realm of the nature spirits. We work with the universal principle of bringing spirit into form. Wherever this principle applies, you will find us. Since Earth is the planet which deals primarily with this particular principle, you will discover that there is a particularly large and active level of nature spirits connected in various capacities with the planet.

Communication is a dynamic which easily falls within the principle of shifting energy into form. Energy as thought is exchanged and translated into word form. The word "communication" is used to describe the exchange of intelligent energy from point A to point B for the purpose of transferring information. Up to now, communication as you know it has been primarily the transfer of intelligent energy between two points within the same level. For example, two people on Earth speaking directly to one another.

I don't wish to appear to be saying that there has been no communication between levels. That would be a false impression. There has been within the soul of each human on Earth a constant link with levels beyond his physical self. But the essence of this communication has been unconscious. Also, there **have** *been some individuals throughout history who have developed the means for conscious communication between levels. But this has been viewed as an extraordinary development by the society surrounding the individual. The time has come for mankind in general to develop the ways and means to bridge the communication gap which has existed between levels.*

This is not a job that is being left solely up to humans. We on the other levels are most eager to work in partnership with you for the pur-

pose of developing the framework needed for easy communication access between levels. For one thing, you must realize that we on the nature spirit level, as is true with the various levels beyond us, need your assistance in understanding your language. I'll give you an example of the communication problems we face with you. We don't work with your set of physical measurements. There is no need for us to use them. For instance, we simply know where something is to be placed or how much of something is to be added for the health of a plant. We don't need to know inches or ounces. But you do. If we are to work with you in a co-creative partnership in the effort to return all that exists on the planet to a state of health and balance, we must then develop ways with you in which our knowing can be translated into inches and ounces. So you see, it is not just your issue, it is our issue as well.

Perelandra is a nature research center, and we nature spirits take full advantage of that fact. There are teams of us connected to Perelandra who work in the spirit of research and development both within the area of nature itself, and how nature as a whole can interface with man in new and better ways. Communication is one of the areas of research that fits into the latter category. We are excited about what has been developed and feel we now have a simple, workable framework for inter-level communication. Don't forget that the frustration you have felt when you've been unable to hear and understand us, we have felt ten-fold when we have been unable to reach or understand you.

KINESIOLOGY

There are two issues in communication to be faced. One is how to ask a question. The other is how to hear the answer. I'm going to deal with how to hear the answer first. After all, that is the biggest psychological barrier we have.

Hearing the answer is simple. We will use kinesiology—muscle testing. With this, we will let the body do the translation work. Simply stated, if a negative energy (that is, any physical object or energy vibration that does not maintain or enhance the health and balance of an individual), is introduced into a person's overall energy field, his muscles, when having physical pressure applied, will be unable to hold their power. For example, if pressure is applied to an individual's extended arm while his field is being affected by a negative, the arm will not be able to resist the pressure. It will weaken and fall to his side. If pressure is applied while being affected by a positive, the person will easily be able to resist and the arm will hold its position.

To expand on a more technical level, when a negative is placed within a person's field, his electrical system (the electrical energy grid contained within his body) will immediately respond by "short-circuiting," making it difficult for the muscles to maintain their strength and hold their position when pressure is added. When a positive is placed within the field, the electrical system holds and the muscles are able to maintain their level of strength when pressure is applied.

This electrical/muscular relationship is a natural part of the human system. It is not mystical or magical. Kinesiology is the established method for reading their state of interaction at any given moment. It is most commonly used today by wholistic physicians, chiropractors and the Touch for Health people.

What does this have to do with "hearing" information from the nature spirit and devic levels, you ask. Simple. If you ask a question using the yes/no format, they can answer your question by transferring a yes (positive) or no (negative) into your energy field. Then you read the answer by testing yourself using kinesiology. All you have to do is learn to muscle test yourself—easier than you think. And learn to ask questions in the yes/no format—trickier than you think.

For now, let's concentrate on learning kinesiology.

If you have ever experienced muscle testing, you most likely participated in a two-man operation. You provided the extended arm and the other person provided the pressure. Although efficient, this method can be cumbersome while standing in the middle of a garden. These arm pumpers have the nasty habit of disappearing right when you need them the most. So we'll be learning to self-test.

The Kinesiology Testing Position

1. *If you are right-handed:* Place your left hand palm up. Connect the tip of your left thumb with the tip of you left little finger (not your index finger). *If you are left-handed:* Place your right hand palm up. Connect the tip of your right thumb with the tip of your right little finger. By connecting your thumb and little finger, you have just closed an electrical circuit in your hand and you will use this circuit for testing.

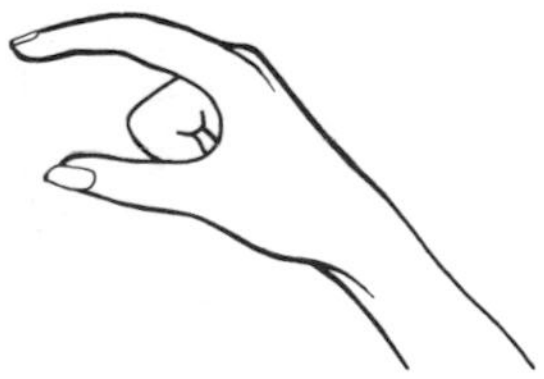

2. To test the circuit (the means by which you will apply pressure to yourself), place the thumb and index finger of your other hand inside the circle you have created by connecting your thumb and little finger. The thumb/index finger should be right under the thumb/little finger, touching them. It will look as if the thumb/little finger are resting on the thumb/index finger. This is the testing position of your two hands.

CRACKING THE COMMUNICATION CODE

Keeping this position, ask yourself a yes/no question in which you already know the answer to be yes. ("Is my name _____?") Once you've asked the question, press your thumb/little finger together, keeping the tip-to-tip position. *Using the same amount of pressure,* try to pull apart the thumb/little finger with your thumb/index finger. Press the lower thumb against the upper thumb, the lower index finger against the upper little finger. If your answer is positive (if your name is what you think it is!) you will not be able to pull apart the top fingers. The electrical circuit will hold, your muscles will maintain their strength, and your circuit fingers will not separate. You will feel the strength in that circuit. *Important:* Be sure the amount of pressure holding together the thumb/little finger circuit is equal to the amount pressing against that circuit with your thumb/index finger. Also, don't use a pumping action in your thumb/index fingers to try to pry your thumb/little fingers apart. Use an equal, steady and continuous pressure.

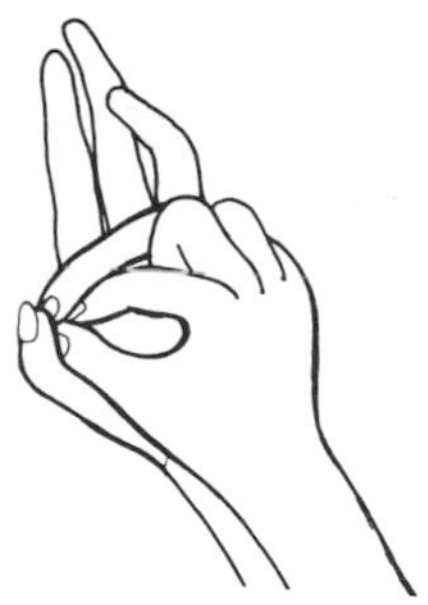

Positive Response

Play with this a bit. Ask a few more yes/no questions that have positive answers. If you're having trouble sensing the strength of the circuit, apply a little more pressure. Or consider that you may be applying too much pressure and pull back some. You don't have to strain your fingers for this.

Once you have a clear sense of the positive response of the circuit, ask yourself a question that has a negative answer. Again press your circuit fingers together and, *using equal pressure,* press against the circuit fingers with the thumb/index finger. This time the electrical circuit will break and the thumb/little finger will weaken and separate. Because the electrical circuit is broken, the muscles in the thumb and little finger don't have the power to hold the fingers together. In a positive state, the electrical circuit holds and the muscles have the power to keep the two fingers together.

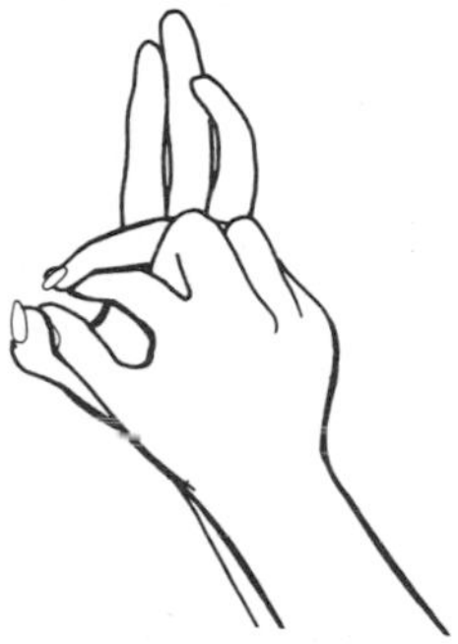

Negative Response

Play with negative questions a bit, then return to positive questions. Get a good feeling for the strength between your circuit fingers when the electricity is in a positive state and the weakness when the electricity is in a negative state. You can even ask yourself (your own system) for a positive response and then a negative response. ("Give me a positive response." Test. "Give me a negative response." Test.) You will feel the positive strength and the negative weakness. Now it's just a matter of trusting what you've learned—*and practice.*

Don't forget the overall concept behind kinesiology. What enhances our body, mind and soul makes us strong. Together, our body, mind and soul create a wholistic environment which, when balanced, is strong and solid. If something enters into that environment which negates or challenges the balance, the entire environment is weakened. The state of that strength or weakness is registered in the electrical system, and through muscle testing it can be discerned.

Kinesiology Tips

If you are having trouble feeling the electrical circuit on the hand you're using, try switching hands—the circuit fingers become the thumb/little finger and vice versa. Most people who are right-handed have this particular electrical circuitry in their left hand. Left-handers generally have the circuitry in their right hand. But sometimes a right-hander has the circuitry in the right hand and a left-hander has it in the left hand. You may be one of those people.

Suppose the testing has been working fine, then suddenly you can't get a clear result or get no result at all. Check:

1. Sloppy testing. You try to press apart the fingers <u>before</u> you apply pressure between the circuit fingers. This happens especially when we've been testing for awhile and become over-confident or very quick in the testing process. I think it happens to all of us from time to time and serves to remind us to keep our attention on the matter at hand. (Excuse the lousy pun.)

2. External distractions. Trying to test in a noisy or active area can cause us to lose our concentration. The testing will feel unsure or contradict itself if you double-check by testing the results again. Often simply moving to a quiet spot and concentrating on what you are doing will be just what's needed for successful testing.

3. Focus/concentration. Even in a quiet spot, one's mind may wander and the testing will feel fuzzy, weak or contradictory. It's important to remain concentrated throughout the process.

4. The question isn't clear. A key to kinesiology is asking a simple yes/no question, not two questions in one, each having a possible yes/no answer.

5. You must *want* to accept the results of the test. If you enter a kinesiology test not wanting to "hear" the answer, for whatever reason, you can override the test with your emotions and will. Back off the testing until you feel you really want to know the answer.

QUESTIONS AND THE UNIVERSE

I've already stated that one of the keys to kinesiology is asking a simple question in a yes/no format. I can go even further with this and say that one of the keys to receiving any information or insight from intelligent sources beyond our conscious selves is the ability to ask a clear concise question regarding the information we'd like to know. I can also say that the biggest stumbling block to the interlevel information flow, besides the fear that we can't "hear," has to do with asking questions.

Over the years, I've learned some pretty mighty lessons in this area. I've found out that there exists in the universe what I call a "cosmic code of conduct." Our worth as free-thinking individuals is recognized and deferred to by all other intelligences. The universe isn't going to just throw truck loads of information at us at will. We must indicate that we wish to know these things. And we must indicate precisely what areas of knowledge we are referring to. It is not enough for me to say I want to know everything there is to know. In order to respond to my desire to know, I must express what it is I wish to know. The universe looks to me to take on my own responsibility for the timing of my growth and expansion. Indicating what I'm ready to learn through the tool of asking a question is how I express my timing to all outside me.

In *Behaving....*, I talk about what it meant for me to accept my position as creator of the garden. This required that I establish my rightful position as co-creator with the nature intelligences. It also required that I recognize my responsibility to do this. To be in any lesser position would place me on a level of the ignorant servant. This is unacceptable to the intelligences I work with and as far as I am aware, it is unacceptable to the universe at large. By accepting our responsibility to make known that which we wish to know for the purpose of expansion and growth is to accept our position as creator of our personal garden.

One consideration within the cosmic code of conduct has to do with timing. Specifically, the universal acknowledgement of our personal timing. This is why we don't get truck loads of information coming at us from out of the blue. The following is an excerpt from a lesson about timing I received in 1984 from a consciousness known to me as Universal Light.

UNIVERSAL LIGHT

The process of evolution is continuous within each soul. And by association so is the concept of timing, since it is so intimately linked to evolution. Therefore if a man can point to only a handful of moments in which timing played a role, he has missed observing and very likely experiencing the many instances of timing in his life. If one were to see his life as a tapestry of design and color, the pattern of the weave comes significantly from timing. As man recognizes and responds to the phenomenon of timing, the weave in his tapestry becomes more dramatic and the color more brilliant. It is his choice. There are a number of phenomena available to him which he can choose to incorporate—at any level of intensity he desires—into his life.

Nothing in the universe, in all of reality, is held back from the individual living on Earth. Each person decides for himself the intensity with which he chooses to live his life. The limitations are his own. How much is available to him is not dictated by the universe. It is entirely dictated by the individual. Most souls who live on Earth, as they struggle through their lessons concerning the relationship of spirit flowing through form, feel that the universe and its truths are being held back from them in one degree or another because they are encased—or enslaved—in the body. This is not only untrue, it is an excuse. To think that something greater than yourself is dictating what you should or should not know, deprives you of the responsibility for self-growth, self-evolution. What is the use of working and seeking to improve, to open and expand yourself when you think you are dictated to by some intelligence, some consciousness greater than yourself, outside of yourself.

The evolutionary process in all souls involves the shifting and expanding of an individual's boundaries and limitations, or what has been termed the "ring-pass-not." Do not think that when we use the word "limitation" we are being judgmental. All souls have some aspect of limitation. There is wise limitation and there is limitation that derives from fear. Wise limitation defines the individual who knows what level and part of reality he can enfold into his life and successfully integrate into his actions in form. Wise limitation admits that knowledge and reality which can be fully grounded by an individual. A wise man understands what he can take into his conscious knowing and what he can ground in action during his life. It is a sign of wisdom when he can say "enough," and give himself time to integrate that which he has come to understand, to successfully reflect it through his body, his actions, and into form. Once successfully grounded, he can shift his ring-pass-not and take in more.

When we garden in conscious partnership with nature, we are not only responding to our own sense of timing, we are also responding to nature's timing in the garden. In the same lesson, Universal Light addressed this issue.

UNIVERSAL LIGHT

Timing has been a major factor in the Perelandra garden, timing and the prevailing logic about what should and should not be done in a garden. Timing within gardens in general has been completely placed to one side and ignored, while the theory of logic has been the principle force. At Perelandra, this has been reversed. Natural timing has come to the fore. Year after year through her observation of timing, Machaelle's concept of logic has changed. What was logical in the garden one year has become illogical the next.

Logic is meant to be active and ever-expanding. Often the individual reaches a particular level of logic and then crystallizes into a static position. Anything that continues to move around him constantly butts up against his static logic. For example, a rock, seemingly on its own, changes position from point A to point B. In a static logic, the intellect dictates that what you just saw did not happen. One of Machaelle's lessons in the garden has been to loosen or decrystallize her logic. That had to occur very early on for her to see the evolution of the garden. When the ring-pass-not expands, so must the theory of logic. In order for all that is new in the ring-pass-not to register consciously, the logic must also expand to incorporate the new information in the ring-pass-not.

Machaelle has also seen that when one works out of timing with nature, a great deal more energy is used than if the job were done in the proper timing. She has retrained herself to observe and try to read the signals of nature's timing. When she saw another timing unfold in the garden, she became confident to look for different timing in herself. Usually the timing precedes her logical notion of what should be, so she has realized that if she waits for the timing the situation unfolds far more effortlessly. In timing there is grounding. In logic and intelligence there often is not.

CRACKING THE COMMUNICATION CODE

I've had another major lesson around this issue of questions and that has to do with the difference between asking a question of the intellect and a question which gives me information for integration. This is a fairly easy thing to distinguish between on paper but a bit tough to begin to discern personally.

You see, we live in an age where we are given deference and approval for the amount of information we know. Our school system honors the student who can stuff a lot of information in his head and then repeat it at the correct moment. Not only do we admire individuals who can do this, we grow up to believe that to live well in society, one must remain intellectually alert. Ask questions. Take in information.

I don't mean to imply that there is something wrong with our being intellectually developed. But I do point out the pitfall that has encouraged us to develop the habit of asking questions for the sake of asking questions. We do nothing more with the answer than file it. This is what I mean by an intellectual question. The more I have developed around this issue of asking questions, the more I have realized what a useless exercise it is for me to ask an intellectual question. What in the world can I do with all that information?

The integration question is one in which the answer is received in right timing and we are able to integrate the information we receive into our life. It can change the way we think, how we perceive the reality around us, how we act, how we move through our daily schedule. When this type of question is asked, we are able to move the answer through a complete grounding process by however the information impacts our life.

I can't give you a formula for distinguishing an intellectual question from an integration question. Obviously, since we are all different, what is intellectual for one is integration for another. But I can give you some hints I've come up with in my own journey through the question issue.

One of the best ways to begin weeding out needless information gathering is to start making it a practice to act on every piece of information we take in. Just the thought of this will give us mental strain. Very quickly, as we attempt to actually respond, time itself will encourage us to be more discerning about the information we are gathering. There simply isn't enough time in the day to respond with some form of action to all the pieces of information we take in. We would die of exhaustion.

I experienced a gradual change around asking questions. At first I continued to ask all the questions that typically popped into mind. As I began to understand the wisdom of taking in only the information I could integrate and use, I became sensitive to what was happening when I asked a question. I could feel some answers move as an energy right into my body system. Other answers I felt bounce off me as a rubber ball off a brick wall. I could hear what was being said to me but the energy behind what was being said didn't come into me. After awhile, I could anticipate the effect an answer would have on me—I could feel whether the energy was going to absorb into me or bounce off—and know that I need not bother to go through the exercise of physically hearing it. I'd just apologize for asking the question and indicate that I need not hear the answer. Further down the line, I realized I could think the question, feel the impact of the answer on me and make a decision whether or not to even open my mouth.

Why am I going through all of this, you ask. Seems a bit overboard doesn't it? Well, through kinesiology I've given you the means to "hear" the answers to all your questions. Kinesiology can open that door for you. And that's precisely what I want to happen for you. But I want to encourage you to use kinesiology as a viable, living tool within your daily life, not as a tool for you to become cosmic scholars. I want you to use it to participate more fully in your life and your environment. I don't want to encourage arm-chair observers. You can easily bog yourself down with information overload and render yourself motionless.

In order to develop the kind of gardening I do at Perelandra, one must ask what seem to be a million questions—all necessary. For your own preservation, it will be essential that you weed out the unnecessary questions. For example, I focus my energy on the design, layout, preparation and timing of the garden. I never bother to ask why this particular design, layout, preparation and timing. I just do it and then I spend the summer observing. By fall, any questions I might have asked in the spring are usually answered simply by my observations. The quality of the answers is greater because I've observed them in action and the results of that action. If I still feel I need input, I'll then ask questions on the basis of my observations.

OVERLIGHTING DEVA OF PERELANDRA

In establishing our partnership with you, I feel it essential to add our overview to this issue of the information which must flow between us. As Machaelle has stated, we on the higher nature levels will not and cannot decide for you what you are to know and when. You must orchestrate this yourself. We take no responsibility for you in this area. If you ask us a question or seek knowledge from us in a particular area, we will answer. We will give you all the information you seek. What you do with the information is completely up to you.

However, the partnership we seek with humans is a partnership of action and co-creative growth. Information is meant to be a dynamic ener-

gy, not a stagnant energy. Although we will give you all the information you seek, we do this in the spirit of action. We seek nothing less. The planet can tolerate nothing less. Too many shifts and changes face us for there to be time wasted on stagnant information gathering.

I point out one additional thing to you. If you humans are only interested in receiving stagnant information, you limit the scope with which we may communicate that information. We are reduced to interacting with you on the mental level. If you physically move with the information you receive, we can then expand our interaction through your physical movements. We can modify movement through intuition, and we can do it in the moment. Through the intuition we can pass along nuances in action that were impossible to pass along to you on the mental level, resulting in a much broader understanding of that which you desire to know. In short, our opportunity for communication with active information is far greater than with stagnant information.

THE NATURE SPIRITS AT PERELANDRA

We wish to join you at this moment because what is being said is of vital importance to us if we are to work directly with you. We ***are*** *action. We* ***are*** *movement. And we dedicate our energy to health, growth and change. We cannot even begin to relate to the human issue of what has been referred to as "stagnant information gathering." We have no understanding of this exercise. Our intent is to interact with you in motion. Our very existence is one of continuous movement. Nature itself is in continuous motion. Where we find humans who are not moving, we back away. We know not what else to do but to move away and tend to our purpose on the planet in separation from the human.*

Regarding our participation in exchanging information with humans: We prefer to do this in a framework of action. As we have said, action is our natural mode of operation. We prefer to interface with you as you work in the garden, for instance. We prefer to communicate through action. If we wish to teach you something about energy and its relationship to form—something which you have indicated to us you wish to know—we will most likely ***show*** *you the information. Demonstrate it to you. This is one reason why those humans who consciously work in partnership with us in their gardens talk about the unusual things they see or experience there. Those unusual happenings have our "fingerprints" all over them and represent times when we have been in communication with the human.*

THE NUTS AND BOLTS OF ASKING A QUESTION

Remember that to use kinesiology successfully, you have to rely on questions in a yes/no format. Short, simple, concise questions. This is easy—and it's not so easy! As thinking adults, we have learned to use compound and compound-complex question frameworks. After all, we don't want to sound like idiots. Simple questions are out of style and consequently we are out of practice. However, with a little bit of thought put to the issue, we can learn to rephrase any question we might have or anything we wish to know into a yes/no format.

I'll give you some common pitfalls to watch out for.

Let's say you want to know if you should remove an old apple tree from your backyard that looks to you to be diseased. You open yourself to the appropriate deva (deciding who is appropriate will be discussed later) and ask, "Should I remove this apple tree from the backyard?" Not, "Gee, this apple tree doesn't look too healthy and I was trying to decide if I should take it down, but the squirrels love it so and in the fall the apples are a nice source of food, but I don't want to risk the other trees and I certainly don't want to kill this one because it has been out there in the backyard for years and it's pretty in its own way...." The first response a nature intelligence would make to you is, "What is your question?"

I call asking a strung-out question like this "mash potatoing." In essence, all you've presented the deva with is a glob of shapeless mash potatoes thus giving no clear avenue for response. If you are faced with an issue that involves many considerations, simply present each consideration separately in a yes/no format. For example, if I were to break down the mash potato question, I would present it something like this:

Should the apple tree in the backyard be removed? (yes/no)
Is the apple tree healthy? (yes/no)
Does this tree's health risk the health of the surrounding trees in the yard? (yes/no)
Is this tree an important source of food for the squirrels? (yes/no)
Is this tree an important source of food for the wildlife in general in the backyard? (yes/no)
(If the tree is to be removed and it is also an important source of food) Should I provide another source of food for the wildlife after the tree is removed? (yes/no)
(If yes, then start listing possibilities one by one.)

Should I provide:
apples? (yes/no)
bird seed? (yes/no)
suet? (yes/no)
pepperoni pizza? (yes/no)

I've not only shown you how to break down a complicated situation into a series of simple yes/no questions, I've also shown how you can build your question process based on the answer to each question. This is how you receive complex information with lots of nuances—allow the answer to the previous question guide you to ask the next question and keep the process building.

Now, let's say you are looking at the aforementioned backyard and everything looks alright but you have some vague feeling that something is wrong. Even this situation can be broken down into a yes/no format.

You would connect with the overlighting deva of your backyard and ask:

Is there something wrong with the backyard? (yes)
Does something need to be added? (no)
Does something need to be removed? (yes)
Is it my child's swing set? (no)
Is it a bush? (no)
Is it a tree? (yes)
Is it the maple tree? (no)
Is it the apple tree? (yes)
(With surprise) Is that sucker sick? (yes)
Should it be removed? (yes)
Soon? (yes)
Has the health of the other trees and bushes been compromised? (no)

(Breathe a sigh of relief and go find someone who will take that tree down for less than $14.85 an hour.)

In essence, what you are doing is playing *Twenty Questions* with a deva. This may seem tedious to you, but this kind of simplicity is an excellent place to begin when learning something new. Don't let false pride and the fear of looking silly get in your way. If you take the time to build your foundation, eventually you will have a broader working relationship between yourself and the nature intelligences, and you'll develop refinements to your technique.

Part of my development has centered around the use of intuition. Once I began to feel comfortable with the *Twenty Questions* routine, I noticed that my intuition began to play into it. I paid attention to this and soon realized that the nature intelligence I was connected with was using my intuition to guide me more efficiently through the questions. I got to the point where, if I walked out into this mythical backyard and sensed something wrong, I would connect with the deva and ask:

Is there something wrong? (yes)

Then my attention might be drawn to the apple tree or I'd get an intuitive hit that the problem was the apple tree, and I would ask, in light of the new input:

Is it the apple tree? (yes)

As you see, I was able to get to the heart of the matter comparatively quickly. But intuition wasn't added until I felt comfortable with the more basic technique. Like any tool, the better we are with the basics, the more proficient we'll be with what develops later.

A Note on Clarity

If you're having difficulty just wording a simple yes/no question, consider this an important issue to be faced and something worth spending the time to rectify. You have not simply stumbled upon a glitch in your quest to communicate with nature intelligences. You've also stumbled upon a glitch in the communication between your higher self and your conscious self. If you can't even clearly word the question, you can't expect an answer. I have met people who cannot articulate a question. In a workshop they will attempt to ask me something and I can't figure out what they are asking—nor can anyone else in the workshop. Usually it turns out that they are frustrated because they can't get any clarity in their own life. Their inability to ask a question demonstrates that lack of clarity.

For those of you who find yourselves in this boat, you have a terrific opportunity to turn that around and develop internal order by putting effort into learning how to articulate a simple yes/no question. In this instance, you are not only developing a tool for communicating with nature, you are also developing the clarity for communicating with yourself. I fully understand that it will take focus on your part and in comparison to someone who finds articulating a simple question easy, it will seem herculean. But if you wish to function consciously with your many levels, you must provide internal clarity and order.

I recommend that you initially devote your attention to learning to ask simple questions and not worry about receiving answers. When you need to ask someone a question, take time to consider what you really want to ask and how it can be most clearly worded. It helps to write down the question. In this way, you can visually see your words. If they don't get across what you mentally want to get across, then play with the wording. Keep doing this until you feel those words accurately get across what you wish to ask. Then go to that person and ask the question. I urge you to continue this process for a fair period of time—even dedicating yourself to the process for awhile. Quite often inner confusion exists because we've not had an acceptable framework for the development of mental ordering. Learning to ask questions gives the mind something tangible to work with. You'll find that as you develop the ability to clearly articulate a question, your inner fog will begin to lift which in turn will automatically begin to lift your outer fog.

Either/Or Situations

I find myself faced with either/or situations quite frequently. This is simple to deal with. Let's say I must make a move and I have two or more options as possibilities. I will open myself to the appropriate nature intelligence. Now, I learned early on that I can't assume that nature knows what is going on inside my head. So the first thing I do when I'm in an either/or situation is to inform the intelligence what I perceive my options to be. I list them all. Example: I receive that the rose bushes need a dressing of phosphorus. I have options available to me as to what I can add to the soil for the phosphorus. I will tell whoever I'm working with that it can either be bone meal, alfalfa meal, rock phosphate or liquid kelp. Then I will ask "Which would you prefer I use?," and go through the list again one by one thereby setting up the scenario in a yes/no format.

Would you prefer
- bone meal? (no)
- alfalfa meal? (no)
- rock phosphate? (yes)
- kelp? (no)

If I get a no on everything in my list, I will double-check myself by retesting. If I still get a unanimous no, then I'll ask:

Is there something else you would prefer that I add? (yes)

I also have Nitro-10, greensand, cottonseed meal, dolomite lime and liquid seaweed. Is it one of these? (yes)

I then relist these fertilizers one by one in order to find the preferred fertilizer.

Another scenario: You get out of bed one morning with a driving desire to wear your yellow and green polka dot shirt. Then you saunter to the closet and as you look for your snappy yellow and green polka dot shirt, your eye catches the purple and orange stripe one and you're overcome with an equal desire to wear this one. Being a responsible person who desires to participate in the universal flow on a daily basis, you say to yourself "Well, which one should I wear?" The 'Well, which one is it?' question is a sure sign you are in an either/or situation. In such situations, I will ask "Does it matter which one of these two shirts I wear today?" (If I get a no, I can exercise free will and make a personal decision based on which shirt attracts me the most. If I get a yes, then I'll shift into a yes/no format and list each shirt separately to find out which one it's to be.

You probably noted that I didn't open to nature in the above scenario. Instead, I connected to my own higher self, since it is on this level that I have housed all the information about myself. All I do is spend five seconds to concentrate my attention into my higher self. If this seems nebulous to you, say aloud:

I wish to be connected to my own higher self.

Focus your attention on what you are saying. If you want confirmation, test yourself using kinesiology.

Am I now connected to my own higher self? (yes)
Am I clear to ask questions? (yes)
Which of these two shirts should I wear?
The one with yellow and green polka dots? (no)
The one with purple and orange stripes? (Yes, but could you upgrade your sense of fashion!?)

FINAL COMMENTS ON KINESIOLOGY

Kinesiology is like any tool. The more you practice, the better you are at using it. You'll need a sense of confidence about using this tool, especially when you are in the midst of planning your garden and you're getting a positive test response on some very strange ideas (that are probably being planted in your intuition by nature spirits). It helps to get over that initial "this-is-too-weird-and-the-damned-testing-isn't-working" stage if you have some confidence in your ability to register a clear positive and negative response. The only way I know over this hump is to practice testing. You will develop clarity in your testing. You'll learn your personal pitfalls. For example, a tendency to be easily distracted will tell you to put some effort into finding a calm, quiet place while you are testing. And you will see the consequences of your answers which will verify your accuracy and build your confidence.

So, what is there we can practice test on? Everything. You could easily drive yourself nuts. What you should wear. What would be healthiest for you to eat for breakfast, lunch and dinner. You take ten separate vitamin and mineral supplements as a matter of course on a daily basis. Try testing them individually ("Do I need vitamin E? B-6? Iron?") to see if you need all ten every day. Or if there are some you don't need to take at all. You are sitting at a restaurant and they don't have tofu supreme on the menu. Is there anything on that menu that is perfectly healthy for you to eat? ("Should I eat fish?" [yes/no] "Should I eat beef?" [yes/no] "Chicken?" [yes/no] "Hagen-Das fudge ripple ice cream?" [Yes!])

The thing is to test everything you possibly can that doesn't place you in a life-threatening situation, follow through on your answers, then look at the results. As I have worked through the years to refine my ability to use kinesiology, I have purposely followed through on answers that made no sense at all to me just to see if the testing was accurate. Doing this and looking at the results with a critical eye is the only way I know to learn about ourselves as kinesiology testers and discover the nuances and uses of kinesiology itself.

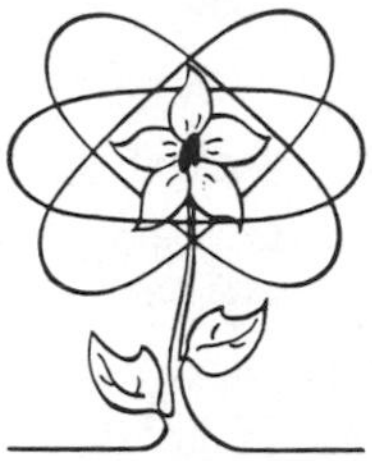

3

ESTABLISHING YOUR PARTNERSHIP

It's time to take the plunge. You've been kinesiology testing everything from here to Aunt Sally's kitchen. You have a fair sense of the positive strong and negative weak sensation in your fingers. Spring is barreling in on you. You are knee deep in the new season's gardening catalogs. And you want to get started in your new partnership.

To get started, I recommend a small, formal declaration on your part. I mentioned in *Behaving....* that this was how I got started and I still feel that this is an excellent way to begin. My suggestions:

1. Go outside. Not only is this a symbolic gesture on your part to physically link with nature, it also might facilitate matters as you direct your attention to nature for the declaration.

2. Direct your attention to nature—to the nature intelligences. If this is too vague for you, just pretend you are speaking into a telephone with nature listening in at the other end. Or sense that nature as an intelligent presence is sitting opposite you waiting for you to say something. The main thing is that you feel free to do whatever you need to do to consciously link yourself with the nature intelligences. Be clear, precise and simple about it.

ESTABLISHING YOUR PARTNERSHIP

3. Say aloud:

I would like to be formally linked with the devic realm.

Wait just a few seconds. You may feel sensations like a wave of energy gently wash over you. You may feel absolutely nothing and this will mean absolutely nothing because you are going to verify your connection with this level using kinesiology. Ask:

Am I now connected? (Then test.)

Once you get over the shock of feeling a powerful and positive test result, go on to Step 4.

4. Say aloud:

I would now like to be formally linked with the nature spirit level.

Again, wait a few seconds then ask:

Am I connected? (Test.)

You'll get another powerful positive result. I know I sound awfully confident about your test results, but remember I am aware of how much nature wants this connection with you and how eager it is to work with you in a consciously communicating partnership.

5. Spend a moment recognizing that you have just opened the phone lines to a new and expanded level. This is a significant time for you and I doubt if you'll want to let it pass lightly.

6. Now that you have their attention—and they probably have yours—it's time to declare the intent of your partnership. If gardening is your focus, simply say aloud:

I now request that we work in a co-creative partnership in the garden and that I be connected to all the nature intelligences involved.

To verify that you have been heard, ask:

Is this declaration accepted? (Test. You'll get another yes.)

If you don't have a garden but you want to establish a partnership, go right ahead. If you have house plants, establish your working partnership around these. You can focus the partnership on a greenhouse or atrium. Or your backyard. Or the semi-precious geodes and crystals you have displayed around the apartment. All you need is one focal point around which you and nature can establish a working relationship. Having a focal point of some kind will allow you to keep the relationship active and this will be essential for the dynamic exchange of information, lessons and ideas you seek.

You are now consciously and actively linked with nature and ready to move on. While you are connected, you may take the opportunity to ask anything you'd like. Just make sure it's in a yes/no format.

If you feel that what you've accomplished is already enough, close out the session. You'll want to get in the habit of closing down a session because 1) it gives your sessions clarity—a beginning when you open a session and an end when you close, and 2) it takes energy on your part to maintain focus during a session and if you are not clear about a session being complete, you might get into an energy-drain situation because of nature continuing to hold its lines open while it tries to figure out what you are doing.

7. To close down a session, say aloud:

   I request that this session be closed.

To verify, ask if the session is now closed. You should have a positive response. If you get a negative, focus yourself on the matter at hand (and not on what has happened during the session!) and make the request again. You'll get a positive result this time.

A WORD ABOUT ETIQUETTE

The easiest way to describe the etiquette I use when working with devas and nature spirits is to say that I treat them as loving, intelligent teachers of the first order who happen to also be my best friends. I am friendly and fully open with them. I will joke and kid around at times. I also try to conduct myself in as considerate a manner as possible. For example, another reason I make it a point to close down my sessions is that in a discussion with a good friend, I would not simply get up and walk out of the room leaving them to figure out if the discussion has ended or not. (I wouldn't do this with a stranger either!) I have discovered over the years that *I* am treated as a good friend and with the most loving consideration. I try to respond in kind. I say "thank you" and "excuse me" and "I'm sorry." I take a moment to acknowledge when something special has occurred between us. I don't just let those moments slip by and even after ten years, I don't take these moments for granted.

I think if in your growing relationship with nature you should get stuck and not know how to respond to a situation, you'll be on safe ground if you consider what you would do if the situation were between you and a good friend—someone you care enough about to put out an effort to not offend.

I don't wish to imply that nature is temperamental and needs to be tiptoed around. But some people don't understand that courtesy is a universal dynamic that is demonstrated on all levels beyond us. And there are some people who, when beginning their partnership, become overwhelmed by the power and majesty they experience from nature and place it on a pedestal for adulation. That's the last place nature wishes to be placed. Good friends aren't placed on pedestals. Others can be taken by the sudden friendly informality they experience with nature and throw all good sense to the wind and act in most inconsiderate and thoughtless ways. I am bringing up the issue of etiquette in an effort to encourage you to develop a sound middle road of care.

PAN

I would like to add to this issue from our point of view. We intelligences within nature do not discern between good etiquette and bad etiquette. Etiquette, as such, is not an issue with us. We exist within the dynamic spirit of love and naturally respond within that spirit. This is extended to humans whenever we have been able to make any contact. We do not try to respond as such, or seek to respond in love. We **are** *love—love in action. Therefore that spirit is the underlying intent with all we do. To act otherwise is alien to us and for the most part causes confusion because we are not familiar with action or intent outside the spirit of love. The human's free will allows him to choose action either within or outside the spirit of love. Nature does not have this choice.*

From our point of view, Machaelle's use of the concept of etiquette is her way of bringing human attention to this issue of action within the spirit of love and our confusion around action outside that spirit. We would say that good etiquette is love in action.

THE ELEMENTAL ANNEX

One of the very first things I was told to do when establishing my partnership with nature was to open what I call the "Elemental Annex"—the nature spirit sanctuary. I set aside an area in the woods near the garden, roped it off and announced that this piece of land was for the exclusive use of the nature spirits. Immediately after this pronouncement, I felt a tremendous rush of energy enter the area and sensed myself surrounded by readiness, action and organization. I also sensed that my gesture of setting aside this piece of land had been accepted as a bridge between the nature spirits and me. From that point in time, our working relationship has been clear and vital—tangible.

I have since moved the site of the garden and a year after that move, I was told to rope off an area near the new garden for the nature spirits. Their shift occurred during the spring equinox in 1984 and was as dramatic the second time as the first.

I strongly recommend that you establish a nature spirit sanctuary. It can be any size and should be in an area where people don't need to enter. It is to be for the sole "habitation" of the nature spirits and traditionally has been regarded as an area where humans are not to enter. The rope is to remind humans to stay out, not keep nature spirits in. Aside from being a tangible gesture of recognition on our part, it also becomes the base of nature spirit operations on your land and can have quite a vibration of activity emanating from it.

How to Open a Nature Spirit Sanctuary

1. Choose a suitable area. If you are gardening, it would be good to have it near the garden.

2. Rope off the sanctuary. Or mark the boundary any way you wish, making sure it is easily discernable.

3. Standing just outside the area, ask that the nature spirits accept this sanctuary and join you in full partnership as you develop your new relationship with nature.

4. If you would like to verify that all of this has happened, open yourself to the nature spirit level (you can now direct your attention to that level by looking directly into the sanctuary) and ask if your roped area has been accepted by them. Then test.

PAN

The nature spirit sanctuary that Machaelle has described to you is more important than ever before. There are areas around the planet that can best be described as sanctuaries which have been established by the nature spirits themselves. Some of these areas have been discovered by humans and are called "fairy rings." If a human stumbles upon such a place, he has described it as enchanted and indeed heightened with a strong and vital energy. This is the energy of the nature spirits he has felt.

ESTABLISHING YOUR PARTNERSHIP

Long ago, when man and nature co-existed on more friendly terms, the nature spirits felt free to establish their area of concentration nearby. These were special points of intense power strategically spaced around the planet through which Earth could be spiritually infused not only by nature itself but by the universe as a whole. But as man's age of development caused him to infringe on the very existence of nature, these points of concentration were either de-activated or moved to safer ground, shall we say. They took on an energy of protection—protection from humans. One must remember that so much of man's modern development has been contrary to the well-being of all that is natural on the planet. This may be extended to include the nature spirits, for their role on the planet is intimately tied into the well-being of all that is natural. The shifting of the points of concentration away from man's proximity has been a retreat by the nature spirits resulting in a significant diminishing of the scope and intensity of the natural power grid around the planet. Consequently, today there exists an isolation between man and the nature spirits, and a planetary environment of despiritualization—form devoid of vital life energy.

The initiation for the reunion between humans and nature must come from humans. The time has long passed where it is appropriate for such an action to be initiated by nature without the conscious participation of the humans who will benefit. The age we are all moving into is one of conscious teamwork, not blind benevolent trust that all will be well.

The benefits of such a reunion are indeed great. The actual operating principles around the notion of spirit and matter perfectly united, which will move man and the planet forward, exist within the dynamic partnership between man and the nature spirits. It is these two who work most directly with spirit and matter united and the problems that arise from this union.

As each sanctuary is made available by man and activated by the nature spirits, it will send out the word that once more man and nature are ready to work together—only now they are ready to work in an equal, co-creative partnership. And as each sanctuary is activated around the world, you will feel, even see, the nature spirits moving out of their protective isolation to re-enter the world at large for the purpose of respiritualizing the planet.

4

BREAKING GROUND

From this point on, much of what I will be doing will be giving you the questions you'll need to ask nature. For example, you are standing in the middle of your one-thousand-square-foot back yard or looking out over your forty acres, shovel in hand, ready to start this garden. You have a clear idea of the size garden you wish based on your needs, desires and the reasonable amount of time you can give to the garden. This is very important for you to have clear in your mind in order to ask the first question. To answer, the deva will want to take into consideration your garden intent and needs and must have that information supplied by you.

Ask to be connected with the deva of your garden. Test to make sure you are connected.

The first question:

> Where should this garden be placed?

(Now I know this is not a yes/no question, but this is the first question. I'll show you how to translate it into a yes/no format shortly.)

Even if you already have an established garden, you have a related question to ask:

> Is this present garden placed in the appropriate spot?

If you get a negative, then you need to consider:

> 1) Are you willing to move the garden area?
>
> 2) Where should it be moved?

If moving the garden is an unwieldy or unacceptable option, you have the right to say "no" to the suggestion. You always have that right. You are the creator of your own garden. But if you wish to establish a partnership with nature, you won't be able to stop with just your "no." You need to make a commitment to do what nature will suggest to you in order to make the present area more workable. To move a garden is an exhausting proposition, I readily admit. But remember, nature would not suggest a move if it did not have good reason. I personally would give serious thought to moving the garden even if I had no idea why nature was suggesting this to me. I'd do it just to find out what nature knows that I'm not seeing.

If you are faced with starting a new garden or moving the site of the old one, you still must deal with the issue of where to put it. There are do's and don't's already established in good gardening practice regarding where one should locate their garden. A southern and eastern exposure. A northern and western protection. On a knoll or rise for good drainage. Etc., etc. Although you may know these points very well, they are not now the issue. The issue is where nature wishes you to place the garden.

I do not suggest you throw out all your learned knowledge. In fact, that will be most useful to you for it will give you the ability to observe different thought, different approach, overall change to a new concept. You'll have a springboard for comparison. When learning, this can be handy. And nature itself will use what you know as the foundation upon which you will build together.

But for the time being, place what you already know to one side and ask the deva of your garden where the garden should be placed. Having asked this question, you need only establish a framework for translating the answer, which you do by breaking down your land area into sections. You can do this visually as you stand there on your land or make a line drawing of the area and indicate each of the sections. Then concentrate your vision into each section and ask:

Do I put the garden here? (Test.)

Keep doing this for all the sections. Once you identify the section and it in itself is a fairly large area, break the section into sub-sections and identify the exact location through the same elimination process.

If at the end you have only one positive response, then you now know where to place the garden. If you have two or more positives, you are being told there is more than one spot and you are being given option. In this situation, I always ask if there is one option better than all the rest. If I get a yes, I'll identify which one by asking the question "Which one is the best?," looking at each of my options and asking "Is it this one?," and eliminating. If I get a no, I give my free will free rein and make a personal choice between the options.

THE OBSTACLE ISSUE

If you haven't already guessed, your partnership with nature can be a constant test of commitment on your part. Issues will come up again and again which will challenge your heart in very fundamental ways. The obstacle issue is but one example. You have gone through the elimination process and have found that the garden is to be right where the ten-year-old oak tree is standing or where you already have a rose bed. You have an immediate heart conflict.

There are some things to think about before you yell "no" and ask for a secondary placement.

1. You asked where the garden should go and this is the answer. You did not give any conditions to nature prior to the question. I don't give conditions because I really want to know the answer no matter what and then I'll deal with any complications that might arise.

2. Nature does not have an emotional relationship with form. It has a godly relationship with form in that it has a divine love for life. It designs and organizes with the intent of divine love inherent in all those decisions. We humans do not have to teach nature how to love properly and respect the world of form. In light of this inherent divine love, it still told you that the best position for the garden is right where that oak tree is standing.

3. The direction nature has given you regarding the garden takes into consideration input, facts, reality, balance and energy from all sorts of levels. The deva has the health and balance of the whole as its primary consideration, not just the oak tree. If I were looking at that oak tree, I'd have to consider that there is a bigger picture involved here.

Still before yelling "no" to taking out the tree or any other obstacle, I'd ask some more questions:

Can this thing be easily moved?
Is it to be moved?
If so, where?

(Do the same positioning process you did with the garden. This time you'll receive the answer in light of the future garden being placed in its position. That potential is now new input when the deva considers your land area.)

If it is not to be moved, is it to be removed altogether?

If yes, then you can pursue the issue by asking if this decision has to do with overall energy balance (if the tree is healthy) and if the tree is actually weakened in energy by its being in this position.

A ten-year-old tree is not easily moved. But if you get a positive answer when you ask if the tree is to remain part of the whole picture of your yard or land, you might ask if you are to plant a younger tree of the same kind in the desired location. If you get a yes, what is most likely being planned for on the part of nature is an energy shift from one form to another. That is, the life energy of the first oak tree will be shifted, prior to your taking it down, to the form of the young tree. This is done on the nature spirit level and is part of that cooperation between man and nature that is available to us. In actuality, you won't be removing a large tree. You will be setting up the vehicle for a complete energy shift by planting the second tree. The spirit and life force of the first tree will remain intact but in a different form.

Participating in an Energy Shift

1. Supply the new form to which the energy will be shifted. Sometimes nature will use a form that is already in the area. For example, you may have another oak tree in the yard and nature will indicate to you that no other form needs to be added and it will use the other oak tree as the receiver of the life energy from the tree to be taken out. (Energy is completely flexible when it comes to size and shape. The life energy from one tree can be received fully in another form without causing overcrowding.)

2. Once the second form has either been added or identified, connect with the nature spirit level. Simply focus attention to it either by calling the nature spirits to you or focusing your attention into the sanctuary area. Make sure you are connected:

Am I connected with the nature spirit level? (Test.)

3. **Initiate the shift** by asking the nature spirits to now shift the energy from the old form to the new.

4. Although this process is immediate and takes a matter of a minute, I do not disturb the old form for about two weeks to make sure the shift fully stabilizes. Before removing the old form, I'll test to make sure all is ready for removal.

There is another wonderful and amazing verification that the energy has shifted which you can do for yourself. Before removing the old form, take a good look at it. Really look at it carefully. Then remove it completely from the spot. As soon as it is away from the area, look where the form used to stand and try to visualize its being there. If the energy was shifted, you won't be able to visualize the form even though you just looked at it less than five minutes before. This is because not only the form but the energy within the form are no longer present and there is nothing before you on any level of reality from which you can draw for a visualization.

Don't panic if you can still see the form. Once again, connect with the nature spirits and ask that they shift the energy even though you have already removed the form. They will do this. Don't assume a mistake has been made on anyone's part. The nature spirits use opportunities such as this all the time for teaching. Show us something different. Give us a new nuance. Change process. Understand that something is happening and remain alert and open for input either through what you observe or what you sense intuitively. Also, you may not have the complete lesson until you do the process with another form to be removed and they show or communicate to you in this scenario again. So don't hesitate to keep moving forward even if you sense you may have made an error and you no longer have any idea what you are doing. If you get information to participate in another energy shift, do it.

For the sake of clarity, let me add that nature does not need our participation in order to do an energy shift. Nature spirits do this all the time—moving energy from one level to another and then into form, or from one form to another. It's an energy dynamic that is as much a part of the nature spirit level as breathing is to us. But I remind you that we are moving into an era of conscious teamwork. In those areas where man and nature interact, such as gardening, landscaping, land management, etc., there is constant opportunity for co-creative partnership and nature will not assume sole responsibility for quality interaction with us. It looks to us to participate in kind.

If, in light of all this, you do not wish to move or shift the obstacle, ask the deva for a secondary position and commit yourself to doing what must be done to stabilize or enhance it. As you become sensitive to working with nature, you'll notice that you won't be feeling a judgmental energy coming from it to you. If you ask for a secondary or alternative decision, you won't feel nature calling you a jerk. It's okay to make that decision, but what nature looks to us for is an understanding that our decisions have implications. An alternative is an alternative for a reason and requires a different approach or different action. If we keep that in mind and remain open to further input from nature, we'll maintain a good, flexible relationship.

DEVA OF THE PERELANDRA GARDEN

Machaelle has touched on an area upon which we would like to expand, and that is garden placement in the context of the whole picture. The purpose of the approach to gardening being presented here is to establish a highly planned and cooperative space where man and nature can work in partnership for the purpose of the enhancement of man's health through the heightened quality of his food and the enhancement of the surrounding land area itself through the radiation of heightened nature energy from the garden. The direction of vibrant, life-giving energy not only moves into the plants and their vegetables. It also radiates out from the garden into the surrounding land and impacts all form within that area. Perhaps it would be easier to visualize what we are saying if one saw the garden as an energy generator. As man and nature work more closely together, the garden energy shifts, clarifies and strengthens, which in turn makes the garden a finely tuned generator. And the life energy contained within all surrounding form is enhanced that much more.

As you can see, a garden where the power of man and of nature have come together in a truly creative endeavor can be in itself a very powerful thing. It has been fairly easy for humans to grasp how this power can impact them personally through the higher quality food they eat from that garden. But humans have tended to miss the powerful impact that garden can have outside itself.

It is for this reason we must be very careful about the placement of such a potential power area within the context of the whole. When you open to us seeking the information of where to place the garden, we will position it where not only the internal garden process is most positively enhanced, but where the external relationship of the garden to the whole is at its most advantageous.

Consider several things: If you are seeking this information from us, by the mere fact of your opening to us you are saying that this garden will be consciously linked in partnership with nature. That tells us that the power potential in this specific garden is great. It is a potential that may not be fully attained for years, since man and nature will need time to work together in a building process, but it is a potential that must be taken into consideration by us on the devic level. There are areas within the whole of your land which are more appropriate than other areas for holding such a power point.

So when we look to place such a garden, we take three questions into consideration. 1) Where on the land is the physical activity of garden growth best supported? 2) Where will the internal movement of energy and the development of a powerful energy environment best be supported? 3) Where will the external movement of power energy into the surrounding environment best be enhanced and supported? We will place a garden in the most positive position in light of these three considerations. And quite frankly, because the energy and the power questions are so important, we may place a garden in an area which looks to you to not be the best growing area (and you may be right), but will better address the power and energy issues. From our point of view, it will be better to improve the form sources available in a specific area for the garden growth process because this can be easily accomplished within the spirit of teamwork between us, the nature spirits and man. Preparing an area with power and energy in mind deals with deeper, more fundamental issues that must be addressed within the intelligent levels of nature alone and removes us from the spirit of teamwork which is so vital a development at this time.

I bring one additional issue to your attention. If a person considers the quality of food both in energy and form to be of importance, then we can assume that he is grasping the relationship between the quality of food and the health of the individual. There is a direct correlation between the two—the health and well-being of the human physical vehicle and the quality of the food fuel introduced into that vehicle. I point this out to emphasize what we in nature see as the internal movement of healing energy within the garden: The healing relationship between the food the garden produces and the physical form into which the food goes. It's a healing dynamic. The external movement from the garden, that is that power energy which radiates into the whole, is also healing—a radiating power energy which has inherent in its makeup the dynamic of healing. As food can transform the physical health of one's body, the radiating energy from the garden transforms the physical health of the environmental form it impacts. So you have an internal healing dynamic and an external healing dynamic. You have learned from the nature spirits that the re-introduction of nature spirit sanctuaries into the planetary whole will serve to respiritualize Earth. On the same order, we say to you here that as these co-creative gardens are established around the planet you will have the seating in of power points which will radiate healing energy into its environment. As these points estab-

lish, they will link with one another forming a healing grid around the planet thus enveloping Earth with its own vibrant, healing energy.

This is one of the potential results we refer to when we say that although nature is powerful beyond your imagination and humans are powerful beyond your imagination, man and nature come together hold the promise of many times their individual power. A potential of this union is the creation of the Earth's own healing energy grid through its gardening system around the planet. And the healing power which will radiate from the gardens and ultimately from the grid formed by the link-up of the gardens will be equally available and usable to both humans and nature because it was created by humans and nature united.

GARDEN SIZE

This is an issue which really should have been settled prior to your locating the garden site, but if you didn't, now is definitely the time. If ever there was a call for sensibility and moderation, this is it. In my travels I've gotten to see plenty of gardens that tend to be either the appropriate size for feeding all of Philadelphia with one burnt-out gardener working it, or the size of a Raggedy Ann baby pool with six eager gardeners pressing the soil to produce enough to feed the aforementioned Philadelphia.

Obviously need is a major factor to be considered. But with the approach we are presenting here, your ability and willingness to maintain responsibility for your end of the partnership throughout the gardening season also becomes a factor. Anyone who has gardened knows that in the spring we have all sorts of energy and excitement to draw on when getting out there to do the necessary work. It's fun to be outside again. Then July and the heat hit and the gardening work is starting to get tedious. I've always heard from the farmers around me that July is the acid test for finding the *real* gardeners. If you've got a garden that still looks nice in July, you're a *real* gardener. If you've got one that looks like it went to hell in a hand basket and ought to be mowed down, you're a fake.

So when thinking about size, I suggest you not just consider your food needs, but also try to make a fair evaluation as to how much energy you really have to give to this project throughout the entire season.

One more thought on this issue: There are all sorts of different gardening methods with books written about each that have different time and space requirements. If I were starting out, I would do a little research in this area to identify the type of gardening practices that appeal to me in light of my own time and space requirements. Then I would connect with the deva of my garden and ask if any one of these practices could be used as the base method for the garden. For example, after all this warning about being reasonable about the size of your garden, I have to admit to you that mine is one hundred feet in diameter and produces enough food to feed Philadelphia. But my garden is primarily a laboratory where we do the kind of research I'm sharing with you in this book, so one hundred feet in diameter is a reasonable size for what has to happen in the research annually. I am the primary human worker. What enables me to garden this space is that I use as my base method Ruth Stout's mulch gardening method. I keep six to eight inches of mulch on the entire garden at all times. It's an ecologically sound and labor-saving process that eliminates watering, weeding, and tilling except to work up the rows in the spring for planting. It is a method that accommodates the size we need for the research work and the fact that there is one human here to do the work. (I highly recommend this method of gardening to anyone, but I especially recommend it to those who wish to have a garden and need to be very efficient about their time in it. Rodale Press carries the collection of Ruth Stout's books on the mulch method. See *Supplies and Resources* for information about her books.)

The issue here is not to press any one method of gardening onto you. The fact is, there is no one right or wrong method. Each has its points pro and con. What's important is to find the method that accommodates you, your needs, the needs of your nature partners and the land. Whatever method or combination of methods you choose, you can be sure nature is going to modify it as you go along so that it can better respond to change and what really is happening in that garden. In essence, the method you choose is just a starting point.

THE GARDEN SHAPE

Gone are the good old days when we went out to that special plot of land, paced off a 30-by-50-foot rectangle, plowed it, tilled it and then staked about fifteen straight rows for planting. Well, maybe those days aren't completely gone but the *assumption* that this is what one does is definitely gone.

At Perelandra, I started out with that rectangle. As the energy of the garden increased and my abilities to work within the partnership improved, I got the word that the garden was not only to change location but size and shape as well. I went from the usual rectangle to eighteen concentric circles, the outermost measuring one hundred feet in diameter.

I also have three paths which spiral to the center. It took four years of fine tuning to finally get the combination of shapes well defined into the garden.

Why bother with this craziness? (Especially when all the existing gardening tools and machinery work best in a straight row garden.) I have been shown and have certainly experienced that shape and energy are related; that a circle has more power than a straight line. One simple way to explain this is to point out the obvious. A circle is a straight line with its two open ends connected, thus forming the circle. A simple straight line has two open ends. The energy contained within the line that is connected and held in the circle is released out the two open ends of the straight line. On a pure, simple energy basis, this is inefficient.

Again, I do not mean to sell you the concept of gardening in circles. What I do at Perelandra may be completely inappropriate for your garden. What I am trying to impress on you is that there are options, and these options should be discussed with nature. Think in terms of your starting point and ask nature for the shape that is best suited for your garden now. Please don't get into a competition with what I'm doing at Perelandra. If you get that the rectangle shape is best for you now, trust that nature knows what it is doing and put in a rectangle. You may or may not get word to change that shape at some point down the road. Simply understand that there is an appropriate shape or combination of shapes that you need to establish for the overall vibrancy and health of the garden, and your source for finding that out is nature.

On a practical level, I suggest drawing on paper all the various shapes you can think of, then connecting again with the deva of the garden (remember issues like the shape and size of the garden are all formulated on the devic level) and testing each shape separately. The one that tests positive is the one for you now. If more than one tests positive you may be getting an either/or choice or you might be getting a recommendation to combine the two shapes into one another for one more complex shape. Simply break this down into two questions:

> Is this an either/or situation? (Test.)
> Are both shapes to be used? (Test.)

The positive result will tell you which way to go.

I really suggest that when regarding the shape issue you test your ideas with nature. I've seen some gardens where the gardener has become entranced with this idea of shape and energy and has laid out the most complicated labyrinth possible. I can tell just by looking at it that this is the work of man's mind. It may be doing all sorts of things on an energy level but those things may not be very helpful to what is trying to happen in the garden. I find nature tends to lean more toward simplicity.

NATURE SPIRITS AT PERELANDRA

We wish to add insight to the issue of shape from our vantage point. We work with the concept of shape and energy constantly. It is an example of spirit and form, energy and matter. There is an intimate and vital relationship between the two. You see and feel this with the relationship between your soul energy and your body. Your soul energy could not function comfortably within the form of a tree and vice versa. There is what can be called "universal appropriateness" when teaming energy to form. Now, don't get us wrong. We are not dealing with judgment here. We are not saying that the form of a tree is too low for the soul of man. But we are saying that there is such a thing as universal appropriateness between energy and the shape it needs in order to function fully within form.

This notion which we bring to your attention is why shape is so important. If we were given the assignment to establish an area such as your garden and we were left on our own to do it, we would immediately know what shape this specific garden was to have for it to function within form. The question is not only essential but basic when considering energy on Earth. Up to now, we have primarily been faced with the individual arbitrarily choosing the form for his garden. He doesn't take into consideration the garden as an energy reality seeking to come into form nor does he understand the relationship of that garden to the whole. So he simply chooses a shape that suits his convenience. Our job, if we may state it this way, is to assist the dynamic process that goes on between energy and its form. If a garden is laid out in an overall inappropriate shape, we are left with, at best, an uphill battle in our work. You are left with a battle in the garden. In order to keep that garden alive, and we mean "alive" not "healthy," you must address a constant demonstration of weakness. In the past, this issue has become so intolerable, so impossible from our position, that we have simply had to leave altogether and release the area completely to the human to do with as he wishes.

Regarding the issue of changing the shape from time to time: Remember that a garden is dynamic, a constant energy flow which shifts and changes on a continuous basis. We read these changes and shifts. We know the nuances. All these nuances are multilevelled and varied because all that is of form within a garden is multilevelled and varied. Everything is in a state of evolution—that is, a state of progressive change. Form must adjust appropriately to evolution. To force form to be static while expecting it to house energy that is dynamic is foolish, to put it simply. It doesn't work and will result in the deterioration of both form and its energy. An unhealthy relationship is created between the two.

We do not wish to scare you and make you believe that you will receive promptings every year to completely change the shape of your garden—or else! We said that evolution is progressive change and form changes respond accordingly—progressively. Once you have established the initial appropriate form, you will receive from us in timing information for a series of progressive changes that will not tax your energy or your patience at all.

The Perelandra garden had a major change in 1979 because it was then that Machaelle made certain personal commitments to the level of research she was willing to explore. This necessitated that the intent of the garden (and its shape) be adjusted accordingly. A major evolutionary step concerning the garden which dramatically shifts the future and its direction requires a corresponding major change in that garden's form.

We point this out so that you won't feel that all the work and effort you will put in to establishing a garden in its proper shape is temporary. In fact, it is the primary design upon which you will fine tune as its progression dictates. There will be some gardens whose initial intent will be consciously changed by their gardeners, as what happened at Perelandra. In these cases, there may be major changes in location, size and shape to accommodate the new intent. But remember, although you as the creator of the garden dictate the intent, you will not be alone in the working out of that new intent. You will have the new information, energy, cooperation and power from our level as well as the devic level behind you. And you will find that the work involved in such a massive change will feel effortless.

5

SETTING UP TO RECEIVE THE DEVIC INFORMATION

The success of the garden rests on information. What goes into the garden? Where do I put it? How many of each should I put in? Do I put rocks in or do I take rocks out? Will there be interplanting? Does that mean flowers or herbs, or what? Basically, you are faced with a piece of land laid out in an unusual shape and now you need to know what to do with it.

All of the information you need is held within the devic level, specifically the deva of your garden. Your job now is to receive the bits and pieces of that information and translate it into useful and usable form. In the past, this has been the big stumbling block for many who have wanted to move into co-creative gardening. But by developing some planning tools for yourself and using kinesiology, this process of getting the specific information from the devic level has become quite simple.

I'll give you as much as I can from my ten years of figuring out how to get all I need from the Deva of the Garden, and the charts and tools I've developed for translating that information into visual form on a small scale—the garden chart.

I start the planning process in early February and I work to have all the necessary charts and information completed by the end of the month. This gives me enough time to order the seeds (which seeds is part of the devic information) and start the early seeds for transplants (again, part of the devic information), so that all I have to do in the spring is translate my planning information into the garden itself.

THE GARDEN CHART

This is an essential tool that will benefit you and the process enormously if you take time to do it well. First, you'll need to draw a scale layout of the garden: its shape, the placement of the rows and any focal points. Make it a simple line drawing and I suggest you do the final copy in black ink. Once you make this layout, you can save yourself all kinds of time next year and the years after by having the original blank photocopied. (Black ink will give you a good, clean copy.) Don't let an 8-1/2-by-11-inch sheet of paper limit you as to the size of your scale drawing. You're going to want enough space to comfortably add all the writing and symbols for the layout of the vegetables. So if one sheet is going to give you permanent eye strain, scotch tape several sheets together (or get larger paper) in order to create your reasonably-sized, easily-workable garden chart. There are photocopy centers that will make large copies of this original for you. The Perelandra chart is on a 14-by-18-inch sheet. Also, consider that you are going to be referring to this chart a lot throughout the season. You may even want to put it up on a wall. It will be very irritating if you have trouble reading it.

Questions You'll Need to Ask

1. Is there a focal point in the garden?
2. If so, where?

A focal point is a point in the garden where something special may be going such as a crystal, a special plant, special herbs, a seating area.... It can be any number of things and is usually considered a position of power within the garden as a whole. At Perelandra, the focal point is the very center of the garden where we now have crystals sitting inside a genesa crystal (to be explained later), all on slate and surrounded by a ring of herbs. The focal point has changed in content but not position over the years. It began as just a natural white quartz rock sitting right in the middle of the garden and has changed as the garden energy changed. (I was told how to change it and when.)

Regarding your focal point, if you have one, don't assume it is in the middle of the garden. Ask the deva of the garden if there is one and if so, where is it to be placed. Then use kinesiology and the elimination process to locate it. (If you find that your intuition is working with you as you ask these questions, don't discount that. Make sure you're connected to the deva of the garden and ask if what you are sensing or "seeing" is correct. If you are open to your intuitive level, nature will use it as part of the communication tools between you. To be sure you are accurate, simply double-check your intuition with kinesiology.)

SETTING UP TO RECEIVE THE DEVIC INFORMATION

Another note on focal points: There is no value judgment placed on whether or not a garden has a focal point. They are there for specific reasons that have nothing to do with one garden being better than another. The important issue here is if a garden is to have one, put it in and position it correctly, and if a garden is not to have one, don't arbitrarily manufacture one.

3. Which direction are the rows to run?
   - North/south?
   - East/west?
   - Circular?
   - Serpentine?

For those of you who know traditional gardening practices, don't assume east/west.

4. How many rows?

With this question, we add a new twist to your kinesiology technique. This is not a yes/no format. It requires a different approach. You are still connected to the deva of your garden. (Test.) Ask:

How many rows are to go into the garden?

1 row? (Test. You'll get a positive.)
2 rows? (Test. Another positive.)
3 rows? (Test.)

Keep progressing in numbers until you test negative. Let's say you test positive all the way up to 15. On 16, you test negative. This means that the number of rows which are to be in the garden is 15. Sixteen is too many and that's why you got a negative.

5. What is the distance between rows?

Are all the rows equidistant? (You'll most likely get a positive on this, but it won't hurt to check.)

How far apart should they be? (Use the same setup as in the above paragraph.)

1 foot? (Test.) If positive, ask:
2 feet? (Test.)

And keep going until you get a negative. Let's say "4 feet?" tested negative. That means 3 feet is your distance. Four feet is too far apart. You

SETTING UP TO RECEIVE THE DEVIC INFORMATION

can get even more precise by asking if the rows are to be wider than 3 feet. If you get a positive, then simply start at 3 feet and add in increments, testing after each increment.

3 feet? (positive)
3-1/4 feet? (positive)
3-1/2 feet? (positive)
3-3/4 feet? (negative) This means that the rows are to be placed precisely 3-1/2 feet apart.

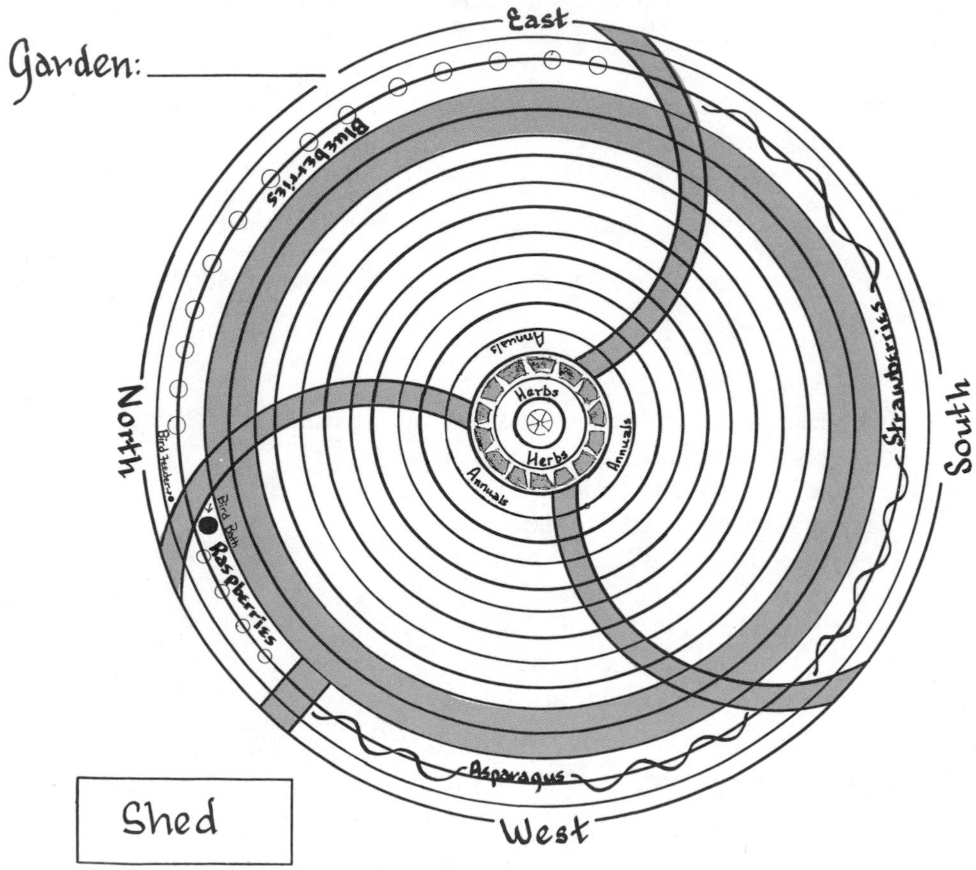

The Blank Perelandra Garden Chart

What has always impressed me with this part of the process is that I haven't had to work the row placement out mathematically in order to get all of them to fit, yet this devic information always fits. At least it has for me. If after placing the rows on your chart you have space left over, check:

SETTING UP TO RECEIVE THE DEVIC INFORMATION

a) The accuracy of your chart's scale.
b) Double-check the number of rows you are to have.
c) Double-check the distance between the rows.
d) Ask if you are to have this space left over. Something may be planned for that space that you aren't aware of yet. If you get a positive and this remains one of life's little mysteries, just keep moving on. Somewhere down the line you will receive clearly what is to happen here. I don't waste a lot of time demanding to know what is going on. I've made it a practice to move on the basis of the information I receive and trust that at some point all of the mysteries will clear up. And they have. Quite frankly, working with the mysteries and then watching them disappear is such fun and so much a validation of the partnership, that I wouldn't want to change this.

If you have more rows than space, double-check your information, including the measurement of the borders of the garden itself. This should clear up any problems.

THE SIMPLIFIED PLANNING CHART

I do not use the blank garden chart during the actual devic receiving process. I use that chart for the final transfer of all the information once I've received it. In essence, it's my final layout chart.

For the actual receiving process, I made a larger chart that serves more as a game board. The Perelandra simplified chart is 14-by-32-inches and its layout has nothing to do with the shape of the garden or the garden chart. You'll notice that the Perelandra garden chart has three sections created by the spiral paths. There are seven rows in each section that are used for the annual garden planting. The other rows make up the large circular path, the focal center and slate circle, the annual flower band, and the outer-most band which is three rows wide and contains all the perennial vegetables, fruit and bushes. The changes in planting which I deal with each year and in which the devic information is referring to occur within the interior seven rows. Each spiralled section contains one-third of each band or row.

So here's how I laid out the simplified chart:

SETTING UP TO RECEIVE THE DEVIC INFORMATION

A. Blueberry (section)	B. Raspberry/Asparagus	C. Strawberry
1.	1.	1.
2.	2.	2.
3.	3.	3.
4.	4.	4.
5.	5.	5.
6.	6.	6.
7.	7.	7.

Herb Band:
Annual Band:
Outer Band:

(Row 1 is the row closest to the center of the garden and row 7 is closest to the perennial band.)

What this does is simplify the garden layout in order to better accommodate the devic information process. If you can simplify your garden layout to this degree, I strongly suggest you do it. You need only make one simplified chart which can be used each year.

THE TAGS

The reason why you can use this chart each year is because you won't be writing on it. It remains a blank board upon which you will work. To work the board, I have made a collection of tags — 1/2-by-2-inch pieces of paper on which I have written the names of each vegetable, flower and herb that I can put into my garden. I also have a handful of blank tags to record new additions as I get that information.

As what goes into each row is identified, I simply place the appropriate tag into the corresponding position on the board. This way, I watch the garden develop and I can more easily see the relationship between the sections and between the rows. The tags also give the flexibility you'll need to correct any errors you might make with the kinesiology, or work with the devic level a bit if you are given several options in specific areas. You'll just be playing with tags rather than erasing and rewriting.

To label the tags, I suggest you wait until you go through your first identification process as to what vegetables, flowers and herbs should go into the garden. That comes a little further down the road and you'll be using seed catalogs for this process. All you'll have to do is transfer the information you get to the tags and you'll be set. For now, it would help if you just made a set of blank tags—about one hundred in number.

SETTING UP TO RECEIVE THE DEVIC INFORMATION

THE COLOR SQUARES

While you're cutting out tags, I suggest you cut out little color squares. As you go through the devic information process, you'll find that each row will have some interplanting pattern. That is, along with your vegetable, there may be flowers and possibly even herbs included. Get some colored paper, colored construction paper will do nicely, and choose six colors. One color each for above-ground vegetables, root vegetables, flowers, herbs, fruits, and one color for rocks, crystals or stones. Mine are about 1/2-inch square.

When you're trying to figure out how to interplant nine gold marigold plants and eleven onions with twenty broccoli plants, these squares come in real handy. Quite often the devic information concerns only the ratio of your interplanting and leaves its pattern up to you and your taste, so the squares allow you to play around and visually see the different patterns.

COLOR SYNCHRONIZATION

The colors I chose for my squares are the same colors I use throughout the entire planning and charting process. My colors are:

red — annual flowers
orange — herbs
green — above-ground vegetables
purple — root vegetables
burgundy — perennial fruits
white — minerals
lavender — roses

When I am setting up a chart where color coding is helpful, I keep the above coding. I do this for several reasons. By keeping the colors consistent, my eye and brain trained to them, I can quickly and efficiently translate this coding from chart to chart, and ultimately into the garden. So even though this may seem a bit much in detail now, further down the road it is a real time saver.

And there's another very good reason. Working with the charts is the microcosm of working in the garden itself. What goes on in terms of energy in the garden is reproduced in energy on the charts. Maintaining consistency in the symbolism I use with the charts greatly enhances this energy building and playing out. As you work with the charts, you'll find yourself becoming more sensitive to what is happening in them and maintaining consistency helps this development. That sensitive interplay between you and the charts will help you feel the building balance and power, as well as areas where more devic information is needed or you've made an error. You'll feel that weakness or instability right from the energy given off the charts.

With this in mind, you may wish to choose your color squares more carefully so that you can easily extend the color symbolism throughout the rest of your work. One consideration will be the colors you can easily get in either pencils or ink for those times you'll be writing in color code.

6

WHAT GOES WHERE

By the time you finish this chapter, you will know what is going into your garden, how many of each thing, where you're going to be putting them and in what pattern, and what color everything is to be. Pretty impressive, isn't it?

I'm going to break this information down to a series of progressive steps.

DEVA OF THE GARDEN CONNECTION

You'll be receiving the content and layout specifics from the deva of your garden. You've worked with this deva already in order to find out where the garden is to be placed and what shape it is to take. Try to remember that the devas hold the architectural information in nature—the blueprints, shall we say. What you'll be getting is the step-by-step read-out of the blueprints for your garden.

The direction and goal of the deva of the garden is to create as perfectly a balanced environment as can be achieved taking into consideration the land upon which the garden sits and its position concerning weather and ecological factors. Each individual aspect of the garden is chosen and placed with this in mind and aims toward the ultimate creation of a wholistically balanced garden environment. It is the quality of that balance which will provide the health and vitality of the garden.

Note: What follows is the overall planning and layout process and as you go through it you may wonder why you would even want to consider putting some of the flowers, herbs and minerals identified for you in your garden. For now, simply concentrate on identifying what is to go into the garden and trust that purpose and reason will be added later.

IDENTIFICATION AND SELECTION PROCESS

Calling in the Devic Plan

1. Get comfortable. Quiet yourself.

2. Ask to be connected to the Deva of the Garden. Test to verify that you are connected.

3. Call in the garden plan. Say something simple like:

> I would now like to receive the devic garden plan. Are we connected for this?

Then test to verify all is set and ready to go.

Selecting Your Vegetables

1. Get a good seed catalog—one that lists the vegetables available to you. This way you won't have to rack your brain trying to remember all the vegetables. Also have paper and pencil handy.

2. Connect with the Deva of the Garden. Test to make sure you're connected. Ask that the garden vegetables be identified now.

3. Using the catalog, go through the list of vegetables one by one, asking the Deva of the Garden:

> Are _____ (artichokes, green beans, lima beans, etc.) to go into the garden? (Test.)

Keep a list of every vegetable that tests positive.

4. Look at your completed list. Let's say your favorite vegetable in the entire world is the artichoke and it's not on the devic list. You have the right as co-creator of the garden to request that artichokes be included. I suggest you ask first: "Can artichokes be included in this garden?" If you get a negative, consider backing off your request this season, trusting that the deva knows something you don't. If you get a positive, add artichokes to your list.

It is during this step that you should make your personal wishes known because they must be taken into consideration for you to receive the proper layout of the garden. Inserting the artichoke information at this point and having the garden layout reflect that inclusion is much easier on everyone than trying to insert a personal wish during or after you get the layout. A lot of erasing will go on at that point. Every vegetable has its unique power and vibration which must be fully adjusted for when included as part of the whole.

5. You now have a complete list of the vegetables which are to go in your garden. You may double-check this list by asking:

Is the garden to include _____?

Then reading the list one by one and testing. Every vegetable should test positive. If one doesn't, test that vegetable again. If still negative, assume you are to remove it from the list.

Identifying the Herbs

1. You are still connected to the Deva of the Garden. Test to be sure.

2. Ask if you are to include herbs in this garden. (Test.)

3. For a positive response: Turn to the herb section in the seed catalog, or use any other source available to you, and go through the list one by one, asking if each is to be included. Keep a list of your positive responses.

4. Double-check the list as you did the vegetable list.

HINTS: The deva didn't include your favorite herb. Again, ask if it can be included as a favor to you. If you get a positive response, add it to the list. If you get a negative response, I again urge you to pull back from this request.

Second: You love herbs. You cook like crazy—especially Italian stuff. And when you asked if herbs were to be included in the garden, you got a negative response. It doesn't mean you can't have herbs. It is only saying that they are not to go into the main garden. Remember that you are building a balanced energy environment and herbs may not be appropriate as part of the package. Ask if you are to have an herb garden separate from the main garden. If so, do the same elimination process you did for locating the main garden and treat the herb garden as a unit within itself, designing and planning it with the deva of that garden.

Identifying the Flowers

1. Make sure you are still connected to the Deva of the Garden. Ask to now receive the identity of the flowers that are to go into the garden. (The requests you make as the first step are important in that they direct the deva as to what information you want. The requests coordinate the two of you.)

2. If your seed catalogs are anything like mine, you have about two hundred pages of every flower known to mankind listed and the idea of going through the pages one by one is exhausting you. I wouldn't tell you to do this. I wouldn't do it myself. I have my limits! Now is the time to call on your intuition. You can approach this list in a couple of ways. One is to simply leaf through the catalog looking at the pictures and casually taking in the names. Notice which pictures you are attracted to and which names stick in your mind. Make a list of all of these. Or, you can spend a little time thinking about flowers. Make a list of all the different kinds of flowers that pop into your mind.

3. The list that you have made is not what is going into the garden. It is the elimination process of all those flowers presented to you in the catalog. To be sure your list includes everything you need, ask:

Does this list include everything I'm going to need? (Test.)

If you get a negative: Ask that the missing flowers be identified and either allow them to pop up in your mind or leaf through the catalog again. Trust that the deva will get this information through to you. Add what you get to the list and once again ask if the list has everything. Keep doing this until the list tests positive. This is the flower list. I suggest you keep it for future reference so that you won't have to go through the elimination process again next year.

4. The list tests positive. Now, go through one by one asking if the individual flower is to be included in this year's garden. Make a list of your positive responses. These are the flowers that are to go into the garden.

Identifying Special Minerals and Crystals

1. Are you still connected to the Deva of the Garden? Request that the mineral and crystal information be given to you now.

2. Ask:

   Are there specific minerals or crystals that are to be included in the garden? (Test.)

3. If positive, go through the same process you've been doing for the vegetables, herbs and flowers. Your seed catalog isn't going to have a working list for you, so I'll give you a fair list right now.

Alexanderite	Moonstone
Amber	Obsidian
Aquamarine	Opal
Azurite	Star Opal
Benitoite	Pearl
Cacoxonite	Peridot
Coral	Clear Quartz Crystal
Diamond	Amethyst Quartz
Emerald	Citrine Quartz
Enstatite/Diopside	Rose Quartz
Fire Agate	Green Quartz
Fluorite	Blue Quartz
Garnet	Rutilated Quartz
Golden Beryl	Tourmalinated Quartz
Hiddenite	Tigereye
Ivory	Tourmaline
Jade	Watermelon Tourmaline
Kunzite	Blue & Red Tourmaline
Labradorite/Spectrolite	Green & Colorless Tourmaline
Chalcedony	Rubellite Tourmaline
Carnelian Agate	Green Tourmaline
Sard	Indicolite Tourmaline
Moss Agate	Catseye Tourmaline
Dendritic Quartz	Opalized Tourmaline
Brazil Agate	Turquoise
Bloodstone	Variscite
Red Jasper	Rhodochrosite
Green Jasper	Rhodonite
Yellow Jasper	Ruby
Brown Jasper	Rutile
Poppy Jasper	Sapphire
Picture Jasper	Smithsonite
Lapis Lazuli	Sodalite
Malachite	Tektites
Malachite/Azurite	Topaz

WHAT GOES WHERE

Before you panic and think you're going to have to get a second mortgage on the house, go ahead and test this list just to see what minerals and crystals the deva is talking about here. You might be pleasantly surprised at the modest results you get. As I've said, I started out with a natural quartz rock in the middle of the garden. Through the years, as the garden energy refined, I have been told to add such minerals as amber, coral, emerald, lapis lazuli, malachite/azurite, clear quartz, amethyst quartz, topaz, tigereye, and rhodochrosite. The size has not been an issue, but quality and clarity have been. So I've bought small but clear stones, and the cost has not been bad at all.

I would suggest you first find out the devic information on the minerals and crystals, then look around your area for a dealer or jeweler who can steer you in the right direction for obtaining the stones on your list. If something is unobtainable either through a jewelry maker, gem dealer or personal jewelry, connect with the deva again with a list of minerals that are available to you and ask for alternative choices. Go through your list, testing each item and record the positive results.

If you would like to understand some of the properties of the minerals you are going to put in your garden, I recommend a fine little book called *Healing Stoned* by Julia Lorusso & Joel Glick. (See *Supplies and Resources* for publishing information.)

APPROACHING THE CHART

Time to work with the simplified chart and the tags you made. You have the full list of what is to go into the garden. Now is the time to find out where to put them.

To simplify the transfer of information from the devic level to you, make sure your chart has the garden rows numbered and that the numbers correspond with the layout of the garden. This numbering can be arbitrary for it is nothing more than a way of identifying each row both to yourself and to the deva. So when you request the vegetables that are to go into row 1, you have a clear picture in your mind where #1 is positioned in the garden, all of the charts you work with correspond to this positioning, and the deva knows precisely which row you are referring to.

At Perelandra, row 1 is actually a circle which is divided into three sections. For clarity, I have identified each row/circle according to its section. Row 1 is either strawberry 1, blueberry 1, or raspberry/asparagus 1. Each corresponds to the section which has these specific perennials. If the layout of your garden is in sections, I suggest you break down your rows accordingly.

The keynote here is clarity. The clearer you are, the easier time you will have in this process of transferring devic information to your chart.

Positioning the Vegetables

1. Make sure you are connected to the Deva of the Garden. Test for verification.

2. Request the positioning of the vegetable information. You can verify that this request was received and all is ready by asking:

Are we ready to receive this information? (Test.)

3. Say:

I'd like to know the vegetables that are to go into row 1.

Again, saying these things is how you order and clarify your own intent and how the deva knows precisely what you are asking for. Saying something aloud requires us to order our thinking that much more. So whenever possible, I suggest you ask the questions and read through the lists aloud.

4. Either read through your vegetable list one by one, testing each vegetable, or go through your stack of tags one by one. If you wish, you may ask with each vegetable:

Does _____ go into row 1? (Test.)

Once you have set up what I have suggested in steps 1 through 3, you are implying this question with the deva and don't have to say it. Simply reading through the vegetables and testing each one implies the question. The positive responses are the vegetables that go into row 1.

5. Place the corresponding tag(s) of the vegetable(s) which tested positive onto the row 1 position of your chart.

6. Repeat this same process for each row. At Perelandra, I repeat the process for each row in each of the sections.

7. Having completed the process, I suggest you double-check your testing. You can do this quickly by reading aloud row by row the tags that are sitting there. Then ask:

Is row 1 correct? (Test.)

Any additions or subtractions? (Test.)

This is a check for your double check. A positive response means the row stands as is. If you got a negative to the first question, ask the second question differently.

Is there some vegetable to add? (Test.)

Is there one of the vegetables to take away? (Test.)

The positive answer gives you indication of the direction to take to correct row 1. If you are to add a vegetable, just test your list again. The positive is the vegetable you missed the first time.

If you tested positive to the second question, test each tag sitting on row 1 by asking:

Should _____ be in row 1?

The negative response tells you what tag to remove. If you got a positive response for both questions, you need to add one and take one away.

HINTS: If broccoli tested positive for rows 2 and 7, then make an extra broccoli tag and indicate broccoli in both rows. Remember, the garden layout is based on energy dynamics, not logic.

If you have some vegetables that had tested positive for the garden but were not placed, read those vegetables aloud and ask the deva if they are to be placed in this year's garden. If positive, ask if you have missed them in the testing so far. If positive again, go through each extra vegetable asking:

Does _____ belong in row 1? (Test)
Row 2? (Test)
Row 3? (Test)

And so on, until you test positive. Then read all the vegetables in that row and ask if it is now complete. Test.

If the extra vegetables test negative for this year's garden, just put the tags aside to be used next year.

Positioning the Flowers.

1. Connect with the Deva of the Garden. (Test.)

2. Go through the same process you used for positioning the vegetables. You'll probably need several tags for each variety of flower. Quite often a specific variety will be placed in more than one position. Also, if you have a focal point in the garden that is outside the row pattern, extend your testing as you go along to find out what is to be included in this space. Treat the focal point as a row and test it exactly as you have been doing for the rows.

3. Double-check your information by reading through the rows one by one as you did with the vegetables. Read and test the vegetables and flowers together for each row.

Positioning the Herbs

1. Connect with the Deva of the Garden. Test for verification.

2. You guessed it. Go through the same process you used for vegetables and flowers.

3. Double-check your information.

HINT: Onions and its family are considered herbs and vegetables, and I have onion tags made for both. When I am positioning the vegetables, I treat onions as a vegetable and when I'm positioning the herbs, I treat them as an interplanting herb. This tag reads "onion herb" so that I can differentiate it from the vegetable. The differentiation will make a difference a little later when we're laying out the pattern the row is to be planted in.

Positioning the Minerals and Crystals

1. Make sure you are connected with the Deva of the Garden.

2. Do this routine again.

3. Double-check your information.

Interplanting with Color

Considering the color of the flowers used in interplanting is another refinement of gardening with energy dynamics. Just as each plant variety in itself has its own energy, so, too, does color. If you have red cabbage interplanted with petunias, you can't assume that means red petunias. It could mean pink or white, or whatever color it takes to achieve the desired energy strength and stability needed in the row with the red cabbage. So now turn your focus to color.

1. Don't forget to be connected with the Deva of the Garden.

2. Address each row individually, as you have been doing all along. If there are flowers in row 1, you can either go through a mental list of the

colors you know this flower comes in, or use your seed catalog as a source for its colors, or make an all-purpose list of the different colors flowers tend to be and use that as the guide for testing each flower.

3. To clearly set up your process, say:

What color is the _____ (flower) in row 1 to be?

Then test through the colors one by one. The positive response is the color. I suggest you write the color on a blank tag and place it on or beside the flower tag. This clear action will aid you when you double-check your work, and save your flower tags since the colors aren't the same year after year.

HINTS: If you get a positive response for two or more colors (This is rare.): Double-check to make sure your positive responses hold. If they do, it just means you are to have more than a single color in the row. (Determining the ratio of each color is explained in the next section.)

If you have two vegetables positioned in a row and there have been two flowers identified for the same row, you'll need to know which flower is to be interplanted with which vegetable. This is simple. Place either one of the flower tags with one of the vegetables—place them in such a way that you are indicating them to be a pair. Then ask:

Do these two belong together?

If you get a positive, you now know how the vegetables and flowers pair up. If you get a negative, reverse the pairing. (Test to verify.) If you have herbs and minerals also indicated for that row, just keep pairing the tags until you get what is to be interplanted with which vegetable.

4. Double-check your work.

Ratio

You know what is to go into the garden, in which rows, what is to be interplanted with what, and their colors. You are progressively building the energy base of your garden by addressing all of these issues. It's a process of refinement. The next step is to find out how many of each vegetable, flower, herb and mineral are to go into each row.

The concept of energy building is really a precision art. Not only are the rows being laid out with an energy balance in mind, but each row's relationship with all the other rows also have an energy balance. It matters to the other rows how many of a particular vegetable you place in any one row. Changing the ratio within a row shifts the energy balance of the garden and the other rows must be adjusted accordingly.

To find the ratio:

1. Yep. Make sure you're connected to the Deva of the Garden.

2. Starting with row 1, address the vegetable first. Ask:
   How many _____ (vegetable) are to be in row 1? Then test, asking:
   One? (positive)
   Two? (positive)
   Three? (positive)

And so on sequentially until you test negative. Go back a number to the one which last tested positive, and that's the number to go into that row.

If you have an herb, flower or mineral in that row, do the same process for them.

How many _____ (flower) go into row 1?
How many _____ (herb) go into row 1?
How many _____ (mineral/crystal) go into row 1?

HINTS: Again, since I use the same tags every year, and each year the ratios are different, I don't write the ratio information on the tags. I keep a row-by-row record of the ratio of everything on a separate piece of paper.

A little time saver (and finger saver) in this process is to not always go through your count sequentially. For example, you have a 30 foot row that calls for broccoli. There's a good chance you're going to have more than 2 plants. I approach the numbering in blocks.

Are there more than 5? (positive)
More than 10? (positive)
More than 15? (negative) This tells me the number is between 10 and 15, and I start the sequential count at 11.
Is it 11? (positive)
12? (positive)
13? (positive)
14? (negative)

I go back to my last positive and I know the row is to take 13 broccoli plants.

For vegetables such as beets, carrots, loose leaf lettuce, spinach, green beans, lima beans (vegetables which have a closer planting) you don't have to deal with precise numbers of plants. That definitely would be tedious. If a row calls for beets, you can approach your ratio in two ways.

a) How many feet in this row is to be planted in beets?
5 feet. (Test)

10 feet. (Test)

And so on until you get a negative on your block count and can begin your sequential count. You can get something as precise as 27 feet of beets.

b) Approach the row not in feet but in segments by asking:

Is 1/4 of the row to be planted in beets? (positive)

1/3 of the row? (positive)

1/2 the row? (positive)

2/3 row? (negative).

The answer is 1/2 that row is to be planted in beets.

Another situation: You got that you are to plant a specific row completely with green beans. You also got that the interplant for the beans is radishes. (For the past five years, I've been given this information at Perelandra.) I don't deal with precise numbers in a row such as this. I approach it as follows:

Is this to be a full row of green beans? (positive)

Is this to be a 1-foot-wide row? (negative)

Is this to be the width of 6 inches? (positive) (Any time you might be considering wide row planting, get this cleared with the deva. It will affect your ratio information.)

How many pounds of seed are to be planted in this row?

1/2 lb.? (positive)

3/4 lb.? (positive)

1 lb.? (positive)

1-1/4 lb.? (negative)

It's 1 pound of seed to be spaced into this row. Now I address the radish interplanting.

Are the radish seeds to be mixed with the bean seeds when planted? (positive)

How much per 1 pound of bean seeds? (You'll notice in most seed catalogs that you can buy radish seeds by the fraction of an ounce and the ounce.)

1/2 oz.? (positive)

3/4 oz.? (positive)

1 oz.? (positive)

1-1/4 oz.? (negative)

The ratio of interplanting is 1 ounce radish seeds mixed with 1 pound bean seeds. If you have more than one row of beans, don't assume this ratio is the same. Test the second row separately.

3. Once you've completed the ratio count for row 1, move on to row 2 and the rest of the rows.

4. Double-check your work by reading the ratio count of each item, row by row. The Perelandra garden row 1 (strawberry section) has chives, leeks and gold marigolds. The ratio is 2 chive plants, 10 leeks, 2 gold marigold plants. I would double-check this row by asking:

In strawberry row 1 are there to be 2 chive plants? (positive)
10 leeks? (positive)
2 gold marigolds? (positive)

This way, if I've made a mistake, I immediately know where the problem is. If I had read the row in its entirety with just one test for the whole row and had gotten a negative, I'd have to go back and break down the row to find the problem.

Hills

Some vegetables traditionally have been planted in hills—a mound of soil with two or more plants. Watermelon, squash, melons, cucumbers are the usual ones. For these vegetables, I'll ask the deva if they are to be planted in hills or singly. If they are to be in hills, I'll ask how many hills and do the kinesiology sequential count. Then I'll ask how many plants per hill.

Changing the Ratio

You have just made the horrifying discovery that, according to your chart, row 6 calls for eight hills of zucchini, three plants in each hill. That's twenty-four plants of zucchini. Now, if you can't imagine the impact twenty-four zucchini plants will have on your kitchen—and sanity—around July you have never gardened before. Trust me, this is a dilemma. You have several ways to approach the situation. No matter what approach you use, keep in mind that the ratio of all the plants in your garden is not arbitrary. It responds to an energy balance and is part of the building toward that balance.

1. Trust in the process and accept the twenty-four zucchini plants. This happens to be the option I would choose. I would be curious to see what twenty-four zucchini plants do for a garden balance. So, my reason would be educational, but then this is the major thrust in my relationship with the Perelandra garden and often leads me to accept the unusual and seemingly impractical.

There would still be this little issue of what to do with the produce from all those plants. You could line up a bunch of unsuspecting city-dwelling friends and let them figure out what to do with their two-hundred-pound allotment of zucchini. Or, you could do something I heard on the radio. Someone discovered zucchini floats. They suggested we haul all the extra garden zucchini in the country to the Great Lakes, stick a stake and a sail on them and float them to Canada.

2. You could also consider returning the extra produce back to the garden in the form of compost. A fair feeding exchange.

3. You could simply refuse to deal with the problem and request that the zucchini ratio be reduced to a manageable four plants. This can be done. But in order to maintain the garden balance, you'll need to go through all the rows again for changes in position, ratio, color, even interplanting. In essence, making a ratio change has an impact on the entire garden. If you don't accommodate the resulting changes, you'll be breaking down the very energy dynamic you're trying to build.

Energy Devices and Generators

What I mean are things like genesa crystals, pyramid/tensor energy posters and devices, copper rods, ionic generators. Anything that is put into the garden for the purpose of shifting, changing or cleansing energy. There are a number of such devices that have been developed which you may be interested in trying.

At Perelandra, the center of the garden includes, beside the quartz crystal, a tensor energy poster and a genesa crystal. The poster generates what is called "tensor energy" but is familiarly known as "pyramid energy." And the genesa crystal is an antenna device made up of four copper circles, two feet in diameter, which when placed together at specific angles creates a ball. This serves as an antenna which attracts to it the life force energy from all form within its range, cleanses the energy, and spins it back out into the environment. (See *Supplies and Resources* for information.)

The introduction of these two devices was gradual and part of the long-range building process of the garden. If you have an interest in something like this, I suggest you check with the Deva of the Garden to make sure the device is harmonious with your garden environment. Also, if you have already done all the chart planning for the year, it would be important to make sure the addition of such a device does not change your chart information. These devices can be extremely powerful. When used as a harmonious addition to the garden, they strengthen and enhance the balance that is already there. When they are out of place, they can throw a garden environment into a state of chaotic disaster. This is not to say that the device itself is a disaster, but when used improperly it can wreck havoc.

A sudden interest or attraction to one of these devices should not be ignored. This could very well be the interplay between the nature intelligences and yourself through the level of your intuition calling attention to something that is to be added to the garden. So check your hits and insights with the Deva of the Garden by asking:

Is my sudden interest in _____ important to the garden? (Test.)

If positive, pursue what you are to do and when.

Planting Position and Pattern for Each Row

Now's the time to use the 1/2-inch color squares you cut out. You have the ratio of each vegetable, herb and flower in the rows but you don't have the pattern of interplanting. This is the final piece of information you'll need for the overall design of the garden.

1. Again, be sure you're connected to the Deva of the Garden.

2. Address each row separately. While focusing on row 1, the very first question to ask:

Does the interplanting pattern matter?

Quite often, I'm given the freedom to design the row as I'd like, as long as I keep the proper ratio. If I get a negative response to the first question, that means I can play with my color squares until I come up with a pattern I like. I have a different color for vegetables, herbs, flowers and crystals. To help clarify, I'll give you an example of a row pattern.

In 1985, row 4 of the strawberry section had 5 brussels sprouts (BS) interplanted with 8 white petunias (P), plus 11 celery (C) with 5 white petunias (P). My pattern was as follows:

2P . BS . P . BS . P . BS . P . BS . P . BS . 2P / 11 C . 5 P

In this one row, I show even interspacing (brussels sprouts and petunias) and cluster spacing (celery and petunias). Since I had full freedom in the patterning, I chose this layout for both practicality and personal esthetics.

If I have two vegetables and their interplantings in one row, as with the example I just used, I will determine direction in the row—for example, north half/south half, or right end/left end—and ask which vegetable is to be planted in which half of the row. To clarify: In the above example, I had both brussels sprouts and celery plus their interplantings positioned in row 4. I determined right side/left side of the row, a direction decision I kept consistent throughout my garden, and asked:

Does it matter which vegetable is planted on the right half of the row? (Positive).

Are the brussels sprouts to be planted on the right? (Negative).

Now I know brussels sprouts is on the left, celery is on the right.

3. Once I have the pattern laid out with the squares, I transfer that information over to paper using the initial of the plant and reproduce the patterning. I find that when it comes time to move that pattern into the garden, it's very easy to visualize when it has been reproduced on paper.

HINT: I even color-code the pattern on paper. Above-ground vegetable initials in green. Root crops in purple. Annual flower initials in red. Herb initials in orange. Again, visually this facilitates matters quite a bit when it comes time to transfer all the information into the garden.

1985 Perelandra Garden Patterning: Strawberry Section

1. Chives (2) Leeks (10) Marigold: gold (2)
C . M . L (10) . M . C

2. Red Okra (4) Petunia (3)
2RO . 3P . 2RO

3. Yellow Snap Beans (16 feet.) Red Basil (6)
3RB . 16 ft. YSB . 3RB

4. Br. Sprouts (5) Wh. Petunia (8) / Celery (11) Wh. Petunia (5)
2P . BS . P . BS . P . BS . P . BS . P . BS . 2P / 11C . 5P

5. Carrots (27 feet) / Green Peppers (3) Red Basil (3)
27 ft. C / GP . RB . GP . RB . GP . RB

6. Snap Peas (17-by-2-feet) / Corn (36 feet)
17-by-2-ft. SP / 36 ft. C

7. Sweet Banana Peppers (3) Anaheim Peppers (3) / Corn (36 feet)
3SBP . 3AP / 36 ft. C

FURTHER HINTS: Sometimes I am told to equally interspace the flower or herb with the vegetable, and in so doing I find I have extra color squares left over in my hand. For example: I have four zucchini interplanted with twelve nasturtiums to be equally spaced with nasturtiums at the beginning and end of the row. I can easily lay out:

Z . 3N . Z . 3N . Z . 3N . Z

I have three nasturtium squares left in my hand to be divided and placed at each end of the row. My first question to the Deva of the Garden:

Does it matter which end gets two nasturtiums? (Positive)

Is it the left end? (Positive)

So now the row pattern reads:

2N . Z . 3N . Z . 3N . Z . 3N . Z . 1N

This may be the most important hint I have given you yet! Transferring the patterning information into the garden can be a bit time consuming and frustrating. The problem of properly spacing the pattern in the row is greatly facilitated if you use poker chips! If you saw the Perelandra garden in early spring, it would look like I'm planting poker chips in all the rows. What's nifty about the chips is that they're convenient, easily movable, easy to see, waterproof, cheap, and come in three colors. In a pattern, one color can indicate the position of a vegetable, another an herb, and the third a flower.

The Garden Chart

You have all the information you need to fill in the large garden chart. As much information as you like can be transferred over. I transfer position, interplanting and ratio, and I color code the vegetables, flowers and herbs. I used to transfer the row patterning onto the chart by using symbols, but found that made the information too intricate to easily read. So I keep the patterning on separate paper.

I have included (on page 75) the complete Perelandra garden chart for 1985 so that you can see what all the information, once pulled together, can look like. In the past, I've been reluctant to flash this thing in public for invariably someone will reach for pen and paper and begin madly copying it to use for their garden. I feel confident that in the context of this book, you realize that it would be useless and counterproductive to ignore all that is being suggested here and reproduce this chart for your garden. But in case you have any doubts, let me assure you that it would be a colossal waste of time and effort and that it would not give you the desired results of a balanced garden environment. It did, however, give *me* a beautiful, balanced, abundant garden in 1985, and a base upon which the garden of 1986 was built.

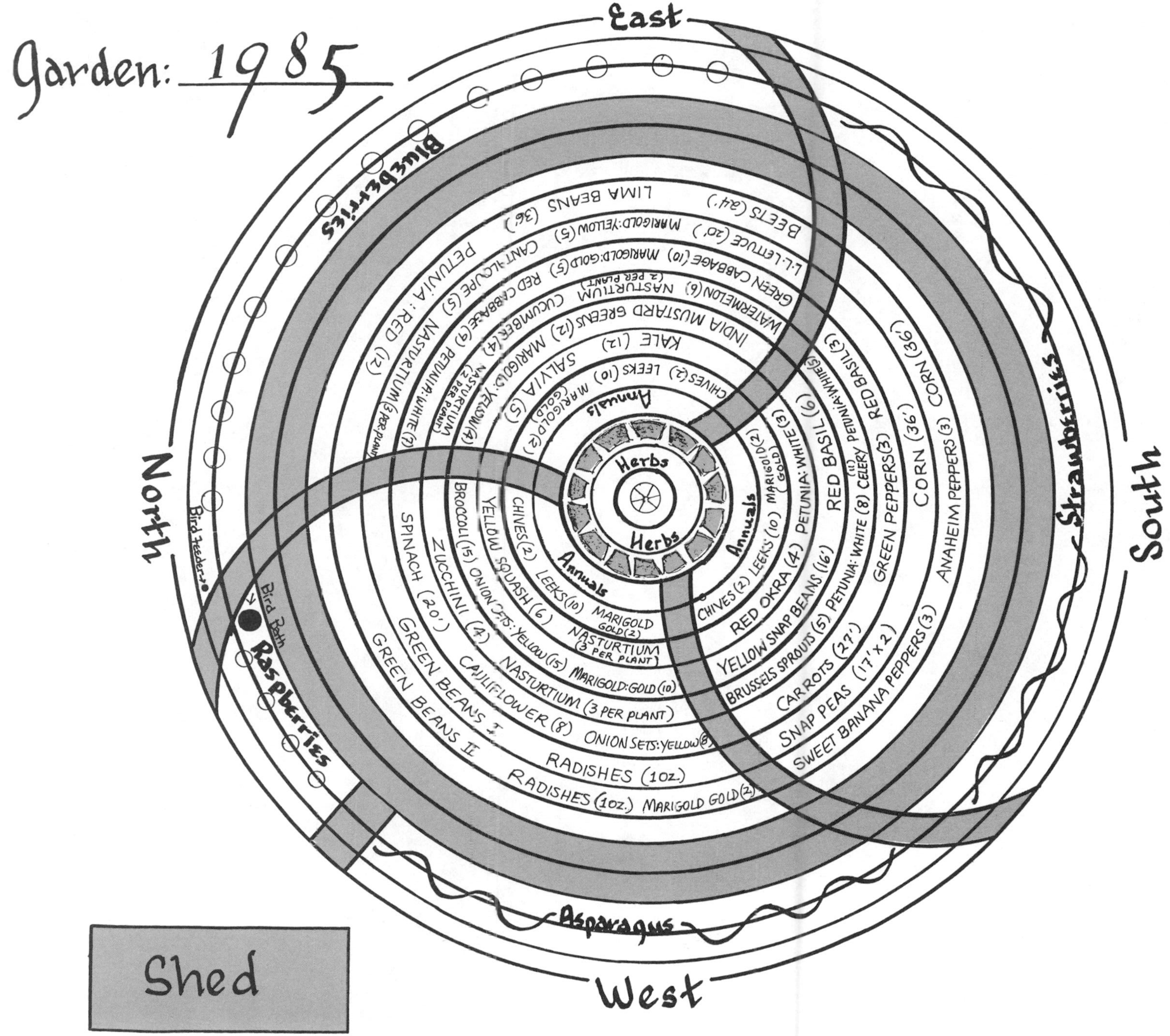
Garden: 1985
East
South
West
North
Shed
Blueberries
Strawberries
Asparagus
Raspberries
Bird Bath
Bird Feeder
Herbs
Herbs
Annuals
Annuals
Annuals
LIMA BEANS (36')
BEETS (24')
MARIGOLD: YELLOW (5)
L.L. LETTUCE (20')
MARIGOLD: GOLD (5)
GREEN CABBAGE (10)
CANTALOUPE (5)
PETUNIA: RED (12)
WATERMELON (6)
NASTURTIUM (2 PER PLANT)
RED CABBAGE (9)
NASTURTIUM (3 PER PLANT)
INDIA MUSTARD GREENS (12)
CUCUMBER (4)
PETUNIA: WHITE (7)
KALE (12)
MARIGOLD: YELLOW (4)
NASTURTIUM (2 PER PLANT)
CHIVES (2)
LEEKS (10)
MARIGOLD (GOLD) (2)
SALVIA (5)
CHIVES (2)
LEEKS (10)
MARIGOLD (GOLD) (2)
PETUNIA: WHITE (3)
RED BASIL (6)
PETUNIA: WHITE (5)
RED BASIL (3)
CELERY (11)
PETUNIA: WHITE (8)
GREEN PEPPERS (3)
CORN (36')
CORN (36')
ANAHEIM PEPPERS (3)
CHIVES (2)
RED OKRA (4)
YELLOW SNAP BEANS (16')
BRUSSELS SPROUTS (5)
CARROTS (27')
SNAP PEAS (17' x 2)
SWEET BANANA PEPPERS (3)
CHIVES (2)
LEEKS (10)
MARIGOLD GOLD (2)
YELLOW SQUASH (6)
NASTURTIUM (3 PER PLANT)
BROCCOLI (15)
ONION SETS: YELLOW (15)
MARIGOLD: GOLD (10)
ZUCCHINI (4)
NASTURTIUM (3 PER PLANT)
SPINACH (20')
CAULIFLOWER (8)
ONION SETS: YELLOW (8)
GREEN BEANS I
RADISHES (1oz.)
GREEN BEANS II
RADISHES (1oz.)
MARIGOLD GOLD (2)

DEVA OF THE PERELANDRA GARDEN

It might simplify one's understanding of the planning stage if one saw his garden as a fine, delicate, gourmet soup in which the eventual success of the soup depends on the lightest and most careful of touches. A pinch of salt would add to the perfection, but a pinch and a half would break the delicate balance the gourmet chef attempts to create and reduce his soup to an ordinary, perhaps even unpalatable experience.

When we work with humans to consciously create a garden environment we approach the task with the lightest of touches so as not to tilt the balance at any given moment. A specific crystal placed in one position may be the perfect pinch of salt, in another position it is the pinch and a half. This applies equally to everything placed into the garden, be it mineral, vegetable or animal.

We might also add that we do not view any particular season as an isolated moment in time. We have an overview of the garden and a sense of direction that can be translated into a span of many years. We see one season as a unit within itself, but we also see how that particular unit connects into the whole, plus what lies ahead in terms of its growth and development toward environmental balance. All of these issues are part and parcel of what we consider when called on by man to help him create the garden of the future.

Each season is a step in the healing process of the garden and its overall environment. Although you may balk at the notion of the twenty-four zucchini plants, as Machaelle has used in illustration, we urge you to seriously consider bearing with us as we move your garden through its healing processes. At this point in time, we of the devic level understand the healing steps in which nature must travel. In the garden environment where man and nature join in partnership, we look to him to help us by implementing those steps. Man will not experience much understanding or logic toward what we are suggesting he implement, for these moves will be beyond present human logic. In time, as we grow together in our partnership experience, man will learn through observation and a new logic and reason will enfold him. For now, as Machaelle suggests, we ask that you trust our input. And see the garden as both a delicate gourmet soup as you approach the individual season and a progressing unit of energy moving through a long-range healing process. Both of these dynamics are fully present in the planning information we give you.

We recognize your right at any time to say "no" to any suggestion we give you. We fully recognize your position as intelligent souls of the universe with the unencumbered right to dictate the direction of your life and environment. We will accept your "no" without hesitation and will adjust our information to you accordingly. But we wish to point out two things to you.

One. Although we can accommodate an arbitrary change in the planning and progression of the garden, it may only serve to unnecessarily slow the healing process your garden must go through.

Two. We of nature are also intelligent life within the universe and for the sake of the evolutionary growth on the planet, we not only ask but demand that humans fully recognize ***our*** *position.*

7

SEED

The issue of selecting seeds can be quite an emotional experience for us gardeners. Quite frankly, I completely skirt the issue by allowing the intelligences connected with my garden to pick their own seeds. I don't make the assumption that seeds obtained from organically grown plants are better for my garden than the seeds from the large seed companies. I also don't make the assumption that organically grown seeds aren't better. As I said, I skirt the issue.

Right about here, I'd like to add an insight I've had about the large seed companies. Nature looks to us to form co-creative partnerships, not manipulative ones. From my interaction with other gardeners, especially organic gardeners because they have developed a fine sensitivity around the quality of all that they put into their gardens, there is a general opinion that the horticultural research and development supported by the large companies is all manipulative and geared toward economical convenience. Case in point is the development of the square tomato so that it can be packed more efficiently and shipped more easily. The result is that we're stuck with a fairly tasteless, but conveniently shipped square tomato.

I point this out to illustrate that I am not insensitive to the opinion held by these gardeners. But my insight is simple. It dawned on me that not all traditional scientists working in the area of plant development are manipulators. And if *I* wanted to dedicate my energy and efforts in this area, I would certainly consider working with a large company for very practical reasons. They have the money to back the research and the money to give me a decent salary. So it seemed reasonable to me that tucked away in these large research centers are scientists with caring hearts who think and work, whether they consciously know it or not, in a co-creative partnership with devic intelligence.

One thing I've learned over the years is that because of the ecological and environmental changes on the planet, we cannot assume that the same plant that flourished one hundred years ago would flourish today. The conditions have changed. The plant most likely needs to be "updated." And this is where sensitive scientific development comes in.

So here we are, back to the original question of what seeds are best for my garden. I have found that the deva of each vegetable knows the quality of all the types of seeds available that will produce that vegetable. I also have learned that each vegetable doesn't have just one "correct" seed. Determining the proper seed not only has to take into account the quality of scientific plant development, but also the conditions of your garden and the environment around that garden. So although I plant the De Cicco broccoli in the Perelandra garden and the choice was made devically, it doesn't mean that the De Cicco broccoli seed is the one for your garden.

Again, I sidestep the issue. I let the deva of each vegetable do the deciding. Up to this point you've primarily worked with the Deva of the Garden. Now you're going to branch out and begin working with the individual devas of the specific plants you have identified for your garden. This is real easy, too.

1. Collect your seed catalogs and have a seat in a nice, warm (because you should be getting ready to order your seeds in late February—early March), comfortable chair. Bring your fingers along. You'll be using them. Also paper, pencil and the list you made of the plants to go into the garden—or your garden chart.

A digression: If you do not have a seed catalog, I suggest you write to Burpee Co. and Parks Seed Company. They will gladly oblige you. I'm suggesting both companies because you should work with at least two lists of seed selections. Their addresses:

W. Atlee Burpee Company	Park Seed
300 Park Ave.	P.O.Box 46
Warminster, PA 18974	Greenwood, SC 29648-0046
Tele: 215-674-4900	Tele: 803-374-3341

I have another address to give you for a very different kind of seed catalog. It is published by the Seed Savers Exchange and is called *The Garden Seed Inventory*. It is an 8-1/2-by-11-inch, 448-page inventory of

SEED

239 U.S. and Canadian seed catalogs It lists nearly 6,000 non-hybrid vegetable varieties that are still being offered commercially and includes the variety name, range of days to maturity, a list of all the companies still carrying that variety, and the plant's description. The book in paperback costs $12. The address:

Seed Savers Exchange
Kent Whealy—Director
203 Rural Avenue
Decorah, Iowa 52101

Back to the seed selection. You are armed with your catalogs and comfortably seated.

2. Let's say the first thing on your list is green beans. Connect with the deva by saying:

I wish to be connected to the Deva of Green Beans. (Test.)

(You may feel a sense of energy washing over you, very much like the sensation you may have felt with the Deva of the Garden. This is just your feeling the actual connection occurring. But again, don't be bothered if you feel nothing. The connection is verified using kinesiology.)

If the test result is negative, check your situation to make sure you are in a quiet place and feeling calm. Check also to see if you need to eliminate any distractions. Focus your attention fully and again request to be connected with the Deva of Green Beans. Test. (You'll get a positive this time!)

As you open to the individual devas, you will be "meeting" them for the first time and may wish to spend a moment getting acquainted before getting down to business. There are a number of ways you can do this. One is to quietly be with the deva. Feel its energy around you and sense its presence. Another is to literally talk to the deva. It doesn't hear—devas don't have ears. But it easily and readily translates the intent of the energy behind your words. You could spend time talking about your feelings about the plant to which the deva is connected. If you wish to enter into a dialogue, simply say what you'd like and then spend a moment being quiet. Quite often, the deva will use your intuition, your sense of visualization, even your ability to perceive emotion to communicate with you. When you have finished and feel comfortable, you can get down to business.

3. For green beans, you'll need to know if you are to plant bush beans or pole beans. Use the same yes/no format you've been using.

Are the green beans to be bush beans? (negative)

Are they to be pole beans? (positive)

By testing the second time, you double-checked your answer to the first question. You can bypass this by assuming a negative on the first question automatically means a positive on the second one. But I would recommend that until you feel very confident about your testing, it might be a good idea to double-check your answers.

4. I'll assume you are using the Burpee and the Park catalogs. Open one to the pole bean listing. Read to yourself or aloud the list. What you are doing here is making known to the Deva of the Green Beans the choice of variety from this particular catalog. The Deva may know the quality of the seed in question but it does not keep a listing of which company carries which seed. Once the list is read, ask:

Is the correct seed available in this list? (Test).

If positive, go back through the list one by one and test until you find the variety that tests positive. The implied question in this testing is:

Is _____ the correct variety?

If you get more than one positive, ask if one would be better than the other. If positive, eliminate your choices to one by asking which is the best, and test again. The positive is your best choice.

If you got a negative result, they are considered equal choices and you get to pick.

5. If, after reading the list from one catalog, you received a negative result to that list, go to your second catalog and repeat the above process, starting with reading the list aloud.

6. Repeat this process for each vegetable, flower and herb that are to go into your garden.

HINTS: At first glance, this may seem like a never-ending chore, but in actuality it goes rather quickly. For one thing, although I may receive twenty catalogs each year, I only use two or three. The lists of varieties offered in the larger catalogs are quite complete and beyond the first several large catalogs, the lists begin to repeat themselves. The effort is well worth it to assure you have the right combination of varieties planted in the garden.

Second: If you have gardened for years, you probably are aware of the specific variety of each vegetable favored by nearly everyone in your area. Word gets around. When I began getting my seed information devically, I was quite surprised at how different my list was in comparison to the favored varieties used by everyone around me.

Lastly: I get the devic information on the seeds each year. I don't assume last year's list to be correct for this year. Changing conditions can have that much of an impact. And so can the evolving healing process that goes on in the garden year after year.

SEED

DEVA OF BROCCOLI

I would like to give you insight into how we of the devic realm view seeds. Humans tend to see them as that which contains a miracle. From a small acorn eventually comes a large oak tree. We of the devic realm can truly appreciate this notion, but we view seeds differently.

When we create on the devic level that which you help bring into form on the physical level, we collect, if we may say it this way, a variety of independent and individual energies which when combined, form one unit of complex but harmonious energy. In my specific case, you have named this unit "broccoli." Every trait and dynamic, seen or unseen by the human eye, has in back of it a specific energy that we on the devic level have drawn into the unit.

Each time a seed is produced by the plant, that full unit of energy, in its most powerful and condensed state, is passed on in the seed. When the plant is assisted and allowed to flourish in the state of the perfect harmony which is inherent in the devically created unit, that perfection also is passed on through the seed.

However, if the plant itself does not develop in form to its full potential, that original devic unit is altered. What is then passed on is not the original unit, but an alteration of that unit. I point this out to show you that there is a relationship between what we of the devic realm create and the quality with which that energy of creation expresses in form.

Now, if left alone without the interaction of humans, the broccoli unit of energy would manifest through the levels of reality and eventually come into form on the planet. There, with the assistance of the nature spirits, the devically created energy would be released from the seed and allowed to develop to its full potential. The combination of the creation, the release, and the development would combine into a more expanded energy dynamic and that would be transferred in total within the seeds from the plant to then be dropped onto the soil, and in right timing, once again be released into form.

For a long time, humans allowed nature to take its own course and for the most part, even when humans became directly involved in their food production, nature was still allowed to take its own course. In recent times however, technology has given man the ways and means to interfere with the process of the devic unit grounding into form through the conduit of the seed. He can either change the timing and development of the plant to such a degree that what is passed on in the seed is an alteration caused by not allowing the form to fully express its own perfect energy. Or, he can intrude his own desires and wishes into the very core of the unit energy, breaking into the devic code as it were, and alter the unit so that the form that develops from this fully expressed energy is also altered. In both cases, what you call "hybridization" occurs and in most cases you are left with a plant in a weakened state that requires, as do most things in weakened conditions, special care.

It is too late in our evolutionary development on planet Earth for man to simply recognize his interference and back out of the picture completely to allow nature to repair itself and once again take its own course. The interdependence between man and nature is too vast and the development of technology too sophisticated to allow such a move.

As has been already mentioned, the coming together in a co-creative partnership is presently the appropriate and sought after move. One does not have to be a scientist to join us in this particular partnership. One need only know how to listen, and then act. I have stated that there are two ways to alter the devic unit. One is to enter the unit itself using specific technologies already present in order to change the combination of energies we created on the devic level. This route is not where our overall partnership can be created. This is where we seek to unite with the scientific community in order to co-creatively repair that which already exists and develop that which must be for the future.

It is the second way a devic unit is altered where the person outside the scientific community can work with us. If physical form can be manipulated so drastically by humans that the devic energy becomes misaligned with its form, it is also possible to work co-creatively with the form to realign it to the devic energy.

In very practical terms, when I am asked to identify the specific broccoli variety that is best suited for your garden, I choose the seed that maintains the strongest connections to that inner devic unit. As Machaelle has stated, there is more than one broccoli variety whose seed maintains a strong connection. Even when left on our own, there would be more than one variety of each plant to accommodate the various conditions in which the plant is likely to grow.

Once the seed is selected, I will work to give you the information upon which you may act in order to assist the development of the form in ways that will strengthen and even alter that complex inner core of energy. In a very real way, we of the devic realm will function in the position of the overseeing scientist and you will function as our assistant with the aid of the nature spirit level. Through a series of gradual and healing changes, the form and the devic unit will be reunited. And once again, the relationship between the devic creation, the encapsulation of that energy in the seed, and the releasing of the original creation into its full form potential will be manifest on the planet.

8

TRANSPLANTS VS. DIRECT SEED PLANTING

Here we go with another emotional issue. In light of the subtle energy fields and stabilizing energy lines which develop around plants as they sprout and grow, is it right to disturb this by moving plants around in the transplanting process? Some feel adamant that all plants should be started from seed in the garden so that none of nature's energy will be disturbed. Others who live in the northern climates have to transplant if they want to harvest their gardens before the first snow fall.

I completely sidestep this issue also. I go through the list of vegetables, herbs and flowers one by one, using this quick process:

1) Open to the Deva of _____. (The deva of each plant.) Then test to verify your connection.

2) Ask:

Is _____ to be transplanted into the garden?

I make a list of all the positive responses. The negative responses are the plants that are to be started from seed in the garden.

3) Release your connection from each deva by one or all of the below:

a. seeing yourself disconnected from the deva.
b. requesting that the deva now release from you.
c. saying "thank you" to indicate you are finished.

TRANSPLANTS VS. DIRECT SEED PLANTING

(It is a good idea that you get into the habit of releasing or disconnecting in a clear manner anytime you have completed working with a deva or nature spirit. This helps them understand what you are doing and keeps the lines of communication clear between you. It is especially helpful when you are calling in the nature intelligences one right after the other in a list.)

I have found through the years that the transplant/seed distinction has more to do with the overall garden timing than anything else. There is a planting rhythm in the spring which reflects the energy building process and relates to weather and insect patterns throughout the entire growing season. (I explain how to get the planting rhythm in Chapter 10.) Because it is based on variables, I get this information annually and do not assume that since broccoli was transplanted last year, it will be again this year.

One of the fun parts of co-creative energy gardening is to adhere to what looks to be totally illogical and somewhat arbitrary spring rhythms and watch how they play out to the garden's benefit throughout the season.

One more thing: By skirting the transplant/seed issue, I do not answer the question about disturbing all those subtle energy fields which form around plants. I know these energy fields exist and that the health and balance of plants are greatly enhanced when these fields are undisturbed. By letting nature make its own choice in the matter, I also make the assumption that whatever is to be transplanted will have its energy fields taken into consideration and established accordingly.

PAN

I will address the energy fields surrounding plant life. The establishment of these fields falls within the domain of the nature spirits. The pattern of the appropriate fields to surround all physical life is established on the devic level and part of the energy unit handed to us in the seed. (I use the word "seed" to describe any primary means of propagation within the nature kingdoms.) Once we receive the energy unit through the seed, we of the nature spirit level "read" the specifics contained within the full devic blueprint and begin the process of assisting it into form expression. As I have said, part of the unit information we receive is the pattern, timing and intensity of the energy fields which are to surround the form.

From the instant the seed moves toward germination, which is initiated on an energy level within the seed, the appropriate surrounding energy environment begins to develop. Those humans who have wit-

nessed this phenomenon either through their own sensitivity or the technology known as "kirilian photography" have developed an understanding of the complex and unseen reality that surrounds form. There is also evidence compiled by humans that when form is physically moved from one location to another, this energy reality is at best damaged. Often, it is destroyed. Both insights are technically correct.

When form, especially plant form, is relocated by humans in an abrupt manner without the assistance of the nature spirit level, the nature spirits will still attempt to re-establish the surrounding energy reality. But the timing of the form and the corresponding development of the energy reality have been thrown off. Consequentially, the re-establishment of the energy reality never has the chance to reach the level of development it would have reached had the plant not been relocated. Sometimes the weakness created by the form and its energy reality being out of sync with one another will prove too intense and result in the death of the plant. More often, however, the plant does not die but continues an abbreviated growth process in a weakened state surrounded by an undeveloped energy reality. The word "runt" accurately describes the resulting growth of such a plant on all its levels.

What I have described is what occurs when humans shift and move form, especially plant form, in response to their own desires and needs without regarding the well-being of the natural plant process. I fully recognize that in order to plant a garden entirely from seed, one must limit his vegetables to only those that are indigenous to his specific area. At one time in Earth's history, this was precisely what occurred. And unconsciously, humans allowed the nature spirits to go about the business of establishing a full, dynamic energy reality around each plant.

As we have all noted and pointed out several times so far, times have changed. Technology has developed which allows humans, with a change in approach and different care, to plant just about anything they wish. A garden, be it vegetable, flower or herb, which is totally indigenous of the area is a thing of the past. We in nature recognize this fact.

It is important to remember that the problem I have been addressing arises from human need and desire, not nature's. Left on our own, the problem does not occur. We know better. Also, we have the power to over-ride human ignorance and arrogance and establish perfection within the nature kingdoms. But to do so, we would first have to isolate humans from the natural processes which exist on the planet thus leaving the human population surrounded with the illusion of form — that is, form which is spiritually devoid and for all intents and purposes, useless. We have the power to do this as well. But we choose not.

TRANSPLANTS VS. DIRECT SEED PLANTING

Instead, we choose to bring the issue to your attention and suggest alternatives, which when worked on by humans and nature spirits together, will solve the problem **and** *establish a new co-creative process which will better address the needs of current times.*

When transplanting information is devically received, that devically created energy unit is appropriately adjusted so that what we on the nature spirit level receive to work with is a blueprint that has included the transplanting timing and development. When the plant is relocated, we have all the tools necessary to completely re-establish its energy reality. The result will be no break in the plant's development (which is the case when careless transplanting takes place), the plant itself will have as part of its devic unit all the protective dynamics needed during the transplanting process, and the form and energy reality will be synchronized.

It is important that the information of what is to be transplanted be given to you devically. Nature spirits can only work with what is received from the devic level. We do not alter or create patterns of life energy. So although the process which Machaelle suggested earlier in this chapter is what can be called a devic process, you can see why I, representing the nature spirit level, would urge you to use it.

9

SOIL

I find soil building and soil work to be one of the more exciting areas of co-creative energy gardening. But then, I spring from the organic gardening tradition and soil emphasis is one of organic gardening's best legacies.

If ever I had to start a garden again from scratch, I would love to use the first year to lay out the shape and build the soil. I would grow nothing. Ask nothing from this piece of land. Every time I say this, when I'm asked my advice or opinion about such things, I'm looked at as if I were just released from a rubber room. "Why in the world," say these people, "would anyone go to the trouble of establishing a garden and grow absolutely nothing during its first year? That doesn't make a lick of sense, lady." Well, I suspect we would reap the benefits many times over when we did begin growing vegetables the second year.

This is just an idea to bat around if you have yet to begin the garden. Perhaps after reading this chapter you might seriously consider doing what I have suspected for some time would be a marvelous experience for both garden and gardener.

Most of us interested in this kind of book already have a garden. I had the Perelandra garden in and working several years prior to my developing a strong, direct and precise relationship I now have with the soil .

There are three issues around soil: 1) How to approach the soil in a new garden. 2) How to build and improve soil. 3) How to work it.

APPROACHING THE SOIL IN A NEW GARDEN

The Perelandra garden is positioned in a field which had been farmed and grazed for many years—since before the Civil War. In the fall of 1979, when I had been told to move the garden to this new area and given its exact location, we had the land plowed and turned for the winter. Then in the spring, the soil was disked, tilled, chemically tested for nutrient deficiencies, given hundreds of pounds of the appropriate different organic fertilizer (such as greensand, dolomite lime, nitrogen, etc.), and re-tilled.

If I had that to do over again, I would not have plowed and turned the soil. I would have broadcast the appropriate fertilizers, put a foot of hay and straw mulch right on top of the land, and let it simmer for that first year. I did something similar to this when I opened the tomato patch near the large garden a couple of years later. The result was a finely-textured, easy-working soil. By plowing, I kicked up a layer of clay subsoil that would make any bricklayer proud and have dealt with the situation for several years.

Now, let me confuse you a bit by updating what I've just said one more time. If I had to do it over again, knowing what I know now, I'd be sitting down with the Deva of Soil and asking what I should do with the soil to properly open this garden. Then I'd do whatever I was told. Since everyone's garden has so many variables, I'm sure all our answers would be different, yet all the answers would work.

To set up this initial session, consider the questions involved and present them in a yes/no format to the Deva of Soil using the following process.

1. Get quiet. Ask to be connected with the Deva of Soil. Then test to verify your connection. (Since this is a new deva to you, you might wish to spend a little time with it before moving on to the matter at hand.)

2. Clarify the purpose of your session by stating that you wish to know what procedures to follow for preparing the soil as you open the new garden.

3. Begin to ask questions. I'll give you an idea of some questions. Keep a record of the ones that receive a positive response. When you finish the session, the combination of these questions and answers will give you the precise procedure you are to follow.

Should the land be plowed? (Just because I feel I made a mistake in the beginning does not at all mean that no garden land should be plowed. I'd leave the issue completely up to the Deva of Soil and if I got a positive, I'd trust in the wisdom of that decision and do it.)

Should the land be disked?

Should it be tilled?

Should the land not be turned in any way?

Should it be aerated (as one would aerate a lawn)?

Should it be hand dug?

Double dug?

Should the soil be tested for fertilizer?

(If fertilizer is needed) Should it be added:

a. on top of the soil?

b. worked into the soil?

(You can receive the precise soil needs from the Deva of Soil and I will give you that procedure in the *Building and Improving Soil* section in this chapter. For now, simply establish if fertilizer is needed and if it is to be broadcast on top of the soil or worked into the soil.)

If it is to be worked into the soil, ask how many inches deep?

1 inch?

2 inches?

3 inches?

And so on sequentially until you get a negative response and go back one number to the last positive response.

Should the soil process begin in:

Spring?

Summer?

Fall?

Winter?

Should the soil sit undisturbed before planting?

Are we talking about days?

Weeks?

Months?

Whatever gets a positive response, find out how many days, weeks, or months by testing sequentially.

(If it is to sit) Should the fertilizer be added before the resting period?

After the resting period?

Is mulch to be added?

Is it to sit on top of the soil?

How thick?

What kind of mulch?
- Hay?
- Straw?
- Grass?
- Leaves?
- Sawdust?
- Black plastic?
- Newspaper? (not the slick color magazine sections)

(If you got several positive responses, you are being advised to have a combination for your mulch.)

Is it to be turned into the soil?
- Plowed in?
- Tilled in?

This list could continue for pages. But what is here gives you an idea of the kinds of questions to ask. Don't let the size of the list scare you. Just start at the top, ask one question at a time, record your positive responses and any issue that will apply to your garden, and at the end you will have all you'll need to know. Also, free your intuition. For as you go along, the Deva of Soil will give you insight and direction. So if you are using the above list as your guide, be aware of questions that might pop up intuitively and go with them. If you have an intuitive insight, you can check its validity by wording the insight into a yes/no question and testing.

HINT: As you ask your questions, think about what is available to you. If you live in the city and are planning to put in a 10-by-15-foot garden in the 20-by-20-foot backyard, you most likely will not have access to or need for a John Deere tractor plus driver to come plow your space. You may not even have access to or any idea of where to rent, borrow or steal a rototiller. That leaves hand digging, aerating, and mulching and not turning your soil at all as reasonable options for you. Your responsibility is to present to the deva the available options. It will choose the best from your list.

4. Look at the list of advice you've just received and coordinate one cohesive procedure from it. This process will make questions you should have asked surface, point out what look to be contradictions in the advice, and call your attention to possible errors. I'll give you some examples. Your procedure as is may say to hand dig the area in the fall, then cover with 10 inches of hay for 6 months before planting. You'll need to know if after 6 months you are to turn the mulch into the soil,

leave what is there, or add more to it. In essence, as you pull your procedure together, you'll discover any gaping holes. Just ask the pertinent questions and fill in the holes.

A contradiction: You had hand digging and tilling as options for turning the soil. You were told to hand dig your garden and not till. Then in the spring, after letting it sit over the winter, you are told to till. Something like this can appear to be a contradiction if you look at all the advice as absolutes. Most likely, what is meant here is to start the process with hand digging, then till later. It is not saying you are only to hand dig and never till—and then reversing it by telling you to till. If you have contradictions, get clarification by asking questions as to what precisely was meant.

Errors: This will especially surface as you attempt to work out contradictions. If after all your efforts to clarify there still is a problem, you simply may have made a mistake in your testing. Go back to the original questions involved and retest.

5. Double-check your procedure by:
   a. reading it aloud, step by step, and after each step testing.
   b. reading the entire procedure, then testing it as one unit.

If you choose *b* and get a positive, you've saved yourself and your fingers some steps. If a negative, go through the procedure step by step to discover which part is not correct. Once again ask the original question pertaining to the step. If you get the same answer, make sure you understand your own question. If you only have a vague idea of what you are asking, clarify it to yourself and re-ask the question. That ought to clear up any problems.

If you straightened out a problem by adjusting the procedure, read the entire procedure through one more time and test it with the deva. A positive will tell you it's correct and you can start working the soil in the new garden accordingly.

DEVA OF SOIL

When humans open a garden, any garden, a note is sounded within the devic level. One mustn't forget that a garden is a manmade invention. Therefore, the sounding of the note indicating that one is to be created must come from humans. When such a thing occurs, the devic level immediately responds by creating the numerous energy units which will eventually be grounded into form.

When a human sounds the note with the intent to work in co-creative partnership with devas and nature spirits, that note is very different in sound, quality and vibration. If I were to use an orchestra as an example, I would say that in the case of the ordinary garden, the note sounded would be that of one instrument. Add to it the intent to co-create the garden with nature itself, and one would suddenly hear a full orchestra sounding a deep and vibrant multilevelled chord.

Nature, on all its levels, will respond in kind. The various energy units we on the devic level create when the single note is heard is very different from the units we create when the full orchestra is sounded. So from the instant you sound the note with the more expanded intent, you will set off creation and movement on a far grander scale.

I point this out to help you understand that assisting a garden into full form once you have sounded the broader note requires a comparable expansion of insight, understanding and action. One cannot sound the orchestra and then respond as if it were a single instrument. The result would surely be frustration on every level.

When we of the devic level "hear" a full orchestral note, we respond as a finely-tuned team and create all the various aspects of a garden reality in balance and harmony with one another. So although that which I would create in the area of soil is completely different from that which the Deva of the Carrot or the Deva of the Garden would create, we are functioning in complete harmony with one another. The quality of detail which is reflected in the energy unit drawn together by the Deva of the Garden regarding what goes into the garden and where must be equally reflected in all the other related energy units.

Obviously, this includes soil. The potential quality of vibrant life energy which is part of the makeup of all that is to grow in your garden must have, as its base, an equal source of life energy from which to draw. This is one of the dynamics of universal natural law—the balanced interrelationship of energy on all its levels. As you concentrate to expand awareness around that which is above ground level in the garden, expand equally to that which is below ground. As you open to and assist the expansion of potential above the ground, remember to open and assist an equal expansion below. The two levels function as a team and your efforts above ground will be greatly eased and enhanced if the team is kept in tandem.

I urge you not to become frightened or overwhelmed by the scope of what is being said to you throughout this book. If you were to begin a relationship with nature without any notion of what this meant or where it would lead, and if you simply followed our insights on a day-to-day basis, you would not feel overwhelmed at all. The expansion of your awareness and our partnership would be organic, gentle and smooth. This Machaelle can attest to for it has been her experience. In this book, you are receiving the benefit as well as the challenge of insight, overview and past experience. By seeing the broader picture, you will have a sense of direction and not have to summon the exceptional blind faith one must have to constantly move forward into the unknown. At the same time, you must deal with the challenge of a quicker personal expansion of awareness which is inherent in being faced with the broad picture.

It might be helpful to remember, as you deal with the challenge of the broad picture, that **you** *are the one who sounds the note. This has deep and practical implications regarding the timing, movement and development of the garden environment. You are also a fully functioning member of the garden team and by the mere fact that you are the one who sounded the note, it has you inherent in its makeup. And you become, on an energy level, a part of the devically created garden unit. Especially in the areas of development, progression and timing, your energy is an equal consideration. If one can see that which is above ground moving in tandem with that which is below ground, then expand this notion to include the gardener. All three move in tandem. The balance of the garden must include the gardener. You will not see a garden team in which advanced practices of soil management are being required of someone just beginning to move into gardening. So as you consider the broad picture, also understand that where you are concerned, you are a part of that broad picture and its balance. I urge you to move forward in confidence, knowing that whatever the degree of the broad picture you connect with and move into, it is a starting point. The overall timing and movement will link into that starting point and will grow and expand from there.*

This brings us full circle to the notion of working with me as you move to open a new garden. The pattern for that movement was set when you sounded the note of your intent. So although the process Machaelle has suggested may seem an outrageous amount of insight and information to deal with on a practical level, remember it was meant only as a guideline and framework from which you and I can begin our communication and working partnership. As I give you the details of the soil blueprint, you will not feel alien to the information because, as I have pointed out, your own energy is a part of that blueprint. And what you receive will be completely consistent and supportive to all other aspects of the garden.

BUILDING AND IMPROVING SOIL

I'm not going to attempt to teach the fine points of soil. For one thing, I don't feel qualified. I'm learning, too. It is a vast area of study that seems as extensive in levels and activity as the universe itself. There are quite a few excellent books written by qualified people, and if you wish to read up on the subject but can't find any books locally, contact the following folks for their catalog and book list:

Necessary Trading Company
New Castle VA 24127
tele: 703-864-5103

I'm going to teach you how to precisely build and improve your soil without knowing what you are doing. You have the best possible expert available to you—the Deva of Soil. All the information is sitting right there. Your challenge is how to get it from that level to you, and like everything else so far, you just need to know what questions to ask. So, here we go.

Fertilizer for the New Garden

In the previous section, you determined whether fertilizer was to be added to the new garden prior to planting anything. Most likely it does. Now's the time to find out what's to be added.

It is important to consider right up front what fertilizers are available in your area and which of them you are willing to use. If you are near sources of manures, it will be essential to find out if you can get them delivered or if you have the means to pick them up. It's very nice if you live in an area that has ample supply of chicken manure, horse manure, cattle manure and llama manure—but if no one will deliver and you don't want a half ton of horse manure sitting in the back of your Mercedes SL, then these really aren't available supplies.

An alternative to animal manures is organic fertilizer such as rock phosphate, bone meal, cottonseed meal, granite meal, leather meal, alfalfa meal, kelp meal and dried blood. I'm steering you away from chemical fertilizers that have catchy names related to the compound in the bag such as "5-10-5." I know that even in this day and age, it's sometimes hard as hens' teeth to find a reasonable organic fertilizer source and you may feel trapped into using chemical fertilizers if that's all your local garden center offers. I give you an alternative. The Necessary Trading Company, whose address I just gave, is about the finest stocked organic fertilizing and supply place I've found. (Just for the record, I am not receiving kick backs from these people. They don't even know I'm referring you to them. I use them myself. They're convenient because they're set up for mail order. And they service the needs of home gardens, commercial gardens and large farms.)

Once you decide on what you're willing to make available to the garden, you're ready to work with the Deva of Soil. One approaches manures differently from the bagged organic fertilizers, so I'll deal with them separately.

Manures

Let's say you have chicken, rabbit, horse, and cattle manures available. (Either you live in a rural area or New York City and are using Central Park as your resource!)

1. Connect with the Deva of Soil. Test to verify your connection.

2. Read aloud the list you are making available. This keys into the Deva precisely what it will be working with.

3. Ask if you are to deal with the garden as one whole unit or, if its design has sections, each section separately. (This is an either/or situation that gets restated into a yes/no format.)

4. If you are to treat the garden as one unit, ask which manures are to be added:

Chicken?
Rabbit?
Horse?
Cattle?

Let's say you got a positive on horse, cattle and rabbit. This means you'll be adding a combination of the three.

5. To determine how much, address each manure separately and ask:

How much _____ manure is to be added?

Here you are going to have to use some common sense. If you have a small garden, the most reasonable measurement to use in the sequential counting may be bushels rather than tons. If you have a three-acre commercial garden, the reverse would make more sense. Whatever you use, make a decision, inform the Deva what measurement you are using, and begin your sequential count. In order to get accurate information, it is vital that the Deva of Soil be clear as to what measurement you have chosen.

Do this for each of the manures indicated.

6. Next questions:

Are the manures to sit on the ground as a mulch?
Are they to be worked into the soil?
If so, how deep? (Do a sequential count in inches.)

Okay. If you are using manures, you now know how much of what kind and how it's to be worked in with the soil.

HINT: You are to get 2-1/2 tons of chicken manure and have absolutely no idea how much in actual volume that is. More likely than not, your chicken manure supplier will know. If he has tons of it to offer, he's been hauling this stuff around the farm a bit and has a fair idea of volume and weight. So don't panic until you talk to your supplier.

If, by chance, your supplier looks at you funny when you ask for precisely 2-1/2 tons, and says something like: "Lady/Mister. How many scoops of this front-end loader do you want dumped into the back of your Buick station wagon?" Still don't panic. Assume he already thinks you're crazy and just excuse yourself. Go to the Buick and pretend you're doing some figuring on a piece of paper. Instead, connect with the Deva of Soil. (Test your connection.) Look directly at the front-end loader in question (you're keying the precise measurement of the loader to the Deva), and ask:

How many loader scoops of chicken manure does my garden need?

Then do a sequential count. Let's say you get 8 scoops. That would be the equivalent of 2-1/2 tons. It also means you've grossly underestimated the volume of 2-1/2 tons and you're going to have to tell this guy you want 8 scoops but will be back tomorrow with a borrowed pickup truck.

Organic Fertilizers

Again, the first thing to do is decide on what you're willing to make available to the garden. If you're using a local garden center as your source, the decision is pretty well made for you. If you are planning to order the fertilizer, you'll probably have a wider selection to work with. In either case, choices will have to be made, and like everything else, I let nature do its own choosing.

For those of you who don't know, let me explain that catchy chemical fertilizer name I gave you earlier. "5-10-5" refers to the chemical analysis of what's in the bag: 5 percent nitrogen, 10 percent available phosphoric acid, and 5 percent water-soluble potash. These represent the major elements most commonly deficient in soil and since I'm recommending you use organic fertilizer, you won't have benefit of the pre-mixed (5-10-5) chemical stuff and will have to create the mix yourself.

Just for the record, let me distinguish between organic and inorganic or chemical fertilizer.

ORGANIC: substances produced by animals or derived from plants.

INORGANIC: includes products derived from natural mineral deposits, manufactured or synthetic products, and by-products of steel mills and factories.

Now, I know I promised you wouldn't need to know what you are doing, but I thought a little bit of explanation would help.

To work with organic fertilizers well, you'll need to have an acceptable source for nitrogen, phosphorus and potash, plus a soil balancer such as lime. Every organic supplier I know has a catalog that lists what it offers for each of these divisions. For example, under phosphate sources you may find rock phosphate, colloidal phosphate and bone meal. Each source has different properties and which to use depends on the makeup and needs of the soil. This is where I let the Deva of Soil take over. With this said, I'll set up the procedure for you.

1. Have your list or catalog ready. In case you want to have an idea of what we're talking about here and are having trouble making a list or don't have your catalog yet, I'll give you a catalog breakdown of organic fertilizers and additives from which you can work now.

Phosphate	Dried blood
Rock phosphate	Cottonseed meal
Colloidal phosphate	Limes and balancers
Bone meal	High calcium limestone
Potash	Dolomitic limestone
Sul-po-mag	Humates
Greensand	Gypsum
Granite meal	Sulfur
Nitrogen	Epsom salts
Fish solubles	Oyster shells
Sugar beet waste	Aragonite

2. Connect with the Deva of Soil. Verify your connection. Then state that you would like to determine what is to be added to the new garden. (Keep in mind that this information is to start the soil building program before you approach the specific needs for planting time.)

3. Begin the questions:

Does it need nitrogen?

Phosphorus?

Potash?

Balancer?

Whatever you received a positive on is the area you'll need to further test. If you need to add phosphorus, read aloud the list of available phosphorus sources. The deva will choose the one that best meets the soil needs.

Continue through the list of needs and identify the best sources you are to use. (I hope you're keeping a record of all the answers you're getting.) When finished, you'll have the combination of organic fertilizers to be added to the soil of your new garden. You've just let the Deva of Soil guide you through a very tricky and sometimes complicated garden issue.

HINT: If your list or catalog includes other items that are considered soil amendments (conditioners and organic fertilizers), read them aloud and ask if any of these are also to be used in addition to what has already been identified.

4. Determining quantity: At this point, the garden can be approached as a whole unit rather than specific rows to be used by specific plants. For each of the nutrients you are adding, ask:

How much _____ (fertilizer) does the garden need?

Begin a sequential count in pounds. Unless you're dealing with a tiny garden, I suggest you start the count in increments of 10 (pounds). In large commercial gardens, we may be talking tons.

HINT: Let's say you've been told your 30-by-50-foot garden needs 86 pounds of rock phosphate, 450 pounds of greensand, 62 pounds of cottonseed meal, and 5 pounds of high calcium limestone. That's all fine and dandy, but now you have to figure out how to spread this stuff evenly over that garden. Some suggestions: Buy a small spreader and figure out how much per square foot each fertilizer is to be spread, set the lever appropriately, dump the fertilizer in, and start walking. The spreader will solve the problem for you. Or, divide the garden into manageable sections, divide the number of sections into each amount of fertilizer (which tells you how many pounds per section is to be spread) and broadcast by hand that amount into each section.

5. You're finished with this particular soil process. Close the session with the Deva of Soil.

Determining the Fertilizers Needed at Planting Time

Each year, after I have gotten the information from the Deva of the Garden where everything is to be placed, I have a session with the Deva of Soil to determine what, if any, fertilizers are needed for each row to prepare for planting. I approach the garden row by row, section by section. To expedite the process, I use a chart. Across the top, I list all the fertilizers I make available. Down the left-hand column, I list all the plant varieties row by row.

I've included a blank chart in the back of the book which you are welcome to photocopy and use. It really does help to expedite things and I find it interesting to keep a record from year to year as to what each variety needs and where in the garden the fertilizers are being added. Because the garden environment is continuously changing, the soil building, and the plants themselves healing, I find the needs are never the same from year to year. The record allows me to observe part of the overall building process that is going on.

By now, you probably have a clear idea of how to proceed with this process. But just to be sure, I'll describe it.

1. Get the chart ready. If the garden is divided into sections, I suggest you make one chart for each section, identifying the section at the top.

2. Connect with the Deva of Soil. Verify your connection.

3. For each plant variety in each row, ask:

Does _____ (plant) in row _____ need any fertilizer?

By identifying the row, you are making sure you and the deva are referring to the same position in the garden. It is essential to maintain this clarity in order for the deva to give you an accurate read-out.

If you get a negative for everything, move on to the next row.

If you get a positive, ask:

Does it need _____?

Read the list of fertilizers, testing each as you go along. (It helps to check the box under any of the fertilizers that test positive. That way you won't have to clutter your mind trying to remember.)

4. For anything that tests positive, you'll need to determine how much. To do this, I first ask:

Is the fertilizer to be added:

Per each plant? (For vegetables such as broccoli which have a lot of spacing between them.)

Per three running feet? (For rows such as beans).

I use three feet because when I'm in the garden applying the fertilizer, it's easy to pace off a row in three-foot increments. Choose whatever is comfortable.

Next question:

How much _____ (fertilizer) will I need per plant/three feet?

For the sequential count, I use measuring cups:

1/8 cup?

1/4 cup?

1/3 cup?

1/2?, 2/3?, 3/4?, 1 cup?, and upward.

So, for a row of snap peas I might test that I am to add, per three feet, 1 cup bone meal and 1/2 cup cottonseed meal. And for brussels sprouts, per plant, I might have to add 1/3 cup alfalfa meal and 1/4 cup cottonseed meal.

HINT: I add these fertilizers, as per instructions, around a week or two before planting. This gives the soil and the fertilizers time to mix and make one cohesive unit before I plant the transplants or seeds.

In a row where the vegetable and the interplanting are mixed (like green beans mixed with radishes), and both need a different fertilizer, just add whatever is needed to the entire row.

Because in this fertilizing process you are only dealing with the specific row area that is to be planted (not the space between the rows), you will need small amounts of fertilizers (which will save money), and a set of measuring cups.

5. Go through steps 3 and 4 for each row and plant variety that tested positive for fertilizer. Be sure to double-check your results.

6. This completes the planting fertilizing process and you can close down the session.

Here's an example of what your information can look like. (C = cup.)

1985 Perelandra Garden Fertilizing: Strawberry Section

1. Chives: per clump	1/3C cottonseed meal
Leeks: per 1 ft.	1/3C cottonseed meal
Marigolds	OK
2. Red Okra: per plant	1/4C bone meal
White Petunias	OK
3. Yellow Sn. Beans: per 3 ft.	1/2C alfalfa meal, 2/3C kelp
Red Basil: per plant	1/8C cottonseed meal
4. Brussels Sprouts: per pl.	1/3C alfalfa meal, 1/4C cottonseed meal
White Petunias	OK
Celery: per plant	1/3C alfalfa meal
White Petunias	OK
5. Carrots: per 3 ft.	1-1/2C alfalfa meal, 1/2C cottonseed meal
Green Peppers: per plant	1/3C alfalfa meal
Red Basil: per plant	1/8C cottonseed meal
6. Snap Peas: per 3 ft.	1C bone meal, 1/2C cottonseed meal
Corn: per 3 ft.	1C alfalfa meal, 1/2C lime
7. Corn: per 3 ft.	1C alfalfa meal, 2/3C lime
Sw. Banana Peppers: per pl.	1/3C alfalfa meal
Anaheim Peppers: per plant	1/2C alfalfa meal

HINT: If you are like I was in the beginning, none of the results are going to make sense. If you are like I am now and know something about fertilizing and what has been advised in gardening books and magazines regarding what should be applied to which plants, some of your results will look outrageous to you.

For seven years I have fertilized according to the advice of the Deva of Soil. The first year was a real act of faith—probably the gutsiest leap into the unknown I've had to take in this gardening process. Everyone I showed the results of the testing that first year and who knew anything about fertilizing said I was crazy and I was going to burn out the garden. (Too much fertilizer actually overwhelms and burns the roots of the plant causing death.) I wasn't nearly as reluctant to make a mistake in the positioning process as I was to burn out an entire garden in the fertilizing process.

SOIL

Finally, during her visit to Perelandra that first year, I showed Dorothy Maclean the charts. (Dorothy is one of the co-founders of the Findhorn Community and has worked with the devic realm for around twenty years.) I told her about my reluctance and pointed out some of the more outrageous results. She looked at me and said, "Why are you even questioning this? Do it."

Well, that was the boot in the butt I needed and the result was as amazing as the information was outrageous. Everything that should have died was healthier than I had ever seen it. The entire garden was noticeably vibrant and healthy. And those fertilizing experts around me just shook their heads in disbelief.

I can't say the fertilizing information has gotten any less outlandish, only that it works—and now seems logical! I find working with the Deva of Soil a magical experience on one hand and a highly technical experience on the other. Like working a huge computer. I enter all the necessary data—10 broccoli and 8 yellow marigold plants are going into row 6 of the strawberry section—and the Deva deals with all the variables and gives me the exact fertilizer read-out. Since adding the Deva of Soil's input to the overall garden process, the garden has visibly and invisibly strengthened and stabilized many times over. It's as if I added the bottom half of the support system—the soil balance. That's why I feel I can't urge you enough to incorporate the devic fertilizer information into your garden process.

A FINAL HINT: As I've mentioned, the Perelandra garden is under a blanket of mulch at all times. This means there is a continuous fertilizing process going on because of the rotting mulch. Therefore, except for the actual planting rows themselves, I don't add other fertilizer on an annual basis. If you are choosing not to mulch, I suggest checking with the Deva of Soil early in the season each year to find out if the garden needs to be fertilized as a whole unit before doing any specific plant fertilizing. If so, use the process for fertilizing the new garden.

DEVA OF SOIL

I wish to continue with the imagery of an orchestra—in particular, the concept of orchestration. As a plant germinates, grows and develops, it passes through a series of stages that when linked together as the full life cycle, create a fine orchestration of movement, sound, pattern, light, intake, release. It crescendos and decrescendos. There are periods in the orchestration where the dynamic is that of a peaceful, still, summer lake. At other times, there is an explosion of life vitality of such mag-

nitude one could liken it to fireworks in the sky. Just as one might sense the orchestration to be almost silent, there is suddenly a reverse and another swelling to a majestic crescendo.

The entire orchestration is created within the devic level of each plant and is part of the blueprint. Once the Deva of the Garden has worked with you to position the various plants into the planting pattern, the blueprint energy of each plant, including its orchestration, begins to fuse into position within the garden itself. It is that fusion which enables me to get an accurate picture of what the soil will have to supply to each plant.

Usually, when humans consider fertilizing plants, they look at it as feeding for the purpose of facilitating growth. In one sense, this is accurate, but much too simplistic. We of the devic level see the soil activity as not just a support system but a comparable and fine orchestration in itself which, when played out, interweaves in harmony with the orchestration of the plant. The two orchestrations, one sounding from above, the other from below, touch and intertwine in a way which creates one larger, fuller and more complex orchestration. When a garden is devically designed and positioned from above and devically prepared from below, the coming together of the two orchestrations occurs prior to seed and plant making contact with soil. This is one of the major benefits of such a garden. The orchestrations are already in place, interwoven, and playing out in perfect timing, and it is into this harmonious environment that seed and plant physically unite with soil.

As you have probably guessed, the information I give you during the various fertilizing processes is given in light of the soil's orchestral response to the specific plants. When a necessary element is missing from its makeup, there will be certain points where the soil will be unable to link appropriately, creating a sudden narrow and limiting shift of the dynamic and dimension in the orchestration. The plant will be temporarily left to move through that point partially or entirely alone, depending on what is missing. Dare I say that the rug has been temporarily pulled from under the plant.

I'd like to make a distinction at this point. The fertilizer information given for a new garden or when the overall health of the garden soil is considered responds to the orchestral development of the soil itself. The information given after the planting pattern is established modifies the basic soil orchestration to enhance and allow the fusion of the soil and plant at the location where they will meet.

If you could physically hear what I have been describing, you would hear one orchestral dynamic in the garden even if absolutely nothing was growing in it at the time. This would be the music of the soil play-

ing out in its unique timing. Add to the garden all of the plants and suddenly you would hear not only the original music of the soil, but a most intricate, multilevelled, multidimensional, balanced orchestral piece into which the music of the soil would now be interwoven. It is this full orchestration which is released into the universe and it is this which is sought by the universe.

Tying Up Loose Ends

I have specifically dealt with the use of organic fertilizers and animal manure in this issue of soil building and improvement. But there are other approaches and practices which you may already be doing or feel inclined to do. In particular, I am thinking about composting and green manure. In both areas, I know next to nothing because they are not practices I use. I mean nothing negative by that. It's just that out of the grab bag of soil building and improving options, we must make the combination of choices that addresses the individual needs of our garden, and composting and green manure are presently not part of Perelandra's needs. I'm going to approach these two practices from the vantage point of knowing almost nothing about them and let you see how I use the devic processes I've been describing to help me get direction as to how to incorporate something new into the garden.

Composting

First I'd connect with the Deva of Soil and ask if composting is to be part of the present soil building practices. If yes, then I'd arm myself with an easy, concise book or pamphlet on composting or look at an organic supply catalog which quite often has incorporated in its section on composting a list of conditions and variables that must be considered for successful composting. With any new addition, I let what is already known about the practice be my guide for asking questions of the deva involved. This gives both the deva and me a mutual framework from which to build. Very often I'll end up with a new practice that resembles the old tried-and-true one but is slightly altered either in timing or by some steps being eliminated altogether with perhaps new steps included.

I am told that the variables to consider in composting are the moisture content, the carbon:nitrogen ratio, aeration, temperature, and activation. I would address each one of these areas with the deva and find out precisely what size pile I should begin with, how much of what (the "what" being those ingredients identified in the information I was using) should be added to achieve the carbon:nitrogen ratio, how much water should be mixed in, how often the pile should be turned for aeration, what the optimum temperature should be, and if anything extra needs to be added to encourage microorganism activity. As far as purchasing anything, I'd go right down the list of options in the store or catalog and test. The positive results would be the combination of stuff suggested by the deva. I would also ask where the pile should be located and get some guidelines as to how to set it up. I know that there is a direct relationship between maintaining all the variables in balance with how one works the pile—the turning, watering, layering, etc. That requires a sensitivity to timing and I would look to the Deva of Soil to give me direction in timing, perhaps checking weekly if anything needs to be done to the pile. I'd do everything that was suggested to me and observe what is happening in that pile in order to learn.

One more area I'd question would be when the resulting soil should be introduced into the garden, what condition that soil should be in, and what process should be used to work the new soil in with the soil already there.

Green Manure

This refers to a fast-growing cover crop of legumes or grasses that is planted in spring, summer or fall (depending on the effects desired), and that conditions, fertilizes and mulches soil.

Again I'd check with the Deva of Soil to make sure this practice is to be incorporated. Then I'd read through a concise source of information about green manure and use that as my framework to ask the Deva of Soil questions. I'd use exactly the same process I used with composting—different questions, of course—and move right through this new area with the deva as my guide. Most organic suppliers have green manuring mixtures and I'd read the list to the deva and let it make the choice as to the best mixture for my garden.

HINT: In both composting and green manuring, or any new practice you are to introduce into the garden, assume that the initial information is the starting point of a building process. I check all of the Perelandra practices on an annual basis in order to get the changes that will facilitate the next step in the building process.

HOW TO WORK THE SOIL

PAN

In each garden, there is a crew of nature spirits assisting the process of soil building and improving. The emphasis of their work is the fusion of the soil building pattern into the soil and assisting the unfolding and movement of that pattern. When humans work the garden soil, they are more likely to interweave with the activity of the nature spirits in the area of unfolding and moving of the soil building pattern.

Now, outside the garden reality, where nature is expected and allowed to naturally move through its processes, nature spirits work in an unhampered manner and unfold dynamics that are quite unlike that which must be unfolded in the garden environment. They are related but different. The garden environment is one area where man and nature come together with mutual needs that are interdependent for a successful conclusion. It is not only appropriate, but vital that man and the nature spirits work together in the garden, and not at odds with one another—and this especially holds true with working the soil.

As has been stated by the Deva of Soil, a pattern of timing and rhythm regarding the soil is formulated on the devic level. This pattern is received by us of the nature spirit level and it is this that we seek to assist into perfect fruition within the soil's cycle. Because we are speaking of the soil within the manmade environment known as a garden, that pattern has inherent in it the co-creative and active partnership between man and the nature spirit level. That partnership is built right into the soil pattern. The specific practices and dynamics need to be unlocked from the nature spirit level, taken into consideration, and appropriately acted upon by man.

Quite often, we observe humans working the soil from the heart, but it is a heart connection based on sentimentality, not appropriateness. Sentimentality springs from heart-felt conclusions which the human has made that usually have nothing to do with pertinent facts. I'll give you an example. We see humans struggling mightily to cultivate tough, heavy soil using only poorly designed hand tools. The results are usually mediocre and don't really allow the soil to fully respond to the growth process of the plants. Despite this, the human will continue to physically struggle with a hand tool. We sense the determination to stick with the struggle based on personal feelings about motorized tools being a disruption to the natural process both in function and sound. We of nature have not been consulted on this issue, yet humans continue to struggle on under the assumption that we have somehow spoken in protest.

On the contrary, we of the nature spirit level look to the celebration of appropriate technology. After all, appropriate technology is the celebration of man and nature come together in creativity resulting in a useful device which allows a task to be accomplished perfectly. We relate to movement and we appreciate fine, well-assisted movement in process. We look to humans teaming with the perfect tool and working with us in an efficient manner for the purpose of unfolding that soil pattern.

Don't get me wrong. I do not for a moment say that the hand tools which have gone through centuries of fine development are to be tossed aside. If I am encouraging humans to respond without sentimentality regarding power tools, I also encourage them to respond likewise regarding the multitude of fine hand tools. The key is to choose what is appropriate, what is necessary to accomplish the task at hand perfectly. I dare say that the indication that the proper combination of choices in both tools and soil work practices is the amount of joy and contentment the human feels in his heart as he performs any specific task.

And this brings me to the second and equally important issue around soil work. Intent and attitude. Behind all human action in the garden comes an infusion of the intent and attitude held by the human at the time of the action. This is one reason why appropriate technology is such a vital issue. If someone is insisting on using an inappropriate tool to do a tough job, he will most likely experience frustration, pain, anger, resentment, impatience.... All of these emotions are infused right into the soil through a conduit—the tool being held at one end by the human, the other end touching the soil. At that point, we of the nature spirit level have a new ingredient to deal with as we attempt to go about our work of fusing and unfolding the pattern. We now have the reality of the emotions grounded by the gardener, the impact of which must be dealt with. I urge you to not underestimate the impact of human emotions, both positive ones as well as negative ones. They are a dynamic force that must be recognized. Out of ignorance, humans leave the resulting problems up to the nature spirit level to deal with.

I am fully aware that what I am now saying is not new. It's been said before—this thing about working in the garden with a positive attitude. I've said it many times before through quite a few people. But the issue still remains and what I have said bears repeating. I strongly urge each human to concentrate on combining the appropriate tool to each specific task and choose the tool within the range of appropriateness that, when used, makes his heart sing. Once accomplished, we will eradi-

SOIL

cate a major stumbling block in the soil building and improvement process. This will, in turn, positively affect every level and aspect of the entire garden process and environment.

10

PLANTING AND FERTILIZING RHYTHMS

SPRING PLANTING RHYTHM

I believe it was the 1981 garden season when it dawned on me to ask if there was a spring planting pattern I should be following that was different from the accepted, well-charted planting times. You know the information I'm referring to. Plant onions early March. Beets and carrots early April. Cabbage family gets planted in mid-April. Etc., etc. I received a resounding "yes."

The next question was how to get the information. I knew where to get it—from the devic level. But I had to devise a way of shifting it from that level to mine. I designed another chart which I use as the framework to get the information. (I've also included a blank of this chart in the back of the book so that you may photocopy a bunch of copies, and use it yourself.) Briefly explained, I listed the four planting months—March, April, May, June. Then I broke down each month week by week. March: week #1, week #2, week #3, week #4. Armed with the new chart and the list of plants to go into the garden, I was ready to work with the devas again. Here's what we came up with.

1. Have new chart, pencil, and list of garden plants ready. Make sure your plant list includes the information of which are to be planted by seed directly into the garden and which are to be transplanted.

PLANTING AND FERTILIZING RHYTHMS

2. For the sake of overall clarity, state that you are opening this session with the devas for the purpose of receiving the planting rhythm you are to use in the garden. Taking time to make this statement, either to yourself or aloud, makes sure everyone involved knows what is going on.

3. Connect with the deva of the first vegetable, flower or herb on your list. Verify your connection.

4. Ask:

a) What month is _____ (plant) to be planted?

Then test each month sequentially. The positive response identifies the month.

b) What week of this month?

Test each week sequentially and where you get a positive, place the name of the plant in the box on the chart.

5. Do Step 4 for the entire list. The only change in this process occurs when you get to a plant that is to be transplanted. There, you'll have two questions to ask:

a) When is it to be planted in the indoor flats? (Identify month and week.)

b) When is it to be transplanted into the garden? (Identify month and week.)

6. When you've completed the list, you'll have the spring planting rhythm.

I've included the 1985 Perelandra spring rhythm chart to give you an idea of what it can look like.

Coding used in the chart:

fl = plant in flats.
g = plant seeds in garden.
tr = transplant time.
(vegetable)1 or (vegetable) 2 = succession planting.
[(vegetable) interpl] = plant in ratio and pattern with a specific interplanting.

1985 Perelandra Garden Spring Planting Rhythm: *March*

#1	#2	#3	#4
Celery (fl) Gr. Cabbage (fl) Red Cabbage (fl) Broccoli (fl) All Peppers (fl)			Mustard (fl) Tomatoes (fl)

April

#1	#2	#3	#4
Kale (fl) Cauliflower (fl) B. Sprouts (fl) Marigolds (fl) Salvia (fl)		Leeks (g) Beets (g) Carrots (g) Spinach (g) Zinnia (fl) Broccoli (tr) Onions (g) [Broc. interpl.]	Lettuce (g) Snap Peas (g) Celery (tr)

May

#1	#2	#3	#4
Gr. Beans 1 (g) Okra (g) Nasturtium (g) Gr. Cabbage (tr)	Zucchini 1 (g)	Watermelon (g) Cucumber 1 (g) Cantaloupe (g) Squash 1 (g) Yellow Beans (g) Red Cabbage (tr) All Peppers (tr) Mustard (tr) Kale (tr) Cauliflower (tr) Onions(g) [Caulifl. interpl.] All Marigolds (tr)	Lima Beans (g) B. Sprouts (tr) Tomatoes (tr) Zinnia (tr)

June

#1	#2	#3	#4
	Corn (g) Gr. Beans 2 (g) Squash 2 (g) Zucchini 2 (g)	Cucumber 2 (g)	

HINT: You'll probably be very surprised at the crazy information you've gotten. Most likely, it will only vaguely resemble the old planting-time charts you've been relying on all these years. I guess it would seem superfluous if I said I am strongly recommending that you follow the new planting rhythm. After all, I'm strongly recommending that you do all the processes in this book. But this particular one is especially fun to see work out. It's one thing to acknowledge that the devic information takes into consideration all sorts of variables. It's quite another thing to actually see how those variables such as soil temperature, weather, and moisture come together. The spring planting rhythm is one of the areas where you'll be able to watch these things unfold most clearly.

Not long ago, I was explaining the planting rhythm process to someone in my area, and she asked, "When do you put in your tomato plants?" I told her the last week in May. That's a solid four weeks after the majority of people in my area begin the tomato sweepstakes (i.e., the race each year utilizing every trick ever devised by mankind in order to be the first in the neighborhood to have the first ripe tomato). She looked at me a little funny and said, "Oh. That's late." Then she asked, "Well, when do your tomatoes come in?" I could tell she was expecting me to say something like the second week of October. Instead, I told her around August 1st. She couldn't believe it. I put my plants out a full month "late" and begin harvesting the same time as she does. That's part of the fun and magic of the new planting rhythm.

NATURE SPIRITS AT PERELANDRA

We wish to point out right here that the planting rhythm not only takes into account the obvious physical variables which Machaelle has listed, but also those which are the higher rhythm and timing that have become part of the energy unit from the devic level. When you utilize the planting rhythms, you work in tandem with us on the nature spirit level as we unfold the garden energy into form in the spring and carry out all the rhythms and timing throughout the entire growing season. Let's just say that when we work together in this, you facilitate our keeping the orchestration of the garden synchronized. When you plant according to arbitrary timing, you tend to move into the garden in a timing and rhythm all your own that has nothing to do with what is really to be played out. We end up having to work around, under, in between, behind, and through you in our efforts to move with the higher patterns. This can become very challenging. Machaelle's success in this area serves as a validation to you of the ease with which a garden can achieve its goals when the orchestration is kept synchronized on all levels.

FERTILIZING RHYTHM

Not long after I instituted the planting rhythm information, I questioned the possibility of a similar rhythm being present in the area of fertilizing. Seemed reasonable. This time I got a qualified "yes."

If there are any perennials in the garden (as there are at Perelandra), the spring or fall fertilizing did have a specific pattern. To discover this, I used the planting rhythm chart and went through the perennials one by one with the devas and identified which month and week I should fertilize. I feel that with these plants and bushes, my more precise fertilizer timing is more in sync with the growth cycle.

Regarding the annual plants that are added to the garden, I don't go through this process. It was suggested to me, and I have since made it a general rule, to add the fertilizer to each row or hill about a week prior to planting. As I mentioned earlier, this gives the soil and fertilizer time to co-mingle and become one homogenous unit.

As I am planting or fertilizing or working the soil on a week to week basis, I do keep one eye on another rhythm—the moon cycles. And that leads me to the next section.

MOON CYCLES

Planting and working the soil according to moon cycles has been around for a long time. The Native Americans were very aware of the benefits of paying attention to the moon cycles, especially when planting. It's a well-founded tradition among organic gardeners and farmers. I treat the moon cycles not as gospel tenets which dictate my movements, but rather a source of free, beneficial energy which, if possible to use, can enhance the garden process. In short, if the best time to plant a row of beans is tomorrow (according to the moon) but it's been raining for three days straight and the bean row looks like a swamp, I'm not going to plant tomorrow.

Each year I make a moon cycle calendar. I get the information from either the *Farmer's Almanack* or the *Hagerstown Almanack*, whichever I happen to purchase first. I can't imagine an area in the country where one can't purchase an almanac, but just in case there is, and you happen to live in it and wish to set up the calendar, here's an address for you:

The Gruber Almanack Co.
111 W. Washington Street, P.O. Box 609
Hagerstown, MD 21741-2530

Both almanacs I've mentioned include a chart titled something like "Best Days For Planting, Weeding, and Harvesting." For the months from March through October, it lists the good, better and best days to either plant above-ground crops, plant below-ground crops, weed and work the soil, and harvest. I use my color coding again to transfer this information onto a calendar.

Green = Plant above-ground crops.
Purple = Plant below-ground crops.
Brown = Work the soil and weed.
Red = Harvest.

I incorporate one other coding which is broken down for you in the almanac chart:

1 = good
2 = better
3 = best

So, if you look at March 28 on my 1986 calendar and see a green 2, that means that March 28th is a better day to plant above-ground crops.

How do I use this information? Simple. In the planting rhythm chart, you have identified which week of what month is best to plant whatever. In 1986, I was to plant lettuce seeds during the fourth week in April. I looked at my calendar for that week and discovered that April 25th and 26th are both green 2 days (better planting days for above-ground crops). In my planning, I'll aim to have the row prepared and ready to go for those two days and, weather and soil conditions permitting, I'll plant then. If variables make it impossible to plant those days, I aim to make sure the seeds are in sometime during the fourth week in April. This way, I keep the rhythm and timing intact—and, whenever possible, I take advantage of the moon cycles as well. As casual as I am about adhering to the moon cycles, it's fair to say that I'm able to coordinate them about 90 percent of the time.

For all you advanced astrology types out there who wish to have the chart included on your calendar for a full year, I'll break down the information so you can get it from the month-by-month calendar in the almanac. Why would I want this information, you ask, for the months of January, February, November and December when I'm not about to do one thing in my garden? Well, I use the moon cycles in my rhythm, too. If I have to set up a meeting to discuss a new idea and I have a choice of days, I'll choose a day with a green number—a moon day for planting above-ground crops. If I'm planning to subvert something, I'll choose a purple day — for planting below-ground crops! Also, as with the garden, I tend to keep one eye on the moon rhythms just to watch how the pattern of my year unfolds in relation to the moon.

So, here's how the moon information breaks down.

Planting above-ground crops: (green)

3 - Cancer (best)
2 - Scorpio (better)
1 - Pisces (good)

Planting below-ground crops: (purple)

3 - Taurus
2 - Libra
1 - Capricorn

Working the soil and weeding: (brown)

3 - Leo
2 - Gemini
1 - Virgo

Harvesting (red)

3 - Aquarius
2 - Sagittarius
1 - Aries

In the month-to-month almanac information, there is a column where the astrological symbols are given to indicate what the day is. (In the front is a small chart identifying the symbols they use.) For example:

January 4, 1986 = Libra = a better day to plant below-ground crops = purple 2 or 2/P.

A full month will look something like this. (B = brown, P = purple, G = green, R = red. Color the numbers for full visual impact.)

JANUARY 1986

Sun	Mon	Tues	Wed	Thurs	Fri	Sat
			1/B	1/B	2/P	2/P
2/P	2/G	2/G	2/R	2/R	1/P	1/P
3/R	3/R	1/G	1/G	1/R	1/R	1/R
3/P	3/P	2/B	2/B	2/B	3/G	3/G
3/B	3/B	1/B	1/B	1/B	2/P	

OVERLIGHTING DEVA OF THE MOON

This, I sense, is a bit of a surprise for you—communicating with the overseeing nature intelligence of a form that is related to but not on your planet Earth. You must understand that all form within your universe and those realities and dimensions which exist beyond your universe are comprised of nature energy. The nature energy which humans experience on Earth is but one set of aspects within the broad scope of the reality called "nature." The very same dynamics which exist within Earth's form reality exist wherever there is form, no matter what galaxy, solar system or dimension. Just as the human spirit is present in one capacity or another everywhere, so, too, is nature. Both may be viewed as two fine gold chains whose links serve to connect all levels of the universe thus giving two distinct energies of continuity within the vast arena called "reality." Perhaps what I am saying will help humans on Earth to see more clearly that their home planet is not at all isolated from all that is around and beyond them. It is a very active and vibrant participant within the larger picture and its links in the universal chain are essential for holding together all that connects before it and after it.

The life energy of the Moon has a special connection with the life energy of Earth. One reason, which I quickly point out, is the proximity of the two spheres. But more important is the relationship between the two spheres that has to do with one being of the other. As I have said, the Moon is related to Earth but not on it. There is a continuous physical interplay between them. Although they would seem to be totally different in physical makeup, they are, in fact, very related, supportive and stabilizing in dynamic. It would be helpful if those who have seen pictures of the moonscape or studied that part of its nature which forms its crust, would release their imagery and preconceptions for the time being and allow themselves to accept that which is naturally of the Moon to be directly related to that which is naturally of Earth, each physically being the extension of the other, and each physically linked within the context of matter.

Visualize the two spheres side by side but not touching. The area I wish to call attention to for the deeper understanding of the Moon's role with natural life energy on Earth is the space between the two spheres. It is here that the dynamic relationship between the spheres occurs. The stability of that which exists within nature on Earth and on the Moon is a direct result of the dynamic relationship which travels between them.

Physically, the Moon is comprised of natural matter that is, as I have said, related to but not on Earth. The reverse is true for Earth's natural matter. It is related to but not upon the Moon. So, technically speaking, each sphere is an extension of the other. Each holds a dynamic beyond that which exists on the individual sphere. Therefore, there is a bond existing between each sphere's natural form. That bond is important to understand, for it is active, not passive and it emits a driving energy which seeks to maintain connection. One might say that the natural form on one sphere actively seeks to reach out to, connect with, and create an extended reality beyond that which it would have experienced had it remained isolated. It is natural law for related form to resonate to, connect with, expand, and experience a broader reality of itself.

It is this relationship that mankind on Earth responds to when he allows the energy of the Moon to co-mingle and become a part of the natural cycle of his planet. What you call "the moon cycles," which relate to rhythm and timing, are but one aspect of the bonding dynamic that occurs between Earth and Moon. When man expands his attention to include the Moon within the arena of gardens and agriculture, he has become a participant in that part of the bonding dynamic. Simply stated, when broccoli is planted according to the proper moon cycle, the plant reaches out to that part of itself which is based on the Moon, which in this example has to do with timing. Not general timing that can apply to any plant, but the specific timing of the broccoli itself. From the vantage point of the Moon, when broccoli is planted on the planet Earth, that energy which is of the Moon resonates to the broccoli reality and seeks to bond with the form on Earth, thus experiencing an extension of its own life vitality.

To say that the relationship between Earth and its Moon is intimate would not at all be understating the facts. The natural bond between the two which I have described is played out between each planet and its corresponding moons no matter what universe or dimension. It is a strong dynamic, these bonds, and will assist humankind most favorably if he not only recognizes their presence but moves within their reality as well. Process is always more easily brought to a successful conclusion when natural law is allowed to function unimpeded.

11

PLANTING PROCESS AND MAINTAINING THE ENERGY OF THE YOUNG GARDEN

DEVA OF THE PERELANDRA GARDEN

The physical planting process of a garden is not the primary issue. What is of utmost importance is attitude and intent. For with the harmonized attitude and intent, the gardener will automatically choose tools, processes, and movements which will coincide with the overall energy dynamic of his garden. So, I will focus attention not on the various physical processes one may have at his disposal, but rather on the underlying attitude and intent.

The imagery of music has been utilized well in this book when describing the energy dynamics of the garden. I will continue with this imagery, but shift it to that of dance. If one is to sense the placement, pattern, rhythms and timing as a complex orchestration, then it would be logical to extend this to include a dance. For when the nature spirits and the gardener move into the garden environment for the purpose of facilitating the fusion of spirit into form and they are being responsive to the multilevelled orchestration which has been co-created by the gardener and the devic level, they are truly moving in dance.

I have specifically chosen dance for in order to participate fully within dance, one must lift his spirit, center his senses, focus his thoughts— in essence, he must strike an attitude that will allow him to hear the music all the way into his soul and move in accordance to that music. It is this attitude I wish to convey for one who wishes to move into the garden in harmony with what is happening there.

For now, I will address the spring garden since there is a special atmosphere present there that changes once the garden is planted and growing. You will recall that all plants and minerals are placed in a precise pattern of balancing vibrations that when translated into sound create a complex and subtle pattern of harmonizing notes. You will also recall that the individual growth patterns of each plant emits a pattern of vibratory sound which weave together creating the overall orchestral movement. The spring planting rhythm is in direct response to this orchestral movement. Each plant with its specific timing, rhythms and patterns moves into the garden environment in right timing, thus introducing its various sounds exactly on cue.

We on the devic level approach the spring cycle of the garden in the spirit of a building process and pattern that spirit into all the information in the blueprint that relates to this time. We do not start the spring in full orchestration. We start carefully, precisely, and introduce a few sounds at a time. We allow those sounds to co-mingle and fully develop their weave in the orchestration before introducing the next related series of notes.

Young plants and seedlings, as with babies, do not respond favorably to loud, full-bodied orchestration. It is simply too much for their systems. Machaelle once likened the early spring planting process to the "Leboyer Birth Method." We on the devic level read from this method gentleness and softness on every level. Full consideration for the open sensitivity of the moment. With this understanding, I would say that this is exactly the atmosphere of the early garden in planting process and the very atmosphere that is part of the devic design. Consequently, why would we encourage full-bodied orchestration in the spring?

Instead, we begin with a gentle, awakening music. Don't misunderstand. It does not begin weakly, but rather simply. And it gradually builds until eventually all the plants' tonal patterns are fully interwoven into the one, full-bodied orchestration.

The building process does not begin when you as gardener start planting. On the contrary, each garden's orchestration begins in what you term "late winter" when we in nature sound the first note of spring. By planting time, the orchestration has been building for some weeks but still can be characterized as simple, gentle and soft in every way. It is important that these young plants be fully enveloped by gentle but stabilized notes. To envision this quality as protective would not be inaccurate. Each young transplant and new seedling is fully encased in perfectly harmonized and gently patterned sound which supports and protects as the new plant acclimates and begins its intonation.

PLANTING PROCESS AND MAINTAINING THE ENERGY OF THE YOUNG GARDEN

You probably thought that I forgot about this issue of the dance. I have not. In order to understand your participation in the dance, you must understand the atmosphere created by the music. You already have the pattern and rhythm of the dance. This is contained in the devic charts. But it is the atmosphere of the music that will now give to you the attitude and intent with which you will move in the garden. Attitude and intent are realities which for humans are based within the heart and mind. This dance which I am trying to describe begins within the heart and mind of the gardener and is automatically translated into appropriate movement. This is not a foxtrot that can be taught to you step by step.

When a small boy is forced to learn the foxtrot for reasons known only to his parents, he will move through the steps with the attitude of detachment. He can learn how to go through the steps, but his mind and heart are elsewhere—and his dance shows it. It is not unusual for those of us within the realms of nature intelligence to sense or observe a gardener moving through the spring planting process—or any gardening process for that matter—in the same detached spirit as the small boy being forced to foxtrot.

If you wish to see that boy move in spirit and true dance, simply place him wherever his mind and heart are. Likewise, if you wish to join in the early spring dance, bring along your mind and heart. Through them, the music will move and you will naturally move with it both within and outside yourself. And you will be most surprised at the ease and grace in which you, your tools, and your young plants and seeds join in effortless movement. For remember, within that movement, carrying and supporting you, is the encompassing energy of the orchestration.

12

SUCCESSION PLANTING

I do very little succession planting at Perelandra. Some years back it was suggested to me devically that I concentrate on establishing one full-season garden with one set of spring rhythms and timing in order to learn the intricacies of such a garden. This move freed up the garden considerably in that I didn't have to throw seeds and plants into the ground early in order to get their production time completed, thus making space available for later plantings. The timing and rhythms that I have described up till now have been my primary focus. Through the recent years, succession planting has been incorporated into the planning a little at a time. You will note that on the Perelandra garden plan there are two rows for green beans (green bean 1 and green bean 2) and they are planted five weeks apart. That's succession planting of sorts. I realize I am not using the same ground for two separate, sequential plantings—the strict definition of succession planting—but this is how the concept was first added into the Perelandra garden. A subsequent refinement around this issue has to do with vegetables such as squash, zucchini, cucumber, etc, where several hills or plants are indicated. Rather than plant all hills at the same time, I was given information that the planting could be staggered, thus assuring production of that particular vegetable throughout the season and easing its inevitable glut in the kitchen. In order to get this information, all one has to do is:

1. Connect with the deva of the specific vegetable in question. Verify the connection.

SUCCESSION PLANTING

2. Ask:

Are there different times in which the individual _____ (vegetable) hills/plants are to be planted? (Test)

If the result is negative, for some reason all the plants should go in at the same time. If the result is positive, then go on to the next step.

3. Refer to the patterning information you did on your garden (back in Chapter 6) so that you'll know where the individual hills or plants are to go. If you have, for example, four hills of zucchini planned, label each hill position A, B, C, or D, and ask:

Does A get planted first? (Test)
Second? (Test)
Third? (Test)
Fourth? (Test).

The positive response is the order of sequence for A. Do the same for B, C, and D. You may end up with something that looks like this:

A = second	or	A = second
B = first		B = first
C = fourth		C = third
D = third		D = second

(Two second plantings and no fourth one.)

HINT: Following this particular rhythm has given me the chance to observe and appreciate the wisdom of the devas to no end. To complete a garden season and have a manageable production throughout is truly magical to me. I enjoy watching such variables as temperature and rain (or lack thereof) interweave with these succession planting rhythms. It's clear evidence to me that somebody sure knows what they're doing — and it's not me because all I'm doing is following instructions!

4. Once you've gotten the order of planting, all you'll need to do is refer to the planting rhythm chart and identify which week each successive hill or plant is to go in.

But we still haven't dealt with the issue of planting fall lettuce where the spring spinach once grew. Using the same ground for an extended growing period for two separate vegetables. Garden greens usually fall into this situation. It just so happens that built into the planning of my garden is, at least, a partial answer to the problem. The spring planting rhythm is such that spinach and lettuce are planted for spring and early summer production, while kale and India mustard are planted for late summer and early fall production. (I didn't have anything to do with that timing.) If I cut the loose leaf lettuce plants even to the ground in the spring, I'll get a second production off the same plants in the fall.

If I really would like a fall planting of any of the early greens, I'll ask the Deva of the Garden if it is in keeping with the rhythm of the garden to do a second planting. If I get a yes, I check to make sure the fall spinach is to go where the spring spinach grew, or if there is to be a little bit of jockeying of position between the available spots. Quite frankly, I've always gotten that the second planting was to be placed where the first one used to be. But I wouldn't want to assume that this is gospel. I suggest you quickly check with the deva involved just to be sure. Then I'll do a fertilizer check and add what is called for to the row in preparation for the second planting. Also, I identify the week for planting the seed. In this way, I assure that I am maintaining the overall garden rhythm.

13

MAINTENANCE

I have to be honest here. Once the garden is planted and the summer eight inches of straw mulch have been spread, I have very little to do except sit around and watch it grow. Because of the mulching, I don't water or weed. Because of the work I've done with the nature intelligences, I don't deal with repelling insects. I've learned that if I just sit back and allow nature to live out its rhythm—which, after all, is the very issue I attempt to facilitate with all that spring information and those charts—the whole garden maintains a life-giving balance that requires no repelling or interference from me. And except for a request here and there for a mid-season pick-me-up, I don't have to fertilize—that's already been done. So I watch and learn.

If I see a row being consumed by insects, which sometimes was the case in the early years, I ask the deva of the vegetable involved if there is something I should do. Remember, the whole garden is approached from the direction of energy balance and it's possible that something unexpected in the overall picture has changed and has impacted this particular row. Also, it's quite conceivable that I made a mistake in translating the information and that's what is causing the problem. If the response to my question is a devic no, I stand back and let whatever is happening happen. And I watch. If I get a yes, then I'll continue asking questions to determine in what area help is needed: fertilizing, thinning, (and for those of you without mulch) watering, aeration or weeding. Once I establish which direction I'm to move in, I'll ask specific yes/no questions designed to eliminate what isn't needed and identify what is.

MAINTENANCE

A point about a row being consumed by something other than yourself: In the earlier years, I would sometimes lose a row—and I was being told to go ahead and let it happen. I've since learned that this is part of the healing and building process which goes on. A garden environment heals gradually and organically. Its healing processes build on top of one another. This concept adds stability to change, and healing is real change. If our body were to suddenly completely heal, if all that was off balance were to magically move to a position of total balance, we would experience spasm on all levels. We would not have given ourselves a chance to integrate all the steps of the change on any level—physical, emotional, mental or spiritual. In order to affect stable change in healing, each step has to be integrated and the next step built on top of that. After all, each step in deterioration, imbalance and poor health was integrated and that downward spiral had a building-block action. Certainly the reverse direction but same concept would be true for the upward-spiraling healing process.

I'm saying all of this so that you won't be tough on yourself or the garden, especially in the beginning. I've been working with the nature intelligences since 1976, and each season has built on top of the previous ones. Then, as I mentioned earlier, in early 1985, the whole garden reached a level of health that allowed everything (insects included) to become life-giving and extend itself in the spirit of friendship with all else in the garden environment. In short, now I don't lose rows. I'm not going to say that I'll never lose a row again. That would not only be dumb, but it would not take into account any future healing the Perelandra garden has before it that will require new process and change. It's just that at this point, it's stabilized.

One maintenance process I do practice is thinning. In the beginning, I did not assume I understood thinning or even the ruling logic behind it. So I opened to (and received) devic direction. As I watched the row in question grow, I kept tabs with the deva on thinning. Basically, I'd connect with the deva and ask, "Now?" Invariably, I'd get a no. The logic that I had learned from reading traditional organic gardening material or from other gardeners was not what was playing out in my garden. Once I got the go ahead, I'd ask for the preferred spacing between plants by 1) asking that question, and 2) doing a sequential testing using inches until I got the desired number. This, too, surprised me. Either it was further apart than I had expected or closer together. Either way, it still wasn't jiving with the traditional logic.

I made it a point to follow these instructions. At first, it was just to see what would happen if I did these crazy suggestions. Once I saw that the vegetables thrived, then I changed my attitude a bit and now I follow these instructions because they work. In time, my sense of logic around the thinning issue changed and I took on a new logic that correlates more closely with what I've been taught by nature. When I consider thinning, I'm operating from this new logic and I tend to open the question to the deva right at the time thinning is to take place. It's become an exercise in verification.

On issues you might be facing that aren't a part of the Perelandra garden, I'd recommend the same approach I used for uncovering a new logic in thinning. Especially for watering and weeding, there might be a different way of looking at them that is blocked from us by our dependence on established thinking. I have no judgment regarding watering or weeding. If they are to be a part of your garden process, then my support is with you in this. But if either are to be practiced, then once again I encourage you to allow the deva and/or nature spirits involved to refine the practice wherever needed.

Okay. The next question is how to find out who to connect with in order to receive the proper information. With some maintenance, it is obvious who to call in. For thinning of spinach, call in the Deva of Spinach. What you are asking for is the blueprint patterning for thinning. For watering, consult the deva of the specific vegetable in question. By identifying precisely which plants need watering, you may be able to conserve water a bit rather than approach the job with one massive watering that takes care of the entire garden whether some plants need it or not.

For weeding, I'd consult with the Deva of the Garden for a general approach to weeding in your garden. Should you be vigilant, moderately vigilant, a little on the loose side, or let the garden become a complete combination of its weeds and the vegetables? (The latter is a recognized gardening approach that emphasizes natural interplanting.) Once the general approach is identified, then related specific information can be gotten from the deva of the individual plant involved.

There's one other area of maintenance which I have used with a light and delicate touch throughout the growing season. That's the mid-season pick-me-up kind of fertilizing. I have used manure tea and foliar feeding. Every two weeks or so, I go through a list of the vegetables or use the garden chart and connect with each deva to find out which plants need a little shot. Because of the earlier fertilizing, this mid-season maintenance is not a huge issue. As I said, I practice it with a light and delicate touch. If you are using manure tea and you discover that broccoli is in need, just ask the deva "How much per plant?" and do a sequential count in quarts. For foliar feeding, I ask if I'm to spray lightly, "mediumly," or heavily.

MAINTENANCE

My basic attitude is to assist the plants by giving them what they need rather than blindly gorge them out with the equivalent of four Thanksgiving meals plunked on top of them.

PAN

Since the thrust of Machaelle's information around this issue focuses on the devic level, I would like to round out the picture by adding insight from the nature spirit level.

In the spring, nature spirits concentrate their efforts on translating the plan of the garden into form. That is, once planted according to the devic blueprint, the garden is the true physical manifestation of the energy that was coalesced into one overlighting plan on the devic level. What you see before you is manifestation in its clearest of examples. Energy has been fused into form.

When the garden is fully planted, the nature spirits enter a new phase of focus. Machaelle has aptly called this "maintenance." From our point of view, maintenance means the carrying through of the growth patterns of all in the garden throughout the entire growing season. If one were to see these two focuses in terms of horizontal and vertical, one could say that the spring focus is vertical. The primary flow of energy movement is vertical—that is, energy is manifesting vertically into form. The second focus is primarily horizontal. The form has been made manifest and now its pattern of growth within form is to be assisted. The various patterns of growth were a part of the overall patterns that manifested into form. So it is no longer a matter of reaching up, as it were, to receive energy patterns. It is simply an issue of reading these patterns which exist within the form energy and assisting their unfolding.

Consequently, if you are at a loss as to which deva to consult regarding maintenance, you may request to be connected with the nature spirit involved with the plant or the process in question. That part of the blueprint is, as I have stated, already accessible to the nature spirits and any of them will be most glad to give you a readout. You may connect with the nature spirit exactly as you have been connecting with the devas. And you may receive answers to your yes/no questions using the same tool of kinesiology. You need not know precisely which nature spirit to consult, only that you wish to connect with the nature spirit involved with the question you are raising. You'll be connected with the right one immediately.

I only raise this as an alternative approach. This is not part of the creative blueprint development, and you may address either the devic level or nature spirit level for assistance. Machaelle has used it frequent-

ly herself and we on the nature spirit level sense that when she is in the garden involved with the dynamics of doing and motion, she feels her proximity to us and addresses such issues to us right on the spot.

I realize her concern for clarity and simplicity as being an overriding issue throughout this book and she has tried not to overload you with the twenty or so options she has learned through her years of practice and research. These you will eventually learn also. For now, starting with one or two options is quite enough, isn't it! Where Machaelle has made a judgment regarding how many sides of an issue to present to you and we of the nature intelligences feel otherwise, we will add our own two cents and allow you to see the give-and-take partnership in love that has developed between us—and which lies ahead for you.

14

FURRED, FEATHERED AND WINGED GARDEN COMPANIONS

Again in 1981, I received the following information: *The garden is inclusive, not exclusive.* Well, that struck me very deeply because I had become accustomed to thinking that if you do A it will produce B which will, in turn, exclude problem C. And problem C usually referred to something furred, feathered, winged—or slimy. In short, that part of nature which falls within the realm of the animal kingdom. This insight was for me a 180-degree turn in mindset and I spent the entire summer repeating it to myself often. I wrote it on the garden-shed blackboard so that every time I hung up my tools, I'd see it. Gradually, as the summer wore on, I could tell that my attitude was shifting from the mindset of exclusion to that of inclusion.

The very first difference I noticed was inside me. I began to sense myself move through the garden without a feeling of burden. Then I began to identify that the burden had been comprised of worry, concern, anger, frustration, a sense of injustice—and it all had been directed to those of the animal kingdom. Now I walked through the garden with the attitude that the bugs, the birds, the rabbits, snakes and slugs were all to be there.

The second change I noted was, I'm sure, a direct result of the first change. I noticed an increase in numbers and activity from the animal kingdom and a corresponding decrease in what we gardeners would call "damage" from that kingdom. A baby rabbit lived for awhile amongst the herbs in the center ring of the garden. I had to be careful when harvesting because of the increased number of snakes. (I'm not sure who was more startled when we met—me or them.) A skunk moved into the space under the shed. Wasp nests were being built everywhere. Tommy the Turtle joined the garden and each year since, he has returned for the summer. He begins in the strawberry patch and migrates from row to row throughout the season. (I know it's Tommy, because he has only three legs.) The general insect population grew to mammoth proportions. Bats and birds began swooping in each day from every angle. Yet with all this action going on, I didn't notice any additional loss of plant or produce.

Since beginning my adventure, I have tithed 10 percent of the garden back to nature just on general principle. To be frank, I don't believe I have ever fully been taken up on that tithing. Now what I observed was that where animal and plant interfaced it was with the softest of touches. At the same time, I felt an air of aggression that had hung over the garden gradually dissipate and eventually it disappeared altogether. What I realized was that I had removed my attitude of aggression toward the animal kingdom when I changed my mindset and this, in turn, changed the collective attitude with which the animal kingdom interfaced with the garden. They no longer had to fight for their life. They could exist within a natural environment without fear of reprisal. Plus, it set into motion the creation of a new balance—one in which the quantity and quality of activity was increased many fold.

Immediately, I received information regarding certain adjustments to this change. A substantial portion of the field just off the east side of the garden was declared a woods' edge and has developed an overgrowth of grasses, cedars and brambles for the protection, housing and breeding of small animals and birds. And a bird feeding station was added in the garden itself.

There is a fence for the purpose of keeping out the neighbor's herd of horses and cattle. They have managed to move through the garden a number of times and have proven beyond a shadow of a doubt that even when they walk along the various spiral paths and stay out of the planting area itself, they still do extensive damage just from sheer size and weight. So although I feel they are a part of my garden's natural balance, they aren't allowed closer than the fence line. But to compensate, they get their 10 percent share (and more) in carrots, corn, stalks and other palatable delights tossed directly over the fence. It saves them the time and effort of banging down the fence and rummaging around for their preferences. The fence excludes nothing else. Deer jump it with ease and grace and lope on through to the other side, jump that fence and head on into the woods. Rarely do I find any evidence of their having been through, save a plop or two.

To give you a further idea as to how my mindset has changed, I can say that I move throughout the garden area with the intent of not doing anything, leaving something around, or setting something up that might damage or injure an animal or bird. I store my tools in a way that they can't cut or damage. I dispose of old seeds carefully because they have been treated or inoculated and I'm not sure what effect this will have on creatures. I check the fence from time to time to make sure it is easily and safely negotiable by all but the cows and horses. I try to stake and rope needed areas clearly so that an animal won't get hung up. In essence, I put considerable effort into providing a safe environment for all. This is another way of demonstrating that the garden is inclusive, not exclusive.

I fear I may be sounding as if this has been an effortless, rosy process, this change of mindset. And that would not only be untrue, it would be unfair to give that impression. The change has been gradual and the lessons constant.

In 1985, I was observing the early spring beauty of the garden. A very large flock of robins had been around for days. In fact, the size of the flock was so big that I spent considerable time each day watching its movements and interaction with the garden area. Eventually, I felt real concern for the earthworm population. The concern grew. I worked to keep my thoughts in check and concentrated on trying to learn through observation what was really occurring. I trusted that all was well, but I couldn't see evidence of this. One day as I was watching, a robin not more than ten feet from me bent its head, yanked one of my prized earthworms out of the ground and gobbled it in less than a second. I was livid and yelled something like, "How dare you eat my earthworm!" Had I had any weapon in hand, I'm sure I would have gone after that robin.

Well, it was obvious that my attempt at containment had just collapsed and I knew I was going to have to get some kind of insight on what the robins were accomplishing (besides devouring my earthworms) in order to rebalance my thinking.

I opened a combined session on March 23, 1985 with the Deva of Perelandra, the Deva of the Garden, the Deva of the Soil, the Deva of the Robin, and Pan. (I figured someone in this group could give me answers.) I asked that all these intelligences speak as one, homogenous voice. Then I requested insight on the increased robin activity in the garden area. This is what I got:

COMBINED NATURE SESSION

The increased robin activity relates to the overall improvement of the health of the garden. Your concern has been the possible imbalance in the earthworm population that might be caused by the increased robin activity. You are not looking at a negative in action, you are looking at a positive in action. Rest assured that there are more than enough earthworms to go around! The soil is not being depleted of earthworms. In fact, the soil is being enhanced by the opening up, scratching and aerating created by the robins.

We could leave your insight at this—our assurance that all is quite well in the Perelandra garden. But we'd like to deepen your understanding since you have taken the time to observe the robin activity and ask us about it.

We'd like to point out a phenomenon which exists within the chain of life that few understand; that is the increase of intensity in life energy when there is full purpose existing within the chain of life. In the case of the robin/earthworm interaction, the attention the robin is paying to the earthworm is enhancing the earthworm's sense of life energy. Being used as food for the robin, of course, adds to the earthworm's experience of purpose. That increase in purpose creates a higher life energy, a more intense life energy, and encourages the earthworm population to multiply. It multiplies not only for its sense of self-survival, but also in response to a sense of purpose beyond itself.

The energy that is created by the interaction between two participants in the grand chain of life is extremely powerful. It encourages life quality with the individuals—a fine sharpening of skills and sensitivities which can be directly related to the challenge of survival, or as we see it, the natural interaction within the chain of life. The species becomes stronger when these skills and sensitivities are sharpened. This is fairly well understood by man in his use of the phrase "survival of the fittest."

What we are emphasizing here is not this aspect of the phenomenon, but rather the heightening of energy when participants are fully interacting within the chain of life that, in turn, enhances the drive to reproduce, to continue the species, to maintain full participation within the chain of life. This second aspect of the phenomenon relates directly to purpose—understanding one's purpose individually and as part of the whole. To use your example of the earthworm/robin activity: The earthworms at Perelandra are not only responding to the balanced environment when they multiply but also the increase in activity provided by the birds, etc. (In this case, the robins.) The earthworms at

Perelandra have the drive to multiply. Their sense of life energy and quality is very high. Their participation in life is one of excitement, purpose, and immediacy.

The flip side of this issue would be the garden where birds are kept out while at the same time, earthworms are purchased from outside the garden environment and introduced into the soil. If we were to describe the quality of life energy among the earthworms in this situation, one could use the word "sluggish." The level of purpose is minimal. The earthworm's response to its own life is also minimal. In this type of garden it would be safe to say that the gardener's overall understanding of energy and its relationship to form is minimal—the quality of life energy among his earthworms reflect this just as all other aspects in the garden would reflect this.

Several years ago, you were given the insight that the garden is inclusive, not exclusive. That insight directly relates to what we are talking about here. By including all members of the chain of life who belong within the balanced garden environment, one encourages and enhances the quality and intensity of life energy within that chain—and within that environment as a whole. Your robin activity is a sign of this enhancement. So, do not fret over what appears to be a rather massive assault on your prized earthworm population. See the robins with new eyes and celebrate with us the acting out of the high intensity and level of life energy that is inherent in the Perelandra garden. The robins, the earthworms, the garden, and you are the better for it!

A note on balance: The Perelandra garden reflects balance on many levels. The activity it calls to itself will be of like reflection—balance. Just as there is out-of-balance activity evident in out-of-balance gardens with or without the gardener's direct assistance to promote this imbalance, there is balanced activity called to and reflected in a balanced garden—with or without your direct assistance. In essence, what we are saying is that as long as you keep your focus on striving for and maintaining the overall balance of the garden and garden area, you can rest assured that the activity called to it will also reflect balance. You've already seen this in relationship to how insects interact with plants. Why would this not work in the very same manner in relationship to how birds interact with earthworms?

Now when I see a robin in the garden, I just say to myself he's giving purpose to the earthworms.

INSECTS

The relationship between the gardener and his insects deserves its own section. As you have probably gathered, my relationship on a direct level is quite nonchalant. I concentrate on getting the garden in the ground in the right position with the correct interplanting and ratio and from then on, I let nature take its course. The insects move in and out creating an intricate pattern that seems to magically weave into the larger fabric of the garden whole. It's extraordinary to observe.

One of the problems in showing this kind of garden to others is that in a day's visit, they see only 1/365th of that weave. They may see the garden right at the time when the cabbage worm is present on the plants and not realize that if they returned a week later, what they assumed would be disastrous would not only no longer be a threat but would no longer even be present. In that short period of time, birds, wasps and various other creatures will have feasted royally on the abundant cabbage worms and the plants are left to continue their growth without missing the tiniest of beat.

Having watched this amazing process year after year, I have been able to change my attitude about bugs from a focus on what they attack, weaken, damage or destroy to a focus of the gift each insect offers to the countless other members of the garden. This, in turn, has allowed me to see the insects' right of relationship to the plant kingdom. It may sound odd, I am sure, but I see the insects as not only an integral part of the environment, but also as part of the garden crops. I encourage their health and vibrancy as I would anything else in the garden. And I look to the garden to draw to it and support a balanced and full population of insects which, in turn, helps to support the overall life of that environment.

Now, on a practical level, this has meant that I have had to learn to coexist with the insects in new ways. If I am going to welcome them into my garden environment, I certainly can't operate in a way that ignores insects' needs. The bird bath is a water source for insects as much as it is for the birds. I welcome dandelions as part of the grassy areas because they are such a good source of nectar in the early spring. I will keep a row of green beans growing long after it has completed its bean production if the bean beetle process is at a critical stage and more time is needed to successfully complete their cycle. In the herb ring I was told to plant costmary, an herb I personally do absolutely nothing with. (I've heard it is used for medicinal teas.) Each year I dutifully fertilize it, and early each spring it becomes completely covered with a billion aphids.

About a week later, an equal number of ladybugs appear in the costmary. Not long after that, there are no aphids and the ladybugs have scattered about the garden. So, I've decided that the costmary in the Perelandra garden is actually a ladybug breeding ground.

I don't remove insects by hand. I try not to interfere with their process at all. If in the process of some pruning I must disturb an egg case, I will try to work around the branch in question or tie the pruned branch to another located in a similar environment.

As soon as the warmth of early spring hits, there are wasps everywhere looking to start nests. For the most part, this is not an issue as long as the nests are not in an area where my presence is deemed a direct threat. Once the larva are laid, the adult wasps become aggressively protective. This seems reasonable to me. I've seen human parents get aggressively protective when their child is being threatened in any manner. So, I'll respect this in the wasps and make an agreement not to have nests where my presence is seen as threatening—like the front door jamb to my garden cabin. After the agreement is made, Clarence or I will keep any nests out of those areas before larva eggs are laid.

When I planted the outer ring of the garden in rose bushes, I wondered how the Japanese beetles would react. I pictured every beetle within a six-hundred-mile range being drawn to the rose ring of the Perelandra garden. Since I don't spray or discourage them in any way, they have total freedom. Well, I do have Japanese beetles. But the number, in light of their freedom is astonishingly low. And they don't *attack* the rose ring. They move rather gently around the ring in a pattern that allows all the rose bushes to blossom fully at different times within the Japanese beetle season. I've also learned that if I allow the beetles to remain on the rose flower they have chosen, they will stay with that flower until it is fully eaten before moving on. They seem to have a memory of the flower and although they may fly around during the day, they will return to that particular flower in the afternoon and stay there for the night. Of course, I am not certain that it is the very same beetles returning to a specific rose. But I am sure that when a rose is hosting beetles, it remains the sole host on the bush until fully devoured. More often than not, the beetles move on to another bush rather than to another rose of the same bush. So if I don't bother them, they take one or two roses on the bush while I get to enjoy the other ten roses on the same bush. The bottom line is that there are Japanese beetles with my roses, but they are no where near a problem. They even feel to be a positive part of the rose environment.

I have found that in the garden insects function as quick dispatchers of communication. If I see a plant or row suddenly overwhelmed, or seemingly overwhelmed, with insects, I'll open to the appropriate deva and ask if the plant balance is off. For example, I may find that a particular rose bush is covered with aphids. When I have inquired, I have been told not to panic, just do the monthly fertilizing as planned and that will rebalance the bush. Once I do the planned fertilizing, the aphids leave the bush within twenty-four hours. Another example: This year we had a shift in timing with broccoli which occurred right after the transplants were placed into the garden. Slugs took over and it wasn't long before the plants had leaf and stem damage. I connected to the Deva of Broccoli and asked if I was to replace these damaged plants with new ones. I was told no. Then I was told to mound dirt to a level above the stem damage, water with liquid seaweed and mulch with oak leaves. I was also informed that the broccoli timing had shifted and that the slugs had facilitated the shift. If I followed instructions, the present plants would reform and continue their growth cycle in the new rhythm. Needless to say, I did follow instructions, and the plants are responding exactly as I was told they would.

In essence, when I look at the role of insects in the garden, I assume balanced interaction. Occasionally when I see something to the contrary, I assume communication and service. At these moments, I'm usually at a loss as to what is occurring, so I'll connect with the nature spirit or deva in question to get direction and insight into what is happening and if I am to assist in any way. In my experience, being asked to assist as I was with the broccoli is rare. Usually I am told there is a change and all is under control. Then I simply stand back and watch a new rhythm take over.

I don't wish to mislead you into thinking that from the very moment I stepped foot into the garden with this new attitude of co-creation, the insect world responded in complete and total balance. As the garden went through its healing processes, the insects adjusted accordingly. Again, they functioned as communicators as to just how far along we were in the healing process. It has taken me ten years to discover the pieces of the puzzle I have given you in this book and to put them into place. Each time I added a new piece, the garden, including the insects, adjusted and struck a stronger balance. I say this in an effort to help you when things appear discouraging and to urge patience. If you stick with the process, you're going to come out the other end and your garden will be as friendly and life-giving as mine.

OVERLIGHTING DEVA OF INSECTS

Within the devic level you will find devas who respond to specific and individual natural form, such as the Deva of the Cabbage Moth, and devas who function from an overlighting position which encompass patterns and processes of entire kingdoms. In this case, I overlight the insect kingdom and wish to give you insight into some of the patterns and purpose which can assist your needed change of consciousness in this area.

Without realizing it, Machaelle has touched upon the overall intent of the insect world in its relationship to humankind. I am speaking here of communication. When the nature kingdoms need to draw human attention to a situation, it will first dispatch large numbers of insects to interact with humans. This may sound ridiculous to you, perhaps even a bit too contrived a notion, but consider this. If nature wished to turn human attention from a focus centered around human cares to a situation occurring within nature that is a result of misguided interfacing between man and nature, what better way to jolt and shift the human attention than through a sudden intrusion, even invasion, from the insect world. From our point of view, it is this world which can be dispatched without creating instantaneous panic. Consider how you would feel if suddenly you were beset upon by a stampeding forest of trees! Or a massive herd of wild beasts! The latter, of course, has been experienced within the human community and perfectly illustrates my point. There would result panic, mass confusion, fear, destruction, and in the case of stampeding trees, shock. This is not the communication I wish to stress here. What I speak of is the communication of sounding an alert, of drawing human attention to nature. It is the insect world which can interface with the human world without creating an immediate destructive result from either party. They can touch humans, pester humans, continuously draw human attention to themselves—and eventually, if successful, draw human attention to a critical situation that is occurring in his environment.

If one were to consider the state of the natural balance within a specific area, it would be a wise move indeed to observe the state of the insect world within that area and the impact of the insects not only upon the rest of the nature but on the human population either in the area itself or residing nearby.

It is true that when nature is out of balance, that imbalance reflects throughout all kingdoms represented in the specific area in question. Therefore, it would be reasonable to assume that it is nothing more than simple logic I am imparting to you. But I am saying more. Yes, the insects would naturally reflect an environment's imbalance. Even more importantly for you, it is the insects who first telegraph this imbalance to humans and they do this long before the natural form within that environment visibly shows the signs of the imbalance. If the communica-

tion lines between the insect world and humankind were to be consciously accepted by man and allowed to operate on the level in which it is intended, the threat of ecological imbalance would be communicated long before a specific area begins the reflective process of sickness, destruction, and eventual removal of natural areas from the planet. If man were to sensitize himself to that which the insects are attempting to telegraph, he would be able to reclaim areas to levels of ecological balance far more easily than he can now imagine possible.

Where insects have interfaced with humankind to such a degree that disease within the human community results, it is not correct to assume that this is a vicious attack by nature. The disease which occurs within the human population is in direct proportion to the seriousness of the imbalance occurring in nature, of which man is a part. They are related. And the key to the natural imbalance is how the disease manifests within the human body. Again, although extreme, the insects are functioning as carriers of communication. In the area of disease, they are manifesting the very problem they wish to communicate symbolically in microcosm within human form.

It might help you to consider what I am saying more fully if I remind you that the human form is natural. It embodies all three kingdoms—plant, animal and mineral—and integrates them into one functioning unit. Keeping this in mind, it is easy to see how nature can reflect in microcosm in the human form exactly what is occurring in macrocosm in the environment around him. All the kingdoms of nature are represented in the human form and available to us at all times. Conversely, the human form reflects the balance of the surrounding natural environment, and that is not only a communication from us of nature, it is the sign of celebration. Man and nature reflecting in balance and in tandem.

If man is to sensitize himself to the communication of the insects, it is important that he view them as messengers of a problem and not the problem itself. When dealing with human disease or nature disease, the insects in question may be conquered or controlled by man and his technology, but the disease itself will not be eliminated until the underlying reason is addressed. In areas where insects appear to be out of control or troublesome, I suggest you draw back and look at the larger environmental picture for the answers you seek. If you are still having difficulty identifying the real problem, look at precisely how the insects are interfacing with human or natural form and there lie the clues you'll need for the answers in the overall picture.

In instances where massive ecological imbalance is being demonstrated in drastic, life-threatening ways either within nature or the human community, understand that this is not a situation where na-

ture is deliberately attacking man out of independent outrage or anger. Humans are not innocent victims being ravaged by some outside, powerful source. Such willful actions are not the way of nature. Where they interface, man and nature are in partnership and have been since mankind joined the life cycle of the planet. Up until now, the partnership has been one of cause and effect on both sides. What is critical at this point is for us to join in a new partnership of co-creativity. Again, remember that the human body is the direct link you have with the natural world. The only way to sever that link is to completely remove spirit from form. But while the link remains, mankind must expect that what occurs in the natural world will be demonstrated in kind within the kingdoms in question contained within human form. This is natural law. What occurs in form resonates in kind throughout all corresponding reflections of that specific aspect of form.

15

THE SOLSTICE AND EQUINOX CYCLE

Annually, there are four important dates that are directly linked with nature. They are:

Fall equinox: around September 21st.
Winter solstice: around December 21st.
Spring equinox: around March 21st
Summer solstice: around June 21st.

Technically, the equinox refers to the two days of the year in which the sunrise and sunset are twelve hours apart giving equal hours to the day and night. The summer solstice is the longest day of the year. And the winter solstice is the longest night of the year.

I observe these four days as nature holidays and use them to take time out, step back, and remember the specific nature process that is related to the equinox or solstice in effect that day. Through the years, the nature intelligences have taught me what each of the four days symbolize for them. Briefly stated, it is the following:

FALL EQUINOX

In nature, this is the beginning day for the next year's cycle. It is the day when the call goes out for that cycle to activate and begin its formation processes on the deepest of energy levels. At Perelandra, the precise moment of the fall equinox is when I, as creator of this garden, initiate the call by verbalizing aloud that I request the next cycle and wish to assist its full unfolding. For this, I usually have just a white candle lit.

NOTE: When I say "precise moment," I mean the precise time of the day the equinox or solstice occurs. For example, 1986's fall equinox was on September 23rd at 2:59 a.m. There is a surge of dynamic energy within the forces of nature at this precise time that is above and beyond the energy of the day itself and I choose to link what I am doing in ceremony with the enhanced energy. The time for the equinox and solstice can be gotten from the almanac, and in most areas they can be gotten from the local newspaper or TV weather report.

It took a while for me to rearrange my thinking about the beginning of the new year not being January 1. And it was a little difficult to still be looking at the growing garden of the present cycle while at the same time calling in the pattern for the next year. But as I moved through the rest of the cycle, I soon learned how appropriate this shift was.

I have incorporated another dimension into this little ceremony, and that has to do with my personal cycle. Each year at the time of the fall equinox, I also call in the next step in my own evolutionary process. I make the commitment to receive and act on that cycle, and I activate this commitment by consciously including it in the ceremony. I have learned from nature that all that exists on planet Earth is grounded fully and completely in form and physical action through the energy of nature. That energy co-mingles with the human dynamics of thought and creativity and serves to fuse into these dynamics the impetus for grounding. It is the natural law of the planet. I have seen this principle demonstrated often and in areas outside the nature environment. It seemed reasonable to me that my personal process would be greatly assisted if I formally and consciously participated in the fusion process between it and the nature energies. My logic was verified by nature and for a number of years now, I have combined my personal cycle with the natural cycle.

I can't give you hard evidence that there has been a drastic change in how I move through my personal cycle each year. I strongly sense that there has been an enormous amount of clarity added to the process, its purpose and direction—and this could certainly be attributed to my conscious participation in the fusion of nature energy through the vehicle of the equinox and solstice cycle.

WINTER SOLSTICE

This is the celebration of the devic level and its role as architect. It is at this moment that I can feel, even "see," the many energies of the next natural cycle come together on the devic level and form one cohesive unit. It is also the moment when I can sense the energies of my cycle as a unit.

For the ceremony, I have a more elaborate setting. This is around Christmas time and to give nature its fair share of the season, I set up what I call a "Life Table." On it, I create a nature setting of greens, nests, nuts, berries, and feather bird ornaments. I also include several jars of canned fruit or vegetables from the latest garden season and handmade crafts to symbolize the creative coming together of man and nature. For the winter solstice, the Life Table candle is lit and at the moment of the solstice, I focus my attention on the devic quality of life.

Just prior to or just after the moment—depending on when I sense it's to be—I draw a card from the Aquarian tarot. Before drawing, I link into the devic level (the Deva of Perelandra) and request that this card symbolize the spirit of the next cycle. Because I combine my process with the nature process, I draw two cards, one to symbolize each cycle. For the second one, the one pertaining to my cycle, I link with my own higher self. (A very simple process. All you do is verbalize the request to be consciously connected with your higher self. You may feel a sense of energy sweep through you which will signal that you are now connected. If you feel nothing, verify its connection by testing, trust the connection has been made, and draw the card. Believe me, that connection is there for you.) I then place the cards on the Life Table. They serve to give the first glimpse at the new cycles.

HINT: I do not even attempt to do the garden charts I talked about in Chapter 6 until *after* the winter solstice. I feel that then the architectural blueprint is complete and its information is accessible to me.

SPRING EQUINOX

For this one, I concentrate on the nature spirit level. At the equinox moment, I sense the transfer of the entire garden reality in energy from the devic level to the nature spirit level. I also sense a shift in the overall dynamic of the garden from one of planning to one of action. Although I may already be working the garden in early March, I use this particular day to consciously recognize that vital devic and nature spirit interaction.

For my personal cycle, I feel the very same dynamic as with the nature cycle: the transfer of energy and the shift of intent from planning to action.

Regarding the ceremony itself, it's another simple moment at Perelandra: the lighting of a single white candle and the conscious focusing on the matter at hand at the moment of the equinox.

SUMMER SOLSTICE

This is the time for celebrating the result of the whole natural process—the devic pattern successfully and fully fused into form with the active assistance of humans and nature spirits. It is the celebration of the coming together of all levels and I experience it as a celebration of joy, sunshine and laughter within each realm of nature.

To prepare for this one, I link into the nature spirit level and am told one or two colors that best carry the vibration and intent of the specific summer solstice being celebrated. (You can get the colors by linking into the nature spirit level, requesting that you be given the appropriate colors, and kinesiologically testing a list of colors. The positive results are the ones.) I then buy ribbon and make bows (combining the colors in each bow) for the garden focal point and all the Perelandra buildings and special places—the Elemental Annex included. This visually unites Perelandra for the solstice. I leave the bows up for the week following the solstice day and carry the intent and celebration of the day throughout the week.

For the day, I light a candle again and at the precise moment I am simply quiet and open. I am quite often given a visualization. Once I "saw" the solstice energies lower into the garden area, then move toward the center of the garden, form into a stem which grew and grew right out into the universe. There a white lotus opened and showered the universe with solstice energy in the form of sparkling lights that looked like fireworks. This visualization accurately describes the quality of celebration I have felt during the summer solstice.

As far as my personal cycle is concerned, by this time I truly have a sense of what I called in and how I am moving, and it is this knowledge that I celebrate. I've always found this to be a pretty amazing process to see unfold. When I call in the cycle in the fall, I have no idea what I am getting myself into. (I do not predetermine or speculate on either the garden's direction or my own at the time of the fall equinox. For both, I clearly put out the call for *whatever is to be* and I leave it at that. In my mind, to predetermine would put me in the position of second guessing or even manipulating the garden or myself in a direction out of pure desire.)

This completes the yearly cycle and, in the fall, I start the whole process over.

OVERLIGHTING DEVA OF PERELANDRA

It is important that one consider the power and impact of action when performed within the state of conscious awareness. The recognition of the nature cycle within the framework of the equinox and solstice rhythm is a perfect example of the fusion of action and awareness. In this particular case, we have two levels of the example. First, there is the recognition of the special dynamic energy activated and released during these four days that is directly linked to the annual natural progression of the planet. Secondly, by taking a moment out to stand back from the day-to-day process and consciously acknowledge the specific stages of that process, one is able to re-infuse his commitment into the process itself. What I am saying is very similar to the relationship the Christmas or Easter festivals have to the Christian. He may struggle on a day-to-day basis to live out his life within his perceived context of Christianity, and his focus throughout the year is on the quality of his response and action within a given moment. The Christmas and Easter festivals serve to allow him to step out of the forest, as it were, where he has been most busy concentrating on each of the trees, and gives him the chance to experience the overview of what he is doing. The result is a revitalization of his commitment to the day-to-day process which, in turn, enables him to step back into the forest and once again work with each tree.

The annual solstice and equinox cycle functions much in the same manner for those individuals who choose to participate. It does not matter if one is actively working in some area of nature. The overriding commitment during these times is to the natural process between spirit and matter which exists throughout the entire planet. Of course, if an individual is actively working in a natural environment, the participation during such moments translates fully into his personal sphere of interaction and directly enhances that process in every way.

The equinox and solstice cycle has existed on the planet since the present establishment of the patterning between the planet, its moon and its relative positioning within the solar system. I say this to remind you that cycles such as this go on around you whether they are recognized by humans or not. The elements of the planet which are already naturally aligned to such cycles receive the beneficial energies they contain. Humans who have no conscious awareness of the equinox and solstice cycle also receive benefit by the mere fact that they are on the planet at the time of these shifts and releases, and by the fact that they are directly linked to the three kingdoms in nature through their physical body.

The energy contained within and released during the cycle, as Machaelle has described, relates to the natural process on all levels. If left alone, if not consciously recognized, that energy is released and results in a general recommitment on the planet to that process. But when humans enter the picture and add to it their free will in the form of a conscious choice to actively participate in the moment, they empower that moment many times over. This, in turn, empowers that commitment not just within the individual but within the planet as well.

To make the point further, anytime an individual fuses conscious awareness to heretofore unconscious action, he empowers the action many times over. Awareness is a vital dynamic within the broad picture of reality. It is not some empty personality trait, as many humans seem to feel. It is a reality itself with its own power and it can be used for the benefit or detriment of humans. It is an aspect of human reality which can be directly linked into the world of nature, thus benefitting both. And it is another example of co-creative partnership.

So as the individual consciously links his awareness into already existing natural cycles, he empowers that cycle to the degree directly proportional to his level of awareness. As his awareness broadens and deepens, the cycle is that much more empowered, and energies released permeate the planet and all that exists on the planet that much more directly and clearly.

In the case of the equinox and solstice cycle, it is most appropriate to consciously include the individual's personal evolutionary cycle because that which is inherent in the process of the personal cycle is precisely that which is being recognized, energized and released in the equinox and solstice cycle. If one were to not recognize this similarity, there would still be beneficial input into one's personal evolutionary cycle. You see, by definition the latter is already a part of the former. Their dynamic process is the same. In order for one's personal process to become physically accessible to him in every way, it must move through the natural laws of the environment in which the individual operates. How one demonstrates his process and progression depends on the level or dimension of reality in which he exists. Therefore, when on Earth, one demonstrates his process in physical action and form. The key to physical action and form on the planet Earth is nature. The framework of the process within nature that relates directly to the translation and fusion of energy or spirit into matter or form is contained in actuality and symbolically in the annual cycle of the equinox and solstice. Therefore, when one consciously includes his personal cycle with the nature cycle, he is, in fact, taking a specific dynamic (his personal cycle) which already is a part of the whole (the equinox and solstice cycle) and bringing it to the fore, thereby spotlighting it and empowering it many times over in those areas that are related to the whole. This same will occur for whatever part of the whole an individual wishes to consciously define and spotlight. Simply by bringing it forward in awareness, the individual empowers it with the prevailing dynamic of the moment.

16

HARVESTING

Now comes the moment of truth. You've done everything possible to keep the garden on balance and it has rewarded you mightily. The aforementioned volume of food for Philadelphia awaits you.

My experience in the harvesting process has been to sense joy and celebration for a job well done. At special times, I can feel all of nature around me, on its various levels, literally celebrate not just the health and balance of the garden, but the resulting incredible production as well. When I approach gardening, it is with my sights set on creating a balanced, healthful environment. I don't consider production. That automatically takes care of itself. So there is always a moment of happy surprise on my part when I realize the green bean row has produced a whole slew of beans. It may sound terribly naive, but I think this probably illustrates best how changed my thoughts, focus and intent are around gardening.

There are days in which the moon cycles are best for harvesting. If I have a choice, I'll use those days accordingly. But really, when vegetables are ready and ripe it's harvest time no matter what day it is. I move into the garden with not just an attitude of celebration but also one of continuation. In fact, the garden process is only half complete. The primary goal of a garden, unless it's for research, is to grow food for human consumption. At this particular point in the process, only the food growing part has been accomplished. Next comes the human consumption process.

I'm making a rather obvious point out of this for a reason. I have met many people who are developing their sensitivities around nature and get caught in a quagmire of sentimentality right about at this point. They've experienced "talking" to and working with the intelligences of nature and consider harvesting a head of broccoli akin to decapitation. Along the way, they have somehow forgotten that the intent of the garden is to grow food for eating. That's why gardens were invented. This intent is incorporated in the overall energy dynamic that is initiated and activated on the devic level. All that is for consumption carries within its pattern harvesting. To not harvest is to cut the process short and not demonstrate in action this particular aspect of the devic blueprint. The goal of the food is to be integrated with, enhance and improve the human vehicle. In simple terms, the plants know this, expect this, and harvesting does not come as a surprise to them.

Now from our point of view, consider the following. The physical body is the vehicle through which a soul interfaces with the planet. The soul has within its makeup endless potential and connects with all of reality and truth. In order for that soul to demonstrate its full potential through the form vehicle, it must have at its disposal a form that is in quality on par with the soul. A lesser-developed physical form simply cannot maintain its stability and efficient level of functioning while being infused with the intensity of energy streaming from the soul operating on full capacity. The soul adjusts to the level of the body and functions on planet Earth in a limited scope that is relative to and on par with the quality of the physical development of its form. It would be quite accurate if one looked at his own body/soul relationship as being in true partnership. As the soul moves through its evolutionary cycles and seeks to expand its conscious presence within form, it will require that the quality of the form be improved to a comparable level. In essence, they move through evolutionary process in tandem.

With the food harvested from the co-creative garden, one has the opportunity to incorporate and integrate the very shifts and changes that go into the garden itself in order to create a balanced environment. So, suddenly the balanced and healthful environment that is reflected outside you in the form of a garden can be fully realized inside your own body environment. The body itself—its cells and molecules—adjusts to the new quality and makeup of the food fuel it is now receiving. The obvious result, beside good physical health, is the development of a vehicle that can support a broader infusion of energy from the soul which then allows the individual to operate on a more expanded and aware level.

Back to harvesting. On a practical level, I harvest with the intent of doing it cleanly, precisely and with care for the parent plant involved. That's the motivating intent behind my movements. I choose between sharp tools or dexterous hands, depending on which will facilitate my intent best. And I try to move with a sense of celebration, not mutilation and murder. Now, to be honest with you there are times when I harvest with the underlying energy that springs from the thought, "Oh my God, what am I going to do with these six bushels of beans?" But at some point along the way, usually after Clarence has finished freezing the six bushels, I remember the celebration around all of this and my thoughts become more balanced.

PAN

The word "celebration" is most appropriate when we of the nature spirit level consider what humans refer to as "the harvest." I also add to this part of the garden cycle the concept contained within the word "bridge," for whenever any element of the nature kingdoms directly interfaces with and is integrated into any other life form or element, that which is integrated serves as a bridge between the two and makes available the life essence of each to the other. Harvesting consciously initiates this dynamic, which is then brought to completion through ingestion.

And this brings me to the third word I would use in describing the dynamic intent contained within the act of harvesting—"service." The overriding intent of a garden is service. Without this, there would be no need to create such an environment. Prior to harvest, the gardener is of service as he works to assist the garden into form in balance. During this period, the garden serves humans in return by creating an environment which shifts and heals all it touches and enfolds. This is true healing service. But the garden's full capacity to serve begins with the harvest. At this point, the human experiences through harvest and ingestion the full notion of serving on all levels. And the partnership that was formed from the very instant he set foot upon the planet is celebrated by man and nature on all levels. Those humans who work with nature in the spirit of co-creativity have acknowledged and successfully demonstrated the link they have with the nature world both physically **and** *spiritually, and nature has responded in kind by producing appropriate food fuel for the physical support of the human spirit on the planet.*

COOKING

All of my friends turned to this section of the book first just to see what I would dare say about cooking. The truth is, by the time I tend the garden (do the research involved), grow the food, harvest it, and get it to the kitchen, I've had it. My personal connection to the process stops at the kitchen door. The process itself doesn't stop, but my attachment to it definitely severs. I know in my heart that to take this food and joyfully and lovingly prepare it continues the quality of the process that was begun way back in February when I started the charts. And I know that there are folks out there who are completely taken by the joy and art of fine cooking. Thank God you exist. For this book, you'll all have to use your imaginations as to precisely how to bring the co-creative garden food cycle to its wondrous conclusion through the vehicle of a meal. I am simply not going to be much help to you in this. Aside from what Clarence prepares, I personally ingest the food by munching and grazing the garden directly. It's one of the perks of being the gardener. When I'm hungry, whatever is the closest edible thing tends to go into my mouth. That's about the height of my culinary interest.

FLOWER ESSENCES

I would like to introduce to you an additional way to harvest a garden. This is the use of the vegetables, herbs and flowers to make what is known as flower essences. By incorporating essence production into your harvest routine, you will add another avenue of the garden's healing service. Already you experience the healing interaction from creating and working in an energy-balanced environment. And there are, of course, the benefits from eating that which is produced in this environment. With flower essences, you create your own collection of homeopathic solutions to be taken orally and used throughout the year by you and your family for specific healing, rebalancing and stabilizing not only on the physical level, but the emotional, mental and spiritual levels as well.

The flower essences have been used in wholistic healing practices in one form or another since man and medicine became a united force. In the 1930s, an English physician named Dr. Edward Bach developed a set of thirty-eight essences which he used to treat the underlying emotional patterns that were the cause of physical disorder and disease in his patients. This set and books on his research and use of the flower essences are still available and used widely throughout the world today. If you are interested, you may write for information and prices to:

Bach Flower Remedies	Official U.S./Canada Distributor:
Dr. E. Bach Centre	The Dr. Edward Bach
Mount Vernon	Healing Society
Sotwell	P.O.Box 320
Wallingford	Woodmere, NY 11598
Oxon OX10 0P2	
England	

There are several groups and organizations which have continued flower essence research and developed additional essences. In our country, the California Flower Essence Society is probably the best known.

Flower Essence Services
PO Box 586
Neveda City, CA 95959

To further explain the flower essences and what they do, I'll give you an excerpt from a session I had with Universal Light in 1984 on a topic he referred to as "horizontal healing."

UNIVERSAL LIGHT

The effect of the flower essences on form (we use "form" to indicate all form, not just human) is directly related to a universal principle: the healing process that occurs on the horizontal level. Although we may not have flower essences per se on other levels of reality, in other corners of this universe, the principle of horizontal movement, or connection, within the same level of reality remains.

To explain: Flower essences are form, are essences of form—flowers—released into another substance which is also form—water—and then given for the healing and balancing of form within a human, an animal, another plant, or even rocks. There is a strong healing quality between like and like. Edward Bach understood this when he shifted from the traditional homeopathic concept (of negative and positive—in other words, two negatives creating a positive) to that of the flower essences (of two positives, or like connecting to like). On a personality level, one finds a healing experience when he relates to a person of like mind and feels, during this communication or interchange, a sense of ease, balance, healing, and understanding. Similarly, the flower essences relate to the body or to form—one might say they are of like mind; they are horizontally connected and related.

Many flower essence practitioners and many people who use flower essences feel that the essences are successful because they respond to the soul, respond beyond the level of form. To put it bluntly, this is not true. Man understands neither the level of form nor the expansiveness within his own level. Flower essences respond from the level of form to the level of form and are highly successful for that reason. The same holds true in any natural healing process—throughout the history of herbs, plants, and healing. The mountain doctor or mountain woman who heals through the use of plants, the witch doctor in Africa who heals through the use of plants and minerals, and the Indian who uses plants, minerals, and crystals have all touched into their "brothers" (all of which are form). They have found a friend of like mind who is able and ***eager*** *to come to and into them for the purpose of healing, balancing, and re-establishing stability.*

To continue:

OVERLIGHTING DEVA OF FLOWER ESSENCES

I am part of what might be called "the healing devas," in that I am a part of a group of overlighting intelligences in nature who focus specifically on the various healing dynamics within and throughout the kingdoms of nature on planet Earth.

When the human soul chose to inspirit physical matter on the planet, we of nature consciously accepted a partnership with humans that related to the development of their physical form and all matters relating to what may best be described as the upkeep and maintenance of that form in every way. In present day terminology, you may say that we have a "contractual agreement" with you humans which was initiated prior to the human soul coming to the planet and was fully activated the very instant the first souls entered the planet's atmosphere. Nature has been completely at your disposal as you took on matter and developed your form. All that comprises human form is extracted from the three kingdoms of nature.

But form development and its maintenance through food, shelter and clothing is only a part of our agreement. In light of the universal law of horizontal healing, we also took on the responsibility to rebalance the human form during times of dysfunction. So in these areas we have the overlighting healing devas who establish the patterns in nature that respond to human form in healing ways and integrate those patterns into the specific blueprint of individual plants, animals and minerals to be recognized, unlocked and used appropriately by humans when needed. I will say to you now that there is contained within nature a pattern of healing which responds and relates to every specific dysfunction within mankind. It is an ever-changing area of service, in that when specific diseases or dysfunctions are eliminated or released as part of the human experience, we devas who work in this area release the complimentary healing pattern that has been held in custodianship within nature. Conversely, when humans introduce and take on a new dysfunctional pattern, we respond immediately and infuse the appropriate balancing pattern within the blueprint of one or more members of the kingdoms of nature.

What you call the "ecological problems" which you now face play directly into the very area of service in which I have been speaking. Simply put, we devas infuse the specific healing patterns in nature on its corresponding devic level. Those patterns are fully integrated. As humans have disassociated themselves from the life balances of nature and moved into a consciousness of manipulating nature solely for their own ends, they have interfered with the successful fusion of that blueprint into its form. Consequently, the healing patterns, although still available, have become cloudy, unfocused, and less accessible to humans.

This brings me full circle to the enormous benefit that lies before those who consciously work to create a garden environment with the attitudes and intent as described in this book. By working the garden with a mindset of co-creation rather than manipulation, one establishes an environment which is raised to a level of life above and beyond the ecological messes surrounding it. This, in turn, allows for the healing patterns to be fully present and a part of the specific forms within the garden environment. The unlocking and understanding of those patterns will be clear and complete and the appropriate form in which the patterns are released will be developed.

It is not an exaggeration (although many will perceive it to be) to say that at some point in the future, the medical world will look to those who have established co-creative gardens to supply the pattern-infused solutions to be used within their own medical arena. These solutions will be recognized for their power, potency, and their ability to quickly get to the heart of a matter in order to return the human to balanced form. Do not underestimate the power and clarity that will be released from each co-creative garden as it establishes its position of balance.

HARVESTING

To address the issue of flower essences: We healing devas look to the plant kingdom as the primary recipients for the infusion of specific healing patterns. This is because the plant kingdom responds to and resonates with the central nervous system in humans. All disorder and dysfunction are reflected in the nervous system, thus making accessible the problems to the plant kingdom. The scope of the nervous system in its various levels of function is no smaller than the universe itself. It is, in the body, the bridge which directly connects and fuses the soul to its form. Since the soul is linked to the universe at large, it is essential that the nervous system have, in form, the same capacity. Eventually, as soul and form balance, the nervous system will operate co-equally with the soul and translate all that is accessible to the soul into and through the body. There will be no separation between the human soul and his body.

As I stated earlier, humans borrowed from the three kingdoms in nature that which was needed for an appropriate form. For the central nervous system, he borrowed primarily from the plant kingdom. And, as I have also stated, it is the plant kingdom which we primarily utilize for the infusing into blueprint human healing patterns. As can easily be seen, it is most appropriate for mankind to look to the plant kingdom for these healing patterns.

It is especially appropriate for the individual and his family to draw from the garden environment flower essences from those specific plants which are useful in aiding and assisting their physical balance. Consider the following: It has been said that the co-creative garden environment shifts, balances, and enhances all that its energy envelops. This includes, of course, those individuals connected with the garden. As it reaches new levels of balance, the garden literally shifts and raises all that it touches to a level relative to that which it is now on itself. The process is continued, but in a different manner, when the food is eaten. Now, those connected with the garden are being affected by its energy from without and within. The physical form is receiving an enormous amount of input from this environment. Aside from the heart influence of the individual, it is the overriding healing impulse received by the body. To continue that impulse in the form of flower essences derived from the very environment in which I speak, is to move along the healing path without missing one step, one beat.

I bring another consideration to your attention. The individual is drawn at specific times throughout his life to live in the location that best serves his higher purpose. This is a truth. It does not discount human free will which allows him to override his inner knowing and establish himself in an environment based on willful desire. When the soul fuses into form it implants its own higher pattern into the nature energy in the body. At this time, like a computer readout, the individual takes on an awareness as to what environment he must be a part of in order for his higher purpose to be fully stabilized and supported in form. This includes the environmental conditions and the food he must have as well as the healing patterns contained in specific members of the nature kingdoms which must be made accessible to him. At various times you will observe individuals, or sense within yourself, a compulsive drive to move or change locations. This is that inner awareness coming into consciousness and, quite often, you will feel the healing power of the new location as soon as you enter it.

Do not misread what I am saying to mean that in a highly mobile society, the individual must strive for permanent roots or a series of long-term roots, or he will loose his opportunity to have needed access to important healing and stabilizing patterns. Remember that I said it is the higher purpose of the individual which fuses with nature thus creating the awareness of appropriate environmental needs. If his higher purpose includes the scenario of many homes in quick succession, roots in many corners of the world, it will result in his desire to move around the planet in directions that place him in the environment which offers physical support and healing at specific times.

Now, people who are drawn to gardening respond to this inner impulse in a very concrete manner. Without realizing it, they create their garden from those plants and minerals which hold the very healing patterns they personally need. Don't forget that the garden is designed on the devic level in the spirit of full environmental balance. It is precisely that balanced energy to which his inner soul/form awareness resonates. Not an ecologically imbalanced or damaged image of this balance. When they expand their gardening awareness to include the production of flower essences, they release from fully inspirited and empowered plants these healing patterns, thus enabling them to enter a new level of personal healing. This is, in fact, a continuation of that which has already begun when they responded to the inner soul/form resonance, settled into a specific location, and established their co-creative garden.

I cannot resist giving you a glimpse into the future, for you see, the relationship of humans to their movement around the planet is directly connected to this notion of their responding to environments which hold for them the very healing patterns they have needed. Humans are presently experiencing much mobility, a great desire to move around the planet, see the world, live in different cultures and environments. At this time in his evolution, it is important that he physically familiarize himself with the planet upon which he lives, for in the future, it will be the planet as a whole, not just one corner of it, that will be the focus of his higher soul patterns and the support for his physical vehicle. Humans are rapidly moving into an era of global consciousness. The drive to be physically present in many different countries and cultures is preparing him for this shift, not just intellectually and emotionally, but physically and spiritually as well. As he travels, his body experiences and responds to new natural patterns, not just new cultural patterns. This exposure opens him to the healing patterns needed in order to expand his physical body balance so that it can fully support the expansion of his awareness of himself and the world in which he lives.

You will note that the emphasis in the present time is one of physical movement around the planet. But the population as a whole is moving into a new era in which movement around the planet will be primarily accomplished on the inner levels through the development and use of the sixth sense. The physical bridge for this era is already being established through the technology of electronics and computers. These technologies are beginning to supply, through the use of physical form, what will be accomplished in the future through the use of the sixth sense. Countries are linking in ways that were never before imagined. Individuals have instantaneous connection and communication with others in areas that used to take days of utilizing the best, most efficient transportation modes to reach. Many have noted that the world is becoming smaller, as they say. Well, it is not really becoming smaller, it is becoming whole.

Once this shift occurs and humans have instant communication through the sixth sense with anyone anywhere on the planet, the need to physically travel will no longer exist. You will see humans physically a part of one environment while at the same time experiencing total access to the rest of the planet.

This will create a change in how the human relates to the environment for physical support and healing. Remember that now the fusion of the higher purpose into form is still, for all intents and purposes, regional. It requires that the individual enter and experience a specific environment for support and healing. In the future, the higher purpose will be global, yet at the same time, not require physical presence in every environment. At that time, the individual will be drawn back into establishing stable, long-term roots in an area that gives him his basic natural support. In the beginning, he will need to pull to him the elements of nature from outside areas that will round out the support for his new global balance. It is quite conceivable that the primary source of global balance will not come in the form of imported food, but rather in the form of flower essences made from ecologically balanced, co-creative gardens throughout the world. The high quality of nature support derived from the plant essences resonating to the greater sensitized human central nervous system will be the most desired form of global natural interchange. And the multitude of co-creative gardens then in existence will link in a new way and respond in global service to human healing.

MAKING FLOWER ESSENCES

Identifying which Plants to Use

Well, you've decided you'd like to dive into this flower essence stuff—or perhaps just get your toes wet. The problem now is to find out which plants from the garden you are to use. This can be an overwhelming moment if you are faced with a hundred different plant varieties. There's a way out of this, trust me.

1. Make a list of every plant (flower, herb and vegetable) in the garden.

2. Connect with (simply by requesting) the Overlighting Deva of Flower Essences. (Test your connection.)

3. Ask:

   Which plants from the garden hold the healing and balancing patterns that would be best for me and my family (my group, my community) to experience in the form of flower essences now and over the coming year's cycle?

I have carefully set up this question so that the deva knows to identify only those plants that apply to you in your current situation or growth. This way, you won't be faced with making sixty essences, only five to be used the first year. Each year, I recommend that you open to this deva and identify more flower essences as they are needed.

4. Read through the garden list, testing each plant. The positive responses are the ones you need now in the form of flower essences. In case you haven't already, make a list of the ones that got the positive responses.

Preparation of Flower Essences

Briefly described, so that you'll have a basic idea of what you are making, flower petals (or in some cases, leaves) are gathered at a certain time of the day, floated in a bowl of water, and exposed to sunlight for a specific amount of time (this is where the energy is released from the petals to the water). The solution is then preserved in brandy (this keeps slimy, green things from growing), and is now ready to store away in a cool, dark place indefinitely. A quart of any one flower essence will probably be enough for one family's use till the children are grown and have their own garden for essence making. They are administered one drop at a time—not a teaspoon, but one drop. (That's how powerful and efficient they are.)

In 1984, I developed the Perelandra Rose Essences, which are a set of eight flower essences, each produced from specific roses grown in the garden, and used to stabilize and balance an individual's body/soul unit during times of transition and transformation. At that time, I received rather precise instructions from the Deva of Flower Essences on how they were to be prepared. I pass along to you these instructions and the deva's comments.

Directions for Co-Creative Flower Essence Preparation

Tools and Ingredients:
- Scissors
- Long tweezers
- 2-qt. clear glass batter bowl (w/handle)
- Glass saucer or plate
- Untreated or distilled water
- Quart canning jars and lids
- Brandy

Best time for selecting flowers: 8 a.m.—10:30 a.m.

Choose flowers that are about one day from being fully open.

DEVA OF FLOWER ESSENCES: At this time you have the flower on the upswing in energy and just prior to releasing its full potency to the environment. By harvesting the flower at this stage, you will allow it to release its full potency to the water instead of the environment.

Clean with hot soapy water all utensils (including scissors and tweezers), the bowl and the saucer or plate, two quart canning jars and lids. Do not touch the inside surface of the bowl or jars after washing.

1. Connect with the Deva of Flower Essences and determine how many flowers are needed to convert one quart of water to full essence solution. Usually this will be just one to five flowers, depending on size mostly.

With tiny flowers, you'll probably need more. Ninety-five percent of the time you will be working with the flower of the plant only. If you sense differently, ask the deva if this is one of the times you are to work with the plant's leaves. If so, ask how many to use and test.

2. Concentrate on making one essence at a time. Cut the flower (or leaves) without touching them. Catch them on the glass saucer as you cut if it is difficult to get a long enough stem for holding. Touching (or sniff-ing) will disperse and change the energy you wish to use for the solution. Do not make a full circle around the garden collecting a bouquet of flowers for all the essences you wish to make. It is important that the different flowers not be co-mingled.

3. In your work area, most likely the kitchen, remove the petals with scissors or tweezers (whatever method is most efficient without touching the petals with your fingers), allowing the petals to fall onto the glass saucer.

4. Fill the large batter bowl (or glass casserole bowl) with one quart of untreated or distilled water.

5. Using the tweezers, lift the petals one by one from the glass saucer, shaking off all stamen, and place them in the bowl of water so that each petal touches the water surface.

6. Do not cover the bowl. Place the bowl, water and petals in a sunny spot in the garden where it won't be disturbed. At Perelandra, I've set up a table for this.

DEVA OF FLOWER ESSENCES: The interaction of the sun's energy directly on the petals and water play an important part in the essence making process. Since sun is important, I suggest that essences be made on a sunny day!

7. At this point in the process, open to and connect with the nature spirit level. Verify your connection. *Without touching the bowl,* place your open hands on each side of it and ask the nature spirits to **release the healing and balancing essence of the petals in full potency to the water.** Allow about fifteen seconds for the process to complete before removing your hands. You may feel the power and energy being released from the petals.

DEVA OF FLOWER ESSENCES: The release will be done etherically, then grounded into the water form by the interaction with the sun. The release of the essence by the nature spirits will occur instantly. The grounding process will take:

3 hrs. . . full sunny day
4 hrs. . . partly sunny day
6 hrs. . . cloudy day (Avoid if possible.)

Although the nature spirit level can ground energy into form instantly, it is preferable, in this case, that the seating of the essence into form be done in "form timing" not "energy timing." The grounding via form timing will more fully resonate horizontally to other form for healing.

NOTE: If bugs falling into the water becomes an issue, a one-layer covering of white gauze will protect the water without interfering with the sun's interaction with the water and petals. No extra time need be added onto the grounding process.

8. After the allotted time, bring the glass bowl—making sure you touch only the handle or the outside of the bowl—back to the kitchen work area. With clean tweezers, remove the petals from the bowl. Remove any foreign matter from the water with the tweezers, being careful not to touch the water with your fingers. It will not effect the potency or clarity of the essence if metal touches or is immersed into the solution as long as that metal is clean.

9. Fill each quart canning jar to just under the 16-ounce mark with brandy. The ratio of brandy to flower essence solution is 40-percent brandy to 60-percent solution or 50-50 percent. There should not be more than 50-percent brandy added.

10. Fill the remainder of each jar (up to the 1-quart mark) with the flower essence solution. Put the clean lids and bands on securely and label the jar or lid with the essence name. You might wish to include the date.

11. At this point, you are finished and may store the jars. It is suggested that they be stored out of sunlight. Also, they may be stored indefinitely and maintain full potency.

12. At Perelandra, I have one more step which I'll share with you in case there is something similar you'd like to do. Remember, my garden has a power center right in the middle which is made up of tensor energy, clear quartz crystal, topaz, and the copper genesa crystal.

The preserved and sealed solution is placed inside the genesa crystal where it goes through an additional shift and stabilizing process. There, each solution is enhanced with tensor energy and quartz crystal and topaz energy. All parts—the flower essence solution, brandy, tensor and mineral energy—are fully coalesced into one stable, fully-balanced unit. The sun is not a part of this step. Therefore, it can be done with or without the sun. This is an energy step. I leave the jars in the genesa crystal for 1 hour. I've also been advised not to place more than 8 jars at a time in the 2-foot-diameter genesa crystal. This step (or any other energy step) should be done on the same day the flower essence solution is made.

Suggestions from a Seasoned Flower Essence Practitioner

I suggest you buy from the local pharmacy a 1/2 ounce dropper bottle for each different flower essence you make. Transfer solution into these bottles, label them, and use them for your day-to-day needs. That way, if you contaminate the solution in any way, you can pour it out, clean the bottle and refill it from your quart stock. Since you are only using the flower essences a drop at a time, it is most unwieldy to try to use them directly from the quart jar, and in the case of contamination, you won't loose the entire quart of solution.

The easiest way to transfer the solution that I have found is with a kitchen baster. I have been told that it is important to store the solution in glass containers, but it is okay to transfer the solution from container to container using clean plastic utensils. It was also suggested to me in the original instructions that for the transfer of the solution to small bottles, the same spirit of cleanliness and care not to contaminate either human to essence, or essence to essence be continued.

For the entire set of utensils, bowls, plates, and jars I use in the flower essence process, I make it a point to use them for this only. I do not use the batter bowl in the kitchen or the baster for that night's turkey.

DEFINITIONS

Well, there you are with perhaps six quart jars of flower essences staring at you, and you say, "Now what?"

There is this little issue of identifying the specific balancing pattern contained within each essence so that you'll have an idea of when to use them and why. Flower essences aren't used like traditional, drug-store-type medicines in that you do not have jars labeled "For colds and flu" as you would find on the store shelves. Flower essences address the underlying causes that may be physically manifesting in your body as a cold or flu. They focus on the emotional, mental and spiritual states we slip into from time to time that cause imbalance and physical stress. So, one can't say that flower essence X is for colds, because the underlying cause from one person to the next can be quite different. Having a cold only means that this is the way you physically process the imbalance created by the underlying emotional, mental, and spiritual issue.

This brings us back to the issue of identifying the healing pattern in each flower essence. The best way I know to get you started and give you an idea of how the definitions sound is to identify some for you. What I've done is ask the healing devas, including the Deva of Flower Essences to identify a list of flowers, herbs and vegetables from the Perelandra garden that would be presently helpful to everyone in general and can be defined for you in this book. So, here goes.

BROCCOLI: Power. Several of these flower essences will deal with the state of power. It is one of the most sought after states today and perhaps the least understood. Consequently, individuals who relinquish their personal infinite power take on the trappings of surface finite power in their misguided attempts to rediscover and reconnect with their infinite power. Infinite power is a complex issue in that it connotes balance on all levels and in every way. Therefore, you will see coming to the foreground in the area of flower essences, those flowers which address various avenues and aspects of power. The movement into a future on the planet rests heavily on humans coming to terms with this broad notion of power.

The balancing pattern contained in broccoli focuses on the power balance which must be maintained when the individual perceives himself to be under seige on any or all of the four levels of his being. (By levels, we mean the physical, emotional, mental, and spiritual or universal.) [Referred to as "p.e.m.s."] *The source of the seige is perceived to be from outside rather than from within. The potential here is for a strong reaction of self-protection. In an attempt to isolate and contain the level from which the threat seems to be occurring, there is a sudden closing down and detachment from any or all of the four levels. This renders the individual powerless, for he has scattered himself to the four winds. The essence of broccoli stabilizes the body/soul unit during this intense time thus enabling confrontation of the perceived seige as a fully functioning and balanced body/soul unit. Broccoli Essence will be especially useful to those going through deep emotional wrenchings such as separation or divorce, those suffering from hallucinations or mental illness that includes hallucinations as part of its pattern, and those experiencing what are perceived to be frightening sixth-sense incidents, experience or expansions.*

Use five flower clusters (one head of broccoli, if left on the plant, creates many flower clusters) to one quart of water.

CAULIFLOWER: In the future, the essence of cauliflower will be known as "the birth essence." Whereas the Perelandra Rose Essences deal with transition and transformation on all levels throughout one's life and death process, the essence of cauliflower holds the stabilizing patterns specifically for the experience of birth. Many of the dysfunctional patterns an individual experiences throughout his entire life cycle are fused into the body and soul during the process of birth. These patterns are a result of the body/soul balance being thrown off center due to the child's refusal to maintain conscious awareness during birth. The essence of cauliflower supports and stabilizes the awareness of both the higher, expanded soul and the conscious child-soul as the two move through birth. With these two levels stabilized in process, the body/soul unit of the child maintains its balance, thus eliminating instances of imbalance which crystalize into the child's body as dysfunctional patterns.

The Cauliflower Essence will not prevent the child from experiencing the kind of birth which is keyed into the evolutionary pattern from its soul level. It will, however, assist his ability to maintain full awareness and to focus on purpose as he moves through the birth.

THE CAULIFLOWER ESSENCE BIRTH STABILIZING PROCESS: The mother should begin this support of the child's process as soon as contractions begin. One or two drops of Cauliflower Essence taken every two hours will provide the necessary internal environment for the child. By concentrating her attention on the baby at the time she is administering the drops to herself, the mother will "telegraph" the vibration of the essence directly to the child. If possible, continue the two-hour rhythm right up to birth. At the first opportunity after birth, place one drop of Cauliflower Essence directly on the lips of the newborn child and another drop two hours after birth. (Two drops of essence concentrate may be diluted in eight ounces of water. Two drops of this solution placed on the baby's lips will be tasteless.) Administer one drop concentrate or two drops water solution each morning for the next two days. This will conclude the Cauliflower Essence stabilizing process.

Use three clusters of flowers per quart of water.

CELERY: Restores the balance of the immune system during times when the system is being overworked or stressed. This essence is particularly helpful during long-term illnesses caused by viral or bacterial infections that overpower and can eventually break down the immune sys-

tem altogether. The essence of celery holds the balancing support for the immune system during such times.

Use six young leaves (not the outer mature leaves) per quart of water.

CHIVES: Power. Chives Essence re-establishes the power one has when the internal male/female dynamics are balanced and the individual is functioning in a state of awareness within this balance. Although the herbal essence of chives would seem to indicate a leaning towards the masculine dynamic, the flower essence holds the pattern for balance between the two, no matter which is predominant at any given time.

Use three flowers per quart of water.

COMFREY: Healing. The essence of comfrey repairs higher vibrational soul damage that may be the result of this or another lifetime. It will sometimes be used in combination with other flower essences that respond more directly to the cause(s) of the damage.

Use 12 flowers per quart of water.

CORN: Traditionally corn has been used for enhancing the spiritualization of Earth and human alike. Specifically, the essence of corn stabilizes the body/soul fusion of an individual during times of spiritual or universal expansion. Rather than focusing on the expansive soul seeking to move through the finite body, Corn Essence balances the individual during those times his conscious being (which is fully of the Earth, responding to an inner yearning) reaches up and out into that vast universal expansion. Quite often, the individual responds to his yearnings by releasing himself from his physical reality and jettisoning into the universe. This vastly limits the usefulness of the experience in his daily physical reality. Corn Essence assists the individual in holding that body/soul fusion, thus allowing him to translate the universal experience into useful, pertinent understanding and action.

Use one tassel (just prior to it being fully open) per quart of water.

CUCUMBER: The essence of cucumber is to be used to rebalance the individual during times of depression. By this, we mean those times when one feels completely detached from his life and perceives it to be a picture show playing out in front of him, but not involving him. The individual has little or no desire to re-enter the picture. Cucumber Essence strengthens the psyche which allows the individual to move from a state of depression to a vital, positive re-attachment to his life.

Use two flowers per quart of water.

DILL: Power. Dill Essence is very useful to those who have released their personal power to others and as a result live through their day-to-day routine having taken on the attitude of the victim. It assists the individual in reclaiming balance in the area of personal power, thus resulting in a shift in his relationship with those around him.

For unlocking this balancing pattern in an essence solution, use the flower of the dill plant just prior to full opening. Use one full flower head per quart of water.

NASTURTIUM: Vital life energy on the physical level. When an individual is working predominately from his head, his physical body will not only atrophy within the muscle structure, but in the area of vital life energy as well. This energy, as a dynamic, is directly connected to the muscle structure. Nasturtium Essence assists in keeping that connection and revitalizing the energy itself when necessary. It has a grounding effect within the individual in that it maintains life vitality in the physical, especially at times when the focus and power on the mental level is pulling that energy to the mental processes.

Use seven flowers per quart of water. Although a mix of colors will be fine, it would be best, whenever possible, to use yellow and cream yellow exclusively or as the predominate colors.

OKRA: There are those, and I refer to quite a large group of people, who insist on seeing or translating their reality in the worst possible light. Neither depressed, for they express strong energy, nor just angry, these are people who have lost the ability to perceive beauty and joy on all levels. Okra Essence restores this ability. Now, it may sound to be a "frivolous" essence—one given a grumpy uncle—but these people live in such an all-encompassing atmosphere of gloom and doom that their attitudes challenge their physical health and well-being. Also, they create such a strong negative environment that they draw to them other negativities which exist beyond their immediate environment. Like attracting like. Eventually they create islands of powerful negative forces that dot the surface of the earth. Although not evil, these people have lost the ability to see the positive.

Use one flower per quart of water.

SALVIA (RED): Emotional stability during times of extreme stress. Salvia Essence is very helpful when an individual is plummeted into an extreme, intense emergency situation, either with himself or someone close, such as sudden injury, an automobile accident, a nuclear accident, or the diagnosis of serious illness—those times when one becomes emotionally broadsided and feels there is nowhere to turn. This essence restores emotional stability which, in turn, allows the individual to think and function in balance as he moves through the most extreme times.

Use twelve individual flowers (not the full spike) per quart of water.

SNAP PEA (GARDEN PEA): *The snap pea is a fairly recent development in the garden pea family, but it carries the balancing pattern that is a part of the overall family vibration. We refer to the situation of frightening, tension-provoking dreams—nightmares. It is especially effective with children and those of child-like minds, such as the mentally or emotionally impaired. The essence of snap pea assists the individual with the translation of experience into positive, understandable process. If an individual is prone to frightening dreams, it is because he has not developed an alternative positive pattern for translating stress or fear. He has only this one avenue. Now, we do not include the occasional frightening dream that all experience from time to time. Rather, we refer to a frequent pattern of nightmares. Snap Pea Essence (or any Garden Pea Essence) supports the individual and allows him to develop alternative, less frightening ways of expressing emotion or experience.*

Because of the support dynamic of this essence, it can also be given to someone who doesn't have frequent nightmares, but who has just experienced one particularly powerful nightmare and is having difficulty pulling out of it. Snap Pea Essence supports and enhances the ability to detach from frightening internal experience.

Use three flowers per quart of water.

SUMMER SQUASH (YELLOW): *Courage. Whereas the Peace Essence in the Perelandra Rose Essence set pertains to the alignment of the individual to the dynamic of universal courage during times of transition and transformation, the courage of the Summer Squash Essence stabilizes the person who experiences fear and resistance when faced with his daily routine. The stability given by this essence during such times will restore the sense of calm courage needed to move forward through the day. Especially helpful to those suffering from shyness or phobias.*

Use two flowers per quart of water.

SWEET BELL PEPPER (GREEN): *Inner peace. Sweet Bell Pepper Essence restores inner balance to the individual who lives and works in a stressful environment. It helps the person move through stressful situations with clarity and inner calm. In today's society, one could say, "Who doesn't have a stressful life?" Humans are presently seeking to understand and integrate ways that will enable them to live a hectic, fast-*

paced lifestyle while remaining healthy and in balance. Sweet Bell Pepper Essence will greatly facilitate this process and a single drop in the morning can be as much a part of the daily routine to release stress as exercising and proper diet. This essence both stabilizes the body/soul balance during stressful situations and restores that balance should a situation throw it off. In short, it may be taken as part of the daily routine, before a specific situation that is perceived to be stressful, or after an experience should the individual be caught off guard.

Use three flowers per quart of water.

TOMATO: Cleansing. Tomato Essence is helpful when infection or disease have become seated in the body. It is particularly useful when the endocrine system is involved. This essence both stabilizes the areas of imbalance and assists the body in shattering and throwing off that which is causing the infection or disease. We use the word "shattering" deliberately, because the Tomato Essence does indeed respond swiftly in the body and in a manner that appears, may even feel, to be shattering. If the immune system has been weakened by the situation, one may need to take Celery Essence in combination with Tomato Essence.

Do not overlook this essence for the small scrape or wound that may potentially develop into a minor infection. It will be useful at these times as well, and could be considered as essential a part of your home first-aid as the bandaid. It may be taken orally or sprayed directly on a cut or scrape with equal effectiveness.

Use five flowers per quart of water.

YELLOW YARROW: Yarrow as a flower essence has been used for protection on the emotional level during times of vulnerability caused by spiritual and psychological growth process. Yellow Yarrow Essence in particular is helpful during these times in that it not only protects one from outside influence during periods of emotional vulnerability, but supports the individual in a way that allows him to soften on all levels so that the integration of his shifts can occur more easily. It protects and at the same time returns one to a state of softness, gentleness. This essence is especially effective for those who respond to their times of vulnerability by throwing up a wall—a wall that impedes their integration process.

Use two flower clusters per one quart of water.

ZINNIA: Restores the individual's sense of playfulness, laughter and joy. Zinnia Essence assists in achieving a balanced and healthful sense of priority while allowing the letting go of those things that need not matter quite so much. It reminds the individual of the balance of a child's laughter and joy, and helps him contact the child within for his balance.

Use four flowers per quart of water. Although any one or combination of the zinnia flower colors may be used, whenever possible use pink and/or cream white. The healing and balancing pattern is particularly clear and strong in these two colors.

ZUCCHINI: Physical strength. The Zucchini Essence is especially helpful during times of convalescence after childbirth, illness or surgery when the body is working to restore physical vitality. It may be taken during an illness as well, for the essence will assist the individual in maintaining as much of his physical strength as possible while going through the illness process.

Use two flowers per one quart of water.

HINT: After making these essences, I discovered the following modifications in the process which gave maximum contact between the flowers and the water. You might find them helpful when you make the flower essences.

CHIVES: Cut the individual flowers from the head. When doing this, be careful not to touch the flowers with your fingers.

CORN: Cut the tassel into its individual stems.

DILL: Cut the individual flowers from the head. Use a clean spoon to skim the tiny flowers from the water's surface after the sun process is complete.

SUMMER SQUASH: Using the tweezers, submerge the flower and allow it to fill with water like a cup. It will remain submerged and be fully surrounded by the water.

YELLOW YARROW: Cut the individual flowers from the cluster. Using a spoon to skim them from the water's surface once the sun process is complete is helpful here as well.

ZUCCHINI: Fill the flower with water as in a cup in order to keep it submerged.

Getting Your Own Definitions for Different Flower Essences

Trust me. Nothing is going to make me grouchier than getting ten requests a day from individuals who feel they need to have the essences of flowers or vegetables not listed above, and are sure the thing I want to do most that day is get their definitions for them.

Let me give you some ideas on how to discern the definitions for yourself.

Pay attention to your intuition. If you sense that you are to make an additional flower essence, your intuition is already working just fine. Let it continue to carry you through the process of learning about this essence. As for a specific framework to follow, I would suggest the following:

1. Open to the Deva of Flower Essences. (Verify your connection.)

2. Ask that the balancing and healing pattern be given you for the specific flower essence.

3. Picture the plant and its flower in your mind. That will be your starting point for the Deva of Flower Essences. It's important now that you not censor or edit your thoughts or impressions. Release your mind to the deva. It will lead you to a single thought or through a series of thoughts, impressions, visuals or sensations. Whatever works best with you. From this, you will get an idea of the balancing pattern the flower essence holds.

I'll give you an example: For cucumber I pictured the cucumber plant and its flowers. Immediately I was struck by the clear yellow color of the flowers and the word that came to mind was "sunshine." Then I felt the sensation of a sunny disposition, which immediately led to a sensation of the opposite—depression. This gave me the direction of the definition and I was off and running with the more precise and complex translation which you have read.

4. Once you get a sense of direction, ask the deva if what you are perceiving is correct. It would be best if you verbalized your perception. (Test.) If you get a positive, you've got it! Write it down before you forget it.

5. If you can't seem to get a handle on the direction, just use kinesiology to test yourself for your need of the flower essence. (For precise steps on how to use kinesiology in this process, read the following section.) Take the flower essence whenever you receive a positive test result (thus indicating you are in need) and pay attention to how you are feeling and what is happening around you. Then pay attention to how you feel after you take the flower essence. Once you use it several times, you'll be able to pick up on a pattern in your life or attitude that will give you the direction for the definition. You'll be functioning as the investigator putting together all the clues. As long as you test for need, you can rest as-

sured that your inner balance is requiring this particular flower essence and can take a drop with the confidence you are doing the right thing.

HOW TO USE THE FLOWER ESSENCES

Perhaps the easiest way to choose the flower essences needed is to look at each bottle and select the one(s) which intuitively attracts your attention. Or you can rely on your awareness of your own inner state and choose among the flower essences based on this awareness.

But sometimes our inner state can be more complex than we realize and perceiving accurate needs can be tricky. I recommend using kinesiology to identify which essences are needed. Here's what you do:

1. Place a dropper bottle of each flower essence in your lap. (This introduces the essences into your environment.)

2. Ask yourself if you need any of the flower essences. (Test.) If you get a negative result, you're fine. Even though you may be experiencing a situation that sounds like one of the flower essence definitions, your balance is holding and you need no additional assistance. Check again later, to make sure you are still in balance.

3. If the result was positive, you need a flower essence. The easiest way to find out which one is to place the bottles one by one in you lap and ask each time:

Do I need _____ essence?

The flower essence(s) that tests positive is the one(s) you need.

Testing for Dosage

1. Hold the bottle(s) you need in your lap.

2. Ask if you need to take the flower essence(s) more than one time. If negative, put one drop from each flower essence bottle on your tongue. Be careful not to touch your mouth with the dropper. If you touch the dropper, wash it well before putting it back into the bottle so that the flower essence won't be contaminated.

3. If positive, you will need to find out how many days you should have the flower essence and how many times a day. This is easy. Use

kinesiology again. With the needed flower essence(s) in your lap, ask yourself:

Do I need this/these 1 day? (Test).
2 days? (Test).

Do the sequential count until you get a negative response. If you need the flower essence(s) for 3 days, you will test positive when you ask "3 days?" When you ask "4 days?" you will test negative. That will tell you that your system is assisted and strengthened by the flower essences(s) for 3 days.

Daily Dosage

Let's say you test that you need to take the flower essence(s) for 3 days. Now using the same format, ask if you should take the flower essence(s):

1 time daily? (Test).
2 times daily? (Test).

And so on, until you get a negative. Most people need to take them either 1, 2, or 3 times daily. Test until you get a negative response. Your last positive response will tell you how many times daily you need to take the essence(s).

Generally, flower essences are to be taken first thing in the morning and/or last thing in the evening and/or in the mid-afternoon. If you wish to be even more precise, test to see if it is best to take them in the morning, afternoon, or evening, or any combination of the three. Just ask your questions in a yes/no format. The more you discover the personal preferences of your own system, the more effective the flower essences will be. As you fine-tune your needs, you will be able to fine-tune the precision of your use of the flower essences.

For dosages over a period of time, add 5 drops of each needed flower essence to 8 ounces of water (spring water or distilled water is preferred), and take one sip from this mixed solution each time you are to take the flower essences. (It is more effective if you hold the sip of solution in your mouth for a few seconds prior to swallowing.) If the glass is emptied before you are scheduled to finish taking the essences, just make the same preparation again.

Dosage Bottles

One-ounce dropper bottles may be obtained from a pharmacy. If a flower essence is to be taken several times a day for a period of time, it may be more convenient to fill a one-ounce bottle with one teaspoon of brandy as a preservative (use more if the essence is to be taken for longer than four weeks or is exposed to high temperatures), plus two drops from each needed flower essence, and spring or distilled water. Shake lightly. Several flower essences may be combined in one bottle, but generally three should be the limit. About 10 to 12 drops from the dosage bottle can be put directly into the mouth (again be careful not to touch the mouth with the dropper).

A note on the water to be used in these solutions: spring or untreated water is best. But if this is unavailable, tap water will suffice. You can also put the drops of flower essences in juice and refrigerate the solution.

Also: *If you are sensitive to brandy, you may use distilled white vinegar as a brandy substitute for preserving your solution.*

Retesting

You may test yourself at any time regarding whether or not you need flower essences. I recommend that you test frequently, even daily, if you sense yourself to be in process or the situation which presently or potentially could throw you off balance is long term.

Surrogate Testing

There may be times when you sense that someone else could be helped by flower essences but does not have them available or is unable to test himself—a child, someone ill, a troubled friend. You can help that person by testing for the essences using a kinesiology surrogate technique which also is quite simple.

1. *Test yourself first* and take any needed flower essences to make sure you are clear before testing anyone else.

2. Physically make contact with the person you are going to test. Have him place a hand on your knee or touch your foot with his foot. Focus on the person for a few seconds. This touching and focus connects his electrical system to yours. Test your connection using the kinesiology technique, asking (aloud or to yourself) if you are fully connected to this person's electrical system. If negative, spend a few more seconds focusing on the individual. If either of you is being distracted, move to a quieter room or quiet the environment you are in. Encourage the other person to keep his mind focused on the hand (or foot) which is touching you. A wandering mind will cause fuzzy test results.

3. If the test for your connection to the other person was positive, you are ready to test for the flower essences. Place the bottles (or box of bottles) in your lap and ask:

Does he/she need any of these flower essences? (Test.)

If positive, place each bottle one at a time in your lap and ask if that flower essence is needed. A positive test response indicates that this particular flower essence rebalances the other person's system and makes it strong. (Remember, you have already cleared yourself of any need for the essences prior to starting the surrogate testing.) Double-check your results by placing the needed bottles in the free hand or lap of the person and ask again if these are the flower essences needed.

If negative, make sure your connection with this person is still positive. Ask:

Am I fully connected to this person's electrical system?

Then retest each bottle individually and double-check these results.

For a baby, the bottles need only be placed on or right next to the child.

When the needed flower essence(s) has been determined, test for how many days/weeks and how many times a day, using the same yes/no testing procedure you used on yourself. *It is important that you remain physically connected with the other person throughout the entire testing process.*

4. If the individual needs flower essences for a period of time, mix the drops in a glass of water or fix a dosage bottle using the dosage mixtures described in *Dosage Bottles*.

5. An important component of the effectiveness of all flower essences is understanding. Therefore make sure that whenever possible the person you are working with knows what flower essences are needed and how they are each defined.

FROM THE "LADY! GIVE ME A BREAK" DEPARTMENT

I am very aware that you are going to have your hands full for awhile working the concepts and ideas presented in this book into your garden process. Also, the garden should go through a few years of its healing process before flower essences are made from its plants. So, if you would like to incorporate the flower essences mentioned in this chapter into your life now, I've gone ahead and developed them from the Perelandra garden. I have included ordering information for these eighteen flower essences and the Perelandra Rose Essences (also developed from the Perelandra garden) in the back of the book.

17

PUTTING THE GARDEN TO BED

The Perelandra garden moves through its growth cycle with grace and ease. By early fall, the whole garden begins to recover from the hot, dry summer days and it takes on a breathtaking beauty. I can tell that its energy is moving toward the winter rest time. Everything has a sense of completion. It's a time that feels very similar to when I meet an older person who has lived well and is now moving through the later years with an air of wisdom and knowing that there are many things in life one need not get in a huge fluff about.

I enjoy this time before the first hard frost which comes around early November. Then, sometime before the winter solstice, I help put the garden in a state of rest for the winter months. I either remove or compost right in the garden all the dead plants, make sure my stake markers are well set in the rows, spread a little hay if needed, prepare the rose bushes for the winter, and clean and oil my tools. I also prepare the bird station with suet feeders and place a heater in the bath so that they'll have access to water throughout the cold days.

I do not attempt to keep portions of the garden producing all year. I know that with a little care and attention, certain cold-weather plants can go on well into the winter. But I have sensed that the rest period of the cycle is as vital to the garden environment as any other period throughout the year. And quite frankly, by this time I need a rest also.

PUTTING THE GARDEN TO BED

When I put my first co-creative garden to bed, I had a most moving experience. For a week, I assisted the nature spirits as they gently removed the energy of each vegetable from the garden environment. It was a very intense time for me. Ten years later, it is still an intense time but in a different way. Rather than concentrate on each plant variety, we now move as a team working with a sense of the garden as a whole. Our combined focus is to shift the garden to its point of rest.

When we are finished, the garden is different but equally as beautiful as it had been throughout the growing season. Its shape is accentuated by the clearly delineated paths and the annual vegetable sections lying under a blanket of straw with nothing sticking up but the bamboo stakes marking the circular rows. It is clearly at rest.

DEVA OF THE PERELANDRA GARDEN

It is appropriate for me to point out here that within the original blueprint of each year's garden is the energy patterning for that garden's completion. How Machaelle puts her garden to bed is her response to that patterning. What is worth noting is her precision and clarity in action. And this is what I would emphasize to those of you who feel drawn to participate in this part of the blueprint.

Now, I should point out that since the garden is by definition a creation between humans and nature, it is quite reasonable to assume that all aspects of the blueprint have built in the dynamic of teamwork between the two. This includes the closing-down portion of the blueprint as well.

However you wish to respond, keep in mind the two words I have already mentioned: precision and clarity. Move with this intent and attitude and allow the energy of these two words to permeate your motions. If you do, you will complete the task in the very same spirit as the garden began so many months before when you translated the blueprint onto the charts. And, equally as important, you will set the tone for the coming garden.

PAN

The closing down of the garden is primarily an exercise in energy, in that what is being done establishes an overall dynamic of attitude and intent for the benefit of the garden environment as a whole. It is not working directly to benefit form, such as fertilizing the soil or transplanting appropriately. Its purpose is to infuse attitudinal energy into that environment which serves to stabilize the rest period and, as mentioned above, set the tone for the coming cycle. Your physical movement that is permeated with the attitudes of clarity and precision, coupled with the resulting winter changes and preparations that you will actually do, are the two ways in which this important attitudinal energy is infused into the environment. It is an energy infusion through the vehicle of purposeful action.

If left on their own, the nature spirits move each growth cycle through to its completion. But in any situation where humans and nature work as a team, it is vital that the teamwork be maintained throughout the entire cycle, including the process of "putting to bed." There are dynamics in this portion of the devic blueprint that are uniquely human and are to be responded to in a human manner. The nature spirits cannot do this for you.

There are no precise steps to give which you may follow in order to accomplish your role in this part of the cycle. More than anything, it is an expression of the human heart and soul translated into precise and clear action centered around the many things a gardener may do that will reflect a sense of completion. Just know that we of the nature spirit kingdom work right along side you focusing on our part of the task which we weave in and out of your motions, and that together, we will successfully put the garden to bed.

18

ENERGY PROCESSES FOR THE GARDEN AND, COINCIDENTALLY, THE PLANET

There are three energy processes I'd like to introduce to you for consideration as part of your gardening practices: the Energy Cleansing Process, the Battle Energy Cleansing Process, and the Soil Balancing Process.

THE ENERGY CLEANSING PROCESS

I first wrote about this process in *Behaving As If the God In All Life Mattered,* but I feel it has such a significant role in the co-creative garden that it bears repeating.

There are all kinds of environmental imbalances and pollution we gardeners have to deal with. All the way through the co-creative garden process, we have continuously considered the issue of establishing an environment that reflects balance on all levels. The Energy Cleansing Process deals with this on the level of thought and emotional energy pollution. This level can function like an X factor. Everything can be going along just fine in the garden and all of a sudden, out of nowhere, there's a horde of something eating three rows of vegetables. I have learned that when this happens, more often than not, it is because there has been a sudden and dramatic shift in thought, intent or emotion either with the gardener himself, or with the family or community connected with the garden.

Before you think I'm exaggerating, let me give you some examples.

In one community I've visited, a well-established rose bed that had been thriving for several years was now dying—and for no apparent reason. The gardeners had looked for all the possible problems and had found nothing. The rose bed happened to be right outside the building where the community's garage and vehicle maintenance crew was headquartered. It turned out that they were in the process of some fundamental organizational changes that were not being accomplished too gracefully. In fact, there were days upon days of heated arguments. Nature functions in the role of the absorber when it comes to ungrounded, raw emotional energy that is released by humans. That is a service to us and it gives us the time we need to learn how to express ourselves emotionally in a completely grounded and balanced manner. We are not out of the problem, in that we still have a great deal to learn in this area, so nature continues to serve us by absorbing these energies. If it did not, we would be constantly battered by our own raw emotional energy. In essence, by performing this service, nature is buying us time. (More will be said on this in the Battle Energy Release Process section.) At the community in question, the roses were absorbing the flying emotional energy from the crew and the energy was winning. The community gardeners had to go to these people, inform them of what was happening, and request that they pay more attention to their process of change. In short, they did, and the roses recuperated to full health.

An odd example: In my childhood home, we had a philodendron plant in the kitchen for at least five years. Now, the emotional environment in that house was not life-supporting or life-giving. At best, it fostered survival. No one talked to anyone else, which gave me the discipline of observation since I didn't use my time to learn verbal communication. I watched a lot—including that house plant. I swear to you, I do not recall it ever growing a new leaf. It didn't die, but it didn't grow either. As time went on, and I realized what a strange thing it was for this plant to never grow a new leaf, I watched it that much more. Till the day I left, I don't recall ever seeing signs of growth.

The fact is, even though emotional energy is invisible, it is no less tangible in its effect on the world of form than insects, heavy rain, or drought. It has a constant impact on the garden environment (not to mention all other components of the environment at large), and can be introduced into the garden by the gardener himself, the family or community connected with the garden, or a national or global occurrence that fosters intense or extreme emotional response by the population.

In order to maintain balance in the garden, this issue must be faced. And this is where the Energy Cleansing Process comes in. It is a simple visualization process which was given me by the nature spirits and devas in 1977. It is designed to remove the stagnant, ungrounded emotional energy that is out of time and place in the environment which has absorbed it, and move the energy back onto the next step of its evolutionary path.

There will be a time when we humans will understand that part of ourselves we refer to as our "emotional body" and will know how to express ourselves on this level in complete and balanced ways. For now, we are all in transition and all learning about these things. So for the time being, we're going to have to rely on such processes and techniques as the Energy Cleansing Process to aid us in cleaning up that which we leave behind during our emotional times.

I am focusing the process on the garden environment, but if you are going to do this process, I'd highly recommend that you include your entire personal environment, of which the garden is a part. Whenever we of the housekeeping department at Cluny did this at Findhorn, which was where I introduced the process, we not only focused on the huge hotel called Cluny (our only responsibility), but we included the entire Cluny property, buildings and gardens as well.

The process itself is a visualization (which takes about thirty minutes of focus to do well) and is based on the energy principle that to move energy from point A to point B, all one has to do is visualize the energy at point A and see it move to point B. That's the power of focus. It is the easiest, most readily accessible tool we have for getting such jobs done. Now, this is not a meditation designed to place you in a euphoric state. It is actual work done with the tools of visualization. You literally accomplish something quite tangible once it's completed.

Preparation for the Energy Cleansing Process

It's important that you be able to close your eyes and easily visualize whatever it is you are cleansing. If it's a room, you'll need to visualize the shape and layout of the room. If it's a house, you must have a clear sense of the layout of the rooms and the shape of the house. For land, a farm or a community, the distance and shape of the outside boundary is important—plus the relative position of the garden, its shape and size, and any of the outbuildings. For anything larger than one room, I would suggest that you sketch a layout of what you are working with. Nothing elaborate is needed. For land, a simple line sketch of the shape of the property with the relative placement of the buildings on the property will do. For a home in the suburbs with a small garden on a small piece of land, a sketch of the shape of the property plus rectangles to locate the house, the garden, and maybe even the dog house, the flower beds and the driveway. Anything you feel will give you an accurate but simple idea of what you're working with.

Attitude: It's a very special moment when we become active participants in the rebalancing of our environment, and it should not be done haphazardly or hurriedly. The biggest mistake we can make is to slip into manipulation. If we forget that we are aiming to act responsibly in this thing we call "life" and that we are choosing to participate as equal partners with the life around us, we can very easily slip from a spirit of co-creation to one of manipulation. Then we would not be participating in a process of balance and gentleness, but one of force and domination. Consequently, the attitude we have as we enter this is vitally important to maintaining a sense of universal balance while going through the cleansing process.

The Energy Cleansing Process

1. Choose and diagram your area to be cleansed. Place the diagram in front of you during the process. (If you need to clarify your visualization of what you're cleansing, you'll be able to look at the diagram and refresh your memory.)

2. Sit or lie quietly. Focus for a few minutes on relaxing your body. When you are comfortable, focus on your inhale and exhale as you prepare to go on.

3. (With your eyes closed.) See a bright white beam of light above your head. This is the Light of the Christ (the term traditionally used to describe that *evolutionary dynamic* contained within us all). See the light rays from this beam move down toward you and totally envelope you in white light. State to yourself or aloud:

> I ask that the Light of the Christ aid me so that what I am about to do will be for the highest good. I ask that this light help me in transmuting the ungrounded emotional energies released by us humans and that I be protected fully during this process. I welcome your presence and thank you for your help.

4. Focus again above your head. See a second beam of light—this time the light is green. (Stay with this focus until you see the light clearly and brightly. The quality of the light simply depends on the quality of your focus. If it isn't very bright, see it brighter. Or will yourself to see it brighter.) This green light is the Light of Nature (or the *involutionary dynamic* contained within us all). See its rays come toward you and also totally envelope you, co-mingling with the white light that is already surrounding you. State (to yourself or aloud):

> I ask that the Light of Nature aid me in the releasing and collecting of the energies absorbed by the nature kingdoms, tangible and intangible, animate and inanimate. I also ask that the Light of Nature aid me so that what I am about to do is for the highest good. I welcome your presence and thank you for your help.

5. State:

> At this point, I ask that any inappropriate, stagnant, darkened, or ungrounded energies allow themselves to be totally released from the intended area. I request this in gentleness and love, knowing that the cleansing and transmutation process I am about to be a part of is a process of life, of evolution—not negation.

6. Visualize the area to be cleansed. (If you're having trouble, look at your diagram.) Visualize the shape of the area, the outside boundaries especially.

7. Visualize a thin white sheet of light forming five feet *below* the lowest point of your area. (If it's a house or land, see the sheet form five feet underground.) See the sheet brighten and become whiter. Focus on it until it is bright and clear. Allow the outside edges of the sheet to extend five feet *beyond* the outside boundary of the area.

8. Once the sheet is fully formed, ask that the Light of the Christ and the Light of Nature join you as together you begin to *slowly* move the sheet up and through the area to be cleansed. See the sheet move slowly, evenly and with ease. (Remember, energy moves easily through form.) Stay focused on the sheet and watch it move through the area. If the sheet begins to sag, stop its movement, and by using your power of focus, lift the sagging area. Once it's even again, allow the entire sheet to continue. As it moves through the area, see the pockets of darkened energy collecting in it. Don't feel you have to fantasize the darkened energy. It will automatically collect in the sheet. All you have to do is recognize its presence.

Allow the sheet to rise to five feet *above* the highest point of the area you are cleansing. The top of the garden shed roof. A tree. The ceiling of your apartment. The highest hill.

9. Using your visualization, carefully gather the edges of the sheet, forming a bundle of white light which totally encloses the collected darkened energies. To the left of the bundle see a gold thread. This thread is from the Light of the Christ. Take the thread and tie the bundle closed. To the right of the bundle is another gold thread that is from the Light of Nature. Take this thread and tie it around the top of the bundle with the first one.

10. State:

> I now release the bundle to the Light of the Christ and the Light of Nature so that these energies can be moved onto their next highest level for transmutation and the continuation of their own evolutionary process.

Watch the bundle as it moves off out of your range of sight. It is important to the clarity of the process that you not try to predetermine where the next highest level is. The universal evolutionary process will take care of that.

11. Now, return your focus to the area you have just cleansed and see, sense and feel the changes. Quite often, a soft white light over the entire area can be seen. As the gardener, especially pay attention to the change in the garden area.

12. *Important:* Focus back on your breathing. Inhale and exhale through your body and out your feet. Repeat this three or four times, each time feeling the exhale exit from your feet.

13. Spend a moment recognizing all the energies that were called together because of your focus, and cooperated with you throughout the process.

The white Light of the Christ.
The green Light of Nature.
The white sheet.
The two gold threads.
The energies that were released.

14. Focus on the nature or the room around you. Sense the environment or the room's walls. The ground or the floor. Feel whatever your

body is touching. Wiggle your toes and fingers. Slowly move your hands and feet. Open your eyes and make a deliberate effort to see the land or room around you. When you are ready, slowly rise to your feet. Walk around. Drink some water, if you desire it. Give yourself a moment before continuing your day. *Be sure you feel completely present to yourself.* If you feel "spacy," put your hands on a tree or rock, focusing on your sensation of touch. Just continue moving your hands over it until you can clearly feel it. Or spend time smelling a flower. In essence, simply ground yourself by restoring your five senses. Focus on being physical.

Energy Cleansing Process Rhythm

It has been suggested to me by Pan that at the present time, in order to keep one's environment balanced, whether it be a garden or an environment that includes a garden or one that has no garden in it at all, the Energy Cleansing Process should be done on a weekly basis. This will keep the level of emotional pollution constantly moving out and from building up again. (A professional therapist, counselor, massage therapist or the like should consider doing the process on a daily basis since that work dictates a high release of emotional energy into the environment.) Also, if you, or someone else in your environment, are going through a particularly difficult time, it may be appropriate to cleanse the area more frequently. Remember, the Energy Cleansing Process not only assists the balance of the natural environment, but also assists our ability to maintain equilibrium on all levels by surrounding us with a balanced support environment and allowing us the opportunity to move through personal process without constantly bumping into collected emotional energy which may or may not have anything to do with the present situation. So if the situation is intense, cleanse more frequently.

Making an Energy Cleansing Process Tape

The easiest way to get through the process, especially in the beginning, is by recording the steps on tape, remembering to give yourself plenty of time to complete each step. (In order to maintain the co-creative balance in the process, it's important that no step be eliminated.) It might be helpful to have the tape machine within easy reach so that it can be turned off while the sheet is rising, giving you all the time you need. If more than one person wants to be involved, have one person read the steps aloud and guide everyone else through the process together. If this is done, it's important that the "guide" person try to be sensitive to everyone in the room and keep them moving through the process as a group.

If all else fails and you want another break, I have recorded the steps and you can order an Energy Cleansing Process tape from us here at Perelandra. The ordering information is in the back of the book.

THE BATTLE ENERGY RELEASE PROCESS

I stumbled onto this process back in 1984, and it was the final touch that shifted the Perelandra garden to its present level of balance as a whole and between the three kingdoms of nature represented in that environment. I really can't say enough about the importance of this process regarding its balancing affects on a garden environment (or any environment) and the insights I was given in order for me to make the necessary consciousness shifts in preparation for doing the process itself.

While doing the co-creative gardening research I observed a level of what appeared to be an antagonistic struggle between insects and plants. It was as if they were doing battle with one another. I assumed that once I understood and implemented all the steps necessary for creating the balanced garden environment, this antagonism would stop. By 1984, I had all the processes and steps I give you in this book fully implemented and still there was this level of tension. I asked why. The sessions I had with the Deva of Perelandra and Universal Light in answer to this question are what follows. The result of putting these insights into a workable format is the Battle Energy Release Process, which I include step by step immediately after the sessions.

I first did the process at Perelandra. I had been told in 1973, by the original owner of our land, that Confederate soldiers rested on this location prior to marching to the Battle of Manassas. I figured that their thoughts and fears as they prepared for battle had to be intense, and having had experience with seeing the effect of thoughts on form, it seemed reasonable to me that the battle-related thoughts had to have an impact on Perelandra.

I set up the process exactly as I have given you, and called for the release of the battle-related energy. Immediately, and I mean immediately, I saw white energy shoot out of every bit of natural form in my view. It looked like steam shooting up. This continued for about twenty minutes and created a cloudy white energy layer about thirty-feet thick that hung about twenty feet from the ground. As in the Energy Cleansing Process, I then requested that the released energy move to its next highest level within the universe. The entire cloud disappeared instantaneously.

I was then told to go into the garden, dig up some soil and hold it in my hands. Not more than two minutes had passed between the final release of the energy and my holding the soil. Now, from working that garden for six years prior, I knew the quality and makeup of my soil very well. Its base is clay. And even with the soil work I had done co-creatively, it was still of the clay character. But when I held the soil in my hands, I saw that this character had changed completely. It was now perfectly loamy in texture. I checked the soil in other areas of the garden and found it, too, had changed.

The garden that year also changed in character. The aggressive interaction I had observed for years was no longer present. And it has remained this way ever since.

After completing the process at Perelandra, I was then asked to go to the Gettysburg Battlefields and do the same thing. I did, and experienced a similar release of energy from the battlefields. The references to the Gettysburg Battlefields in the sessions are in regard to the work I did there.

I think it's fair to say that just about every square inch of land on this planet has at some point in history experienced war or battle. Whether the specifics are known or not, it would not hurt to assume the need for the release of battle energy from your garden, land or lot and do the process. Unlike the Energy Cleansing Process that needs to be used on a regular basis in one's life for the continuous check of emotional or stressful energy, the Battle Energy Release Process needs only to be used one time within a specific land area since it deals with the results of an historic event.

UNIVERSAL LIGHT

1. The Relationship between Nature and War

You have been absolutely correct in that there is a connection between nature and military history. There is a healing role which must be addressed in that area in which military touches nature.

Remember the concept of horizontal healing: like healing like, form healing form. When war is waged, it is not simply a matter of moving form, of creating strategy of form against form, man against man, equipment against equipment. When war is waged, energy is moved on all levels. The many sounds of war (we use "sounds" figuratively and literally) are echoed throughout the universe on all its levels. Up to this time, the movements of man through the instruments of war (battles, fighting) have been appropriate. It has been one structure in which man can grow, change, and move forward. It has not been the only structure in the arena of global government available to man, but surely it has been the most widely used.

ENERGY PROCESSES FOR THE GARDEN AND THE PLANET

You know that nature serves as a buffer for man on Earth in regard to the universal energies that flow to Earth. Were it not for nature, those energies would hit man directly, shattering him. Universal energies, by nature, are more homogeneous than the energies of Earth. This, of course, relates to the fact that Earth is of form: energies are in their most differentiated state. Consequently, it is essential that nature serve as the intermediary, as it were, between the souls who reside on Earth in a state of individuation and the larger, more encompassing, homogeneous energies of the universe that are available to them. If one were to relate the principle of war to a concept with which you are familiar, one would say that war, as a framework of change for man, is conceptually similar to the healing form known as homeopathy, that is, negative creating positive. War, by nature, uses negative tools and disciplines—negative in that they are designed to negate life and position for the sake of advancing someone else's life, position, land.

We do not indulge in the traditional value judgment of this. As a foundation, a framework, we do not see war as wrong; we see it simply as a framework. However, war as a framework for progression, change, growth, is no longer appropriate. The developments in warfare have far unbalanced that relationship of negative creating positive. Now the negative (the tools, the weaponry, the bomb) is so negative, so strong, that it would indeed be difficult for positive to rise out of the rubble. Consequently, we see the traditional war framework as simply inappropriate.

When regarding nature in light of war, one must look at several levels, aspects, functions and roles which nature has played. Since we have mentioned the role of nature as the buffer between universal energies and man, we will go on and talk about a role that nature plays of which man is not aware: the buffer between man and universal energies in the other direction—war being a particularly prime example of the need for this buffer.

War on Earth is, as a framework, not alien to change and growth processes in the universe. Energy has moved and frameworks have been created in similar ways; however, because of the differentiated form that war takes on Earth, it is, in its impact on the universe, extremely powerful in its most dense, most intense way. Consequently, it has been important that nature absorb this intensity and serve as a buffer between Earth and the universe so that the balance of the universe would not be unnecessarily tipped due to the intensity of the individuated warfare.

We speak here of the specific power that is created when one takes the whole, and clearly and fully separates it into all its parts, coordinates it, and moves it as one unit (of its many different parts) in one direction for one cause. World War II is an example of this principle on its broadest level: it was not just one country against another; it was countries against countries—the whole was larger than ever before. There were more individuated parts than ever before, and they were all successfully (albeit not easily) brought together as one unit and moved forward for one purpose.

The impact of this beyond Earth was great. Without the buffer of nature, the universe would have indeed tipped, meaning its balance would have shifted to such a degree that its sense of natural timing would have been thrown off and it would have needed a period of time to regain its balance. Nature absorbed this intensity and released it to the universe as a less intense and more easily absorbable energy form. Not only was the universe not tipped, but the knowledge, information, and growth experiences occurring within the framework you know as World War II were picked up and used simultaneously in various situations throughout the universe.

One could look at what we have been saying as the vertical role between man and war, nature, and ultimately, the universe. Because man has not understood the principle of energy, he has also not understood the impact of war on an energy level, on the energy around him. Although up until now war may have been an acceptable framework, that does not mean that (like any framework) it is without implications on an energy level. All action, all intent, moves energy. This is a law man is only beginning to understand. Consequently, he has gone through thousands and thousands of years of functioning within that framework without understanding the implications of the framework except on the basest of levels. We do not use the word "basest" to mean it as a value judgment; we mean it in a form context. Reworded, one might say he has not understood the implication of his actions except on the level most "of form."

When war is waged, the coming together and the release of intense, basic emotions occurs. It is the eruption of emotion. Man cannot sustain his life within that intensity, for when the battle is over, the intensity of the battle remains. We are dealing with the very same principle you deal with in the Energy Cleansing Process: how emotions remain within a room after grief, or after a battle between husband and wife. Multiply that by five-hundred thousand, and you can imagine the intensity we are dealing with on the war level. In order for man to survive, to continue living, to move out of the framework of battle and continue moving forward, he must be buffered fully from this intensity.

As you know, nature will absorb energies but, on the whole, will not transmute them. Consequently, this enormous body of intense energy created in battle throughout the history of man is being held by nature.

It has always been meant to be a temporary assignment, but as one well knows, temporary (in terms of time) on one level can mean quite a different thing on another level. Man has the ability to transmute, to change energy from one level to another; however, what you are about to do is to go as the representative of man back into the area, or field, of battle to touch in with nature and to release that which has been held for the sake of man—to release these energies from nature, transmute them, release them from Earth, and allow them to take their balanced, healthful position within the context of the universe. Once this is done, this aspect of battle will become useful to, and usable by, the whole.

Confronting these intense energies which have been held by nature, you are not acting in the role of the absorber. In fact, you are not acting in the role of the transmuter; you are acting in the role of the conductor, the orchestrator. You will ***facilitate*** *the transmutation process and the release of these energies into their rightful place in the universe. This work will go on outside you. You will neither move the energies through nor serve as the absorber. That has already been done by nature. Consequently, you will be fully protected. Your understanding of the dynamic of energy will allow you to facilitate fully the processes that must go on without, shall we say, getting in the way of the process. This is a technical process within the laws of nature.*

Once these energies have been released from an area of battle, it will then be appropriate to facilitate the rebalancing and healing process within nature by the use of flower essences. We recommend that you remove the energies, test to make sure the area is clear, and then connect with the overlighting deva of that area to receive insight on the flower essences that could be used within the nature spirit level to facilitate the healing process within nature. Of course, simply left alone nature would balance; but by facilitating the process, you once again step into the role of man taking responsibility for his own actions and working co-creatively for the healing of Earth. Not only will these actions actually facilitate the healing process within the realm of nature, but they will also symbolically sound a note of man taking on his own responsibility for the destruction that he has created within nature. So instead of it taking years, possibly, for the rebalancing of nature within the area, you will leave the area of battle having cleansed the emotions (the energy that has been held within nature all these years) out of the realm of nature and given back to nature precisely what it needs for its own rebalancing—that is a good day's work.

UNIVERSAL LIGHT

2. Insights on the Battle Energy Release Process

The Battle Energy Release Process you are conducting is not a surprise to nature (in terms of your entering an area and activating this process). Nature is alerted, anxious and eager to cooperate with you in releasing these energies. It has been essential that a representative of man work in co-creative partnership with nature in releasing the energies. This is a Pan/Christ function—nature and man working together in harmony for the purpose of shifting the imbalances within the realm of nature into balance.

Nature is fully capable of releasing these energies (we do not wish to confuse this with the concept of transmuting energies), but nature does not have within it the tool to transmute human energy from one level to another: it can only absorb and release. Consequently, these energies could have been released at any time, but there has been a higher timing involved. Mankind had to change and grow to a level where he could then turn around and take responsibility for the impact he has had in nature (as well as other areas) due to his own actions.

That growth within man implies his change in energy from Piscean to Aquarian. Since he is now entering that period of active change, it is obvious that now is the time he is capable of taking custody of the energies which have been held by nature, and releasing them into the universe so that they may take their rightful place within the universal change from the Piscean to the Aquarian Age. The energies that are being released on battlefields are not isolated from this change; timing has been essential in the development of the Battle Energy Release Process, so as you move into the battlefields themselves, you will find that nature will not be surprised by your presence. It has been waiting for man to return and take custody of that which it has been holding for so long for his benefit.

We warn you that as you move into the battlefield areas themselves, you will experience a greater amount of energy than you experienced at Perelandra. This is one reason the battlefields will have to be approached not as one unit, but from the angle of their being a collection of many different smaller battles all coming together to create a single larger one. If you attempted to release the entire battlefield area with all of its parts as one whole, you would truly run the risk of being overwhelmed. That is not a necessary experience for you to have, so we urge you to approach any battlefield as a collection of smaller battles all carried out within one well-defined geographical area.

Regarding the fact that energies released from nature form appear white, these energies have not been transmuted by nature, but by history: Historical experience, the review and understanding of war; the healing (there have been generations of healing) that has occurred within the families whose husbands and sons experienced that war; and the healing that has occurred as those who experienced the battles firsthand moved from lifetime to lifetime, dealing with their role, their deaths, in that war (they themselves serving in the transmutation process). So as you see, this is not just a collection of energies held by nature untouched since the battle. Those energies have automatically been transmuted because of the continuing evolution of those souls who were a part of the battle and the continuing evolution of the families who were either attached to those surrounding the battle or affected by the battle.

If in the future you choose to enter areas of more recent wars where the energies held by nature have not been transmuted by those touched by that war (we think specifically of Viet Nam), you will have to alter the process you are using in order to accommodate the untransmuted energies.

Recently you have considered the notion of nothing you experience ever remaining forever on the back burner: how, somewhere down the road, you will have to face everything—all emotions, pain, experience—and fully and completely ground those experiences within you, understand their purpose, and transmute them. The transmuted battle-related energies fit within this area of thought, this notion of nothing remaining forever on a back burner. What you are experiencing now by viewing the white, transmuted battle energies is one result of looking at everything on the back burners—bringing it forward, dealing with it, grounding it, and transmuting it. That process within an individual soul does not remain isolated within the soul. As each man who died at the Battle of Gettysburg grounded his own experience, that energy was transmuted.

This only serves to give you another example of the power which man's actions have, the power man has within himself, and the broad implications of his actions. If man can act in such a way that he can create a huge, massive body of traumatic energy that needs to be held within the realm of nature so that man himself will not self-destruct from its rawness and intensity, then he also has the power to transmute it. It works both ways. Man on Earth has the tendency to see only how destructive he can be; he does not have self-confidence about how constructive he can be.

The question arises: If man has had the ability and has actually transmuted this energy that has been held within nature, then why have these areas remained ecologically unbalanced? The issue here is not primarily the negativity of energy, although the initial impact on nature was this intense negativity: the massive cloud of raw emotional energy released in war and absorbed by nature initially threw off the natural ecological balance. However, the energy of the Battle of Gettysburg has been transmuted, and what remains and continues to throw off the ecological balance is not negativity. The simple fact is that a large body of man-made energy is being held in custody by nature. In essence, nature has been willingly and eagerly performing a service for man at a cost to its own balance and development. While these areas have maintained this service, the ecological balance has never been able to be retained or rediscovered. Once the areas release this body of energy, there will be a strong and evident move toward re-establishing an ecological balance.

We emphasize that the role of nature in this area of service has been a willing and cooperative role, not something that was forced on nature. Nature is an intelligence which can willingly choose its position within the evolutionary process of man on Earth. It could have refused this role; however, had it refused, man would have been in a lot of trouble. He would not have had the healing time he needed in order to evolve to the point where he could then come back and take full custody of these energies. As we have said, nature has buffered man from these energies; it has been an important and necessary service.

Regarding the question of nuns praying over battlefields, they have laid groundwork upon which you are building. The feeling to which they are responding—the major feeling, as we see it—is the one they receive from the energy being held. They are responding to this service. Although they wish to release these energies, this "stigma of war," from these battlefield areas, it has not yet been time, and they have not had the wherewithal to do this. Consequently, their prayer and emotion, the direction of their prayer, has been more aligned to the holding pattern and has helped achieve a Pan/Christ balance within that pattern. They are, in essence, women who intuitively understand that something within man needs to happen in these areas in order to balance the horror of war. They have responded with prayer and their response has not gone unheeded or been ineffectual. If one could see the energy of their prayer, one might visualize it moving from them into the massive energy being held by nature, and that in itself has had a healing effect. However, we repeat, the effort by the nuns has not served to release this energy from the realm of nature, because they have not understood the role of nature in this. Consequently, they have not been able to respond with a process that would release the energies from nature.

ENERGY PROCESSES FOR THE GARDEN AND THE PLANET

At this time, we would like to move on to a related matter: to expand on the notion of how an individual soul can affect the impact of history by looking fully and completely at his role within history.

The concept of history has several levels. One level can best be described as simply what happened: A leading to B leading to C creating D. When looked at sequentially, it is quite easy to see how one act in history can affect future acts, movements, and changes. However, these things of the future and these acts of the past are not static; their impact is constantly changing. First of all, historians look back at events and judge and re-evaluate them—that alone changes the impact of history. You may have a specific event which for a number of years carries a particular impact on history. Then suddenly, this event is viewed differently and re-evaluated. From that point on, its impact will indeed change. It may change again and again, depending on how many times it is viewed differently and re-evaluated. Each time it changes, its impact on the present and on the future also changes.

What man does not fully recognize right now is the impact of the souls who were involved in a particular event as they themselves evolve, re-evaluate, change, and look at things they have put on the back burner. As they go through this process, they activate a transmutation process within the event itself.

One might say that history itself goes through an evolutionary process. It is a fluid, moving phenomenon. No one can say within his own life, "Well, I have done that, so now it's over and I never need look at it again." If his personal role in a specific event is incomplete and ungrounded, he will have to look at it again—and again and again. Each time, if he so chooses, he can change his evaluation of the event and his role in it, and thus change the impact, the energy around the event itself.

Another point is that emotions are inherent in every historical event. When individual participants of an historical event place things from that event onto their personal back burners, it is usually in the area of emotions. We would have to say that the principal area preventing, or interfering with, the forward evolution of history comes from the level of the emotions that participants have placed on back burners. As man evolves within himself, he will have opportunity to recall those emotions.

Now, he often places emotions on the back burner so that he can move forward at the time. One can say that the phenomenon of placing emotional reaction to an historical event on the back burner is very similar indeed to the phenomenon of nature absorbing the emotional energy released during war. If nature did not do this, man would not have the space to evolve and grow in order to get to the point of being able to come back and take full custody of what nature has been holding. Quite often, the emotions experienced during the outplay of historical events are so intense and raw that in order to continue, man must place these emotions on a back burner. But they were never meant to stay there—just as nature was never meant to hold battle energies forever—and must be brought back up when he is ready for those emotions to ground fully through him, to be transmuted and released. When that happens, the body of emotion inherent within the historical event itself will also shift. As each man takes custody of his own emotions within the historical event, the general body of the event will shift.

We do not view placing events on the back burner as an escape, but as survival. There are some experiences within each man's life that must be placed on the back burner until he has the full opportunity and wherewithal to fully ground those experiences through him, transmuting whatever energies need to be transmuted and completing his role on the impact of an historical event (any past event or experience within a person's life, within any lifetime).

The consideration of history as a fluid, evolutionary process is another example of how everything that is, everything that exists on Earth, is an active participant in this change from the Piscean to the Aquarian Age. Everything moves, shifts, and evolves. Just as separating truth from insanity within the area of war alters the body of information regarding war that is available to this universe and beyond, so, too, does the fluid, evolutionary process of history change that body of information available to this universe and beyond. These changes are not just for the benefit of Earth. All of these changes are for the benefit of the whole—this universe and that which is beyond.

UNIVERSAL LIGHT

3. Insights on the Battle Energy Release Given after the Gettysburg Battlefield Work

Each battlefield, each battle, each war, is a microcosm reflecting the position of the universe. So often people think war has been an ugly blot on the history of Earth, that it has reflected the ugliness of man on Earth. Well, we do not see it that way, in those judgmental terms. All the wars that have occurred on Earth throughout history have reflected a universal mindset, not a mindset unique to Earth alone. This is another reason how and why the evolution of specific areas of Earth affect the entire universe and beyond. If the effect can flow from the planet Earth out through the universe and beyond, then one must con-

sider that the effect also flows the other way—from beyond the universe, into it, and to Earth. It is a two-way flow, involving evolution and effect.

The work accomplished at Gettysburg [Wednesday, March 7, 1984] *has sounded a clear, strong note throughout the universe and beyond that; indeed, the mindset of souls, of all that exists, has truly begun to change and is changing. That which has been rippling throughout the universe (this change in terms of problem-solving, this movement from violence to non-violence) was clearly grounded within the arena of form.*

Remember that a battle is a microcosm of the universal mindset that is acted out in the arena of form, and it is not that Earth has acted out universal wars or battles. One must not try to superimpose the form reality of a battle onto other arenas and areas of the universe. What we are suggesting is that man on Earth, in tune with and in touch with the evolution of the universe, taps into the prevailing mindset and interprets that into the arena of form. Up to now, the primary interpretation has been battle, war. Although he is not acting out some universal war that is clashing well beyond his own sense of vision, he is showing very clearly in a form-like manner the implications of the universal mindset were it to be translated into form.

Now, a change takes preparation, and the preparation for the change from Piscean to Aquarian in the arena of war has gone on for some time. There have been many questions arising in people's minds. There has been the realization that since the dropping of the atomic bomb in 1945, war on Earth has been inappropriate. This became the catalyst of an intense period of preparation within the mindset of all souls to move from the old way of doing things to the new. Preparation is not the thing that strikes the tuning fork; it is what gets man to the point where he can strike the tuning fork.

The change from the old to the new, from the Piscean to the Aquarian, begins in the heart. It is a shift in attitude, in how one perceives something. Man has had to go through years of challenge, thought, and struggle in preparation for that shift in attitude, and attitudes have begun to change. But just as a battle is a microcosm of universal thought acted out in the arena of form, it can also serve as a microcosm of a massive change in attitude come together and acted out within its arena (such as a battlefield)—again within the framework of form.

The preparation on Earth up to this point has required that man change his attitude about different realities and events that have occurred around him. For example, his vision about war has expanded so that if one were to break down the components of war and look at just one component—say, death—I think it would be easy to see how man has changed his attitudes. The narrow vision from which he has worked has been that a man dies and that's that; there is nothing more, nothing further. He dies, rots, and goes to earth. Over the years, a large group of humans on Earth have shifted their attitude and understanding of what death is. With that one shift in attitude alone, one can re-enter a battlefield area and view it from a completely different perspective.

Death is just one component of war. There have been many components that have changed, that have gone through a preparation period. What you did when you re-entered Gettysburg was to take the various components that have changed, create a framework called the "battle energy release process" using those new attitudes, and therewith release the remnants of the old. You created new form, new structure, and released the remnants of the old which happened to be held within the nature kingdoms. Again, we would like to point out that neither this change in attitude about death nor this collection of attitudes surrounding war is unique to Earth—they are universal. Just as man on Earth is not isolated from the universe, we can also say that this collection of attitudinal changes is a result of man's dance with the universal flow, interpreting that which is within the arena of form. Had there not been a universal transition in progress, and had not man on Earth prepared himself to join in this transition, it would have been impossible for you to effect an efficient framework to accomplish what you did Wednesday. You would have, in essence, superimposed a framework onto the situation and struck an alien note. The Gettysburg battles were fully connected to the universe, so a man-made structure outside that connection simply could not have accomplished any kind of energy move. Again, it would have been an alien structure. Wednesday you tapped into that which is the universe, translated it into structure, and enacted it within the framework of form, thus completing the whole picture. The universal microcosm, acted out within the framework of war, has now changed.

Remember that war is a collection of universal thought patterns come together within the structure of form and acted out in a microcosmic way. At Gettysburg, you took that collection of thought patterns (which had changed since the battle), created new structure, and through the framework of form released the final energy of the old that was being held within the nature kingdoms. Gettysburg was fought within the framework of one understanding. You reflected within yourself the many changes within that framework which have occurred within man on Earth and within the universe. You reflected those changes through the form of the process you performed throughout the battlefields, the result of which was the final release of energy that had been held by nature since the battles.

The principle of horizontal healing plays a strong role in what occurred Wednesday and in what we are saying. The energies of the transition were grounded into a framework of form (The Battle Energy Release Process). Because that intent, attitude, shift, and change were translated and grounded into form, their effect on what was released in battle, in form, was far greater and far more efficient than anything else that could have occurred. This process demonstrates the principle of horizontal healing (form healing form being just one demonstration thereof) and is a fine example of how new attitudes can be translated into the structure of form and used to heal, change, and shift the results of old attitudes.

This brings us to the word "love." What greater love is there than empathy, compassion, and understanding. The impetus to all the changes that have occurred, are occurring, and will occur regarding the concept of war lie within the areas of empathy, compassion, and understanding—to use one word, love. As the energy of love expands within man, how he views what is around him shifts and changes. At the risk of sounding trite and using that well-worn concept, we would say that the basis of what occurred Wednesday rests within the area of love.

The preparation for what occurred lies within the area of man's growth in understanding love. The changes in man's attitudes toward history, death, decision-making, nature, his connection to the universe, the universe's connection to him, the dynamic of man's and nature's reality (known as energy)—all those attitudinal changes center around his shift in empathy, compassion, and understanding; his growth in love; his ability to open himself to something greater, wider, and broader.

If one were to see Wednesday's result as a fully vibrating tuning fork, one would also have to see that what struck the tuning fork to make it vibrate fully were attitudinal changes brought about by empathy, compassion, and understanding—i.e., love. At the same time the tuning fork began to vibrate fully and completely, the universe was infused with an enormous rush of energy that also can best be described as the energy of love—that is, empathy, compassion, and understanding. It is no wonder that what may have appeared to you to be a small act (when compared to the universe) had such an impact on the whole.

UNIVERSAL LIGHT

4. The Battle Energy Release Process from the Vantage Point of Nature

The role of nature in battlefield areas such as Gettysburg has been to hold a vast energy while man has consciously and unconsciously worked to transform that dynamic into something less traumatic until the change has reached the point where he may return to an area such as Gettysburg and reclaim the energy. We will talk about the effects of releasing such energy. To hold the energy is a voluntary decision on nature's part, in its service to mankind. But there has been a cost to both nature and man.

When nature holds such a vast body of energy as at a battlefield, its own perfect balance is tipped. When nature places its balance to one side, its entire physical makeup reflects this shift in intent. Nature voluntarily has shifted its intent—from existing within the laws of spirit flowing fully and perfectly through form—to existing off balance. When that occurred in Gettysburg, for example, the entire physical makeup of nature changed there. It was an all-encompassing ecological shift of every cell and molecule. Everything within the environment of the Gettysburg battlefield shifted its makeup, function, and purpose to a position that was slightly at odds with the surrounding environment. It created an environment of stress, an environment of slight abrasion. We say slight because had nature reflected a dramatic change on all levels, in proportion to what it had absorbed, the nature kingdom itself would have been destroyed there. The environment would have been destroyed.

Imagine the entire environment of Gettysburg to be a set of gears. Each gear went slightly out of alignment in relation to the other gears and this created a slightly abrasive situation with an immediate physical change in the environment. The soil shifted, the health of the trees changed, the basic overall health of the environment went from a position of strength to a position of vulnerability, very much like a human body under stress. As the years progressed and nature in the area continued to function off balance, its physical form continued to deteriorate. The makeup of Gettysburg shifted as the town grew, more people came, and technology changed, and the environment did not enfold these changes into a balanced ecology. Very much like the domino effect, an increasingly more complicated and complex imbalance occurred, one imbalance building on another imbalance and so on. The co-creative relationship between man and nature simply could not exist.

In a co-creative relationship man and nature work in partnership and when there is a change, for example in appropriate technology, nature has the agility and the ability to incorporate that change into its own environment with balance. We are assuming that the changes are used appropriately, and that man is working in partnership with nature and not with manipulation. When the environment itself is off balance, a co-creative relationship in technology between man and nature simply cannot exist. In the area of Gettysburg the changes in the town, the farms, and the technology reflected in an imbalanced way in nature there.

Many people feel that in order for man to be responsive to nature, he must live what you call the simple life—a life devoid of advancement, technology and change. That simply is not true. Technology is one of the areas where man and nature come together in partnership most clearly. Man acts on his ideas and from the elements of nature invents a new form, thus he creates technology. Nature has always been an eager and full participant in the development of form through the art form of technology. The key is to work in technology co-creatively with nature. An ecological balance in technology must also be maintained. The laws of ecological balance are not excluded from the arena of technology. As man enters an environment bringing with him development and growth, the nature of that environment is designed to envelop and cooperate with those changes.

When nature absorbed the energies released from the intensity of battle, its balance tipped. Added to that, man has not understood his co-creative relationship with nature. These two factors are holding nature back in its evolution on Earth.

The battlefield of Gettysburg instantaneously changed in response to the work you did there. The most dramatic and important change was the shift in the flow of nature energy in the area from imbalance into balance. It is as if the dominos dropping were falling to the right. That was the direction of imbalance, shall we say. What you did was go back to the first domino, set it up, and tip it to the left. That is the familiar direction of a balanced evolutionary flow. This is a dramatic change, and although there were many instantaneous shifts within each cell of nature in that area, there was not a complete restoration to full balance. It had taken a long time for the battlefield area of Gettysburg to establish its complex, difficult position of imbalance. Now that the energy is moving in the proper direction, balance will more quickly be restored. But certain aspects there will need more time.

When nature is moving in imbalance, although there is an irritation, a grinding of the gears so to speak, people become very used to it, they acclimatize themselves to that environment. The attitude of the people flows in the direction of imbalance. Now nature has shifted into a flow of balance. But little has been done to attain support for that shift from the people in the environment. Nature will continue to flow in the direction of regaining its balance, but balance will take longer to achieve because of the lack of support from the people there.

If people were to shift their attitude towards nature, the environment could shift into perfect balance instantaneously. That is the power of man's relationship to nature. When he takes responsibility as a co-creator, the evolutionary flow of nature responds. Just as man develops far more quickly and fully when his environment supports him lovingly, so does nature.

There is always the possibility for physical change to occur instantaneously, according to the attitude of the people involved. The Battle Energy Release Process is timely now because people are beginning to change their attitudes toward the environment. Your work in the battlefield areas will be received, albeit on an unconscious level, by a less alien society. The changes in man's general attitude towards ecology over the past ten to fifteen years have not gone unnoticed. As the people in the Gettysburg area continue to grow, the environment which has already shifted into the direction of balance will move more quickly.

The Battle Energy Release Process

1. Connect with the overlighting deva of the battlefield and ask to be given insight as to the appropriate location(s) for your work. Or go to the location on the battlefield or land area you intend to clear that intuitively attracts you. If the land area includes your garden, do the process from there.

2. Open a coning of energy. That is, call to you:
   a) the overlighting deva of that specific battlefield or land area,
   b) Pan—representing the nature spirit level,
   c) the white light of the Christ energy (mankind's evolutionary energy traditionally known as Christ energy),
   d) your own higher self and the higher selves of anyone working with you in this release process.

The calling together of these energies creates a larger vortex of energy called a "coning." Spend a moment acknowledging and sensing the presence of each "member" of your coning. This will clarify and ground it. (Verify the presence of the coning using kinesiology by asking if the coning is formed and activated. If you get a negative, start the coning formation over again and this time really focus on what you are doing. Then retest.)

3. Present yourself to the overlighting deva of the battlefield or land/garden area as a representative of mankind who has come to nature in the spirit of love and co-creativity to take custody of the battle energies held by nature and to facilitate this release process.

4. **The Release:** Ask nature to now release all battle energies *with gentleness and ease.*

Watch or feel the release process. It may be completed in a few minutes or need a longer time period such as a half hour. The energy will be released from all surrounding natural form and rest as an "energy cloud" right above the battlefield or land. If you have no sense of this happening, simply trust that it is occurring and continue on.

5. When the process is complete, request that the released energy now move to its next highest level within the universe. Do not attempt to predetermine where that might be.

6. Spend a moment feeling/receiving the changes that have been made in the battlefield or area. Note your sensations, intuitive insights and what you see in your mind's eye. This serves to fully ground the completed release process.

7. To close the Battle Energy Release Process: "Dismantle" the coning by recalling or focusing your attention on its members individually and requesting that they each now release from the coning. (Test to verify that the coning is now dismantled and de-activated.)

SUGGESTION: I mentioned in the introduction to the Battle Energy Release Process that I did this as the final balancing process for the garden. This is true because I needed to unravel the whole co-creative garden balancing process to that final point, forcing me to observe that there was still an aggression problem and ask the question, "Why?". But I don't recommend that you wait. I suggest you do it as soon as possible. It will favorably impact the entire process of establishing the balance in your garden.

The best time of the cycle to do the Battle Energy Release Process is before you even begin to get the devic chart information in late winter. The impact of the process is so great that it could require adjustments in the blueprint. The overlighting deva of your garden will immediately note the shift in the garden environment and adjust the blueprint accordingly. If you have already begun the growth cycle and feel drawn to do the process anyway, I'd go right ahead. Its impact may not be fully accounted for in the blueprint until the following year but, in the meantime, it will favorably affect the blueprint already in process.

THE SOIL BALANCING PROCESS

This is the last energy process I use and it is as valuable as the other two. It's an extension of the soil work presented in Chapter 9 and it may be used by itself or in conjunction with the Energy Cleansing Process and the Battle Energy Release Process.

I was taught the Soil Balancing Process to use with the nature spirit and devic levels during those times when I am faced with what seem to be impossible soil-balancing jobs. For example, after doing the Battle Energy Release Process at Gettysburg, I was told to stabilize that work by balancing the soil for the entire battlefield. Now, there are three ways one can approach this kind of request. 1) Say "You're crazy!" and walk away. 2) Find out how much fertilizer is needed from the deva and schlepp bags of the stuff everywhere—thus creating a lot of attention and eventual problems with the U.S. Park Service. 3) Work with the devic and nature spirit levels and do the nifty balancing process I was taught.

Another example: Soil balancing in areas that are inaccessible because buildings are sitting on top of it. Now, I can hear you asking, "Why would someone want to fertilize and balance the soil beneath their basement floor or underneath a high-rise apartment building?" Don't forget that this soil is the true base upon which the building sits. And when concerned about ecological balance on all its various levels, that base becomes important. Let me explain this further: You have just bought an old house which you plan to restore. Either as a matter of good sense or because you might feel some strange "vibes" in the house, you do the Energy Cleansing and/or Battle Energy Release processes and can immediately feel that an impact has been made. The house feels light, perhaps even free. Let's assume that one of the families who had once lived in the house was a little strange. Strange to the point that the emotional and mental energy they created actually altered the physical environment of the house. That can truly happen (as was pointed out in the Universal Light sessions for the Battle Energy Release Process) and does quite frequently. That's what you felt when you decided you had better do one of the energy processes.

But carry this thought further. Emotional energy is absorbed by the environment. What you released from the house was absorbed not only by the house itself, but the land it sits on as well. If the emotions are traumatic or out of balance, it can literally throw land physically out of balance also. In order to absorb and hold this energy, the molecular structure of the land and any form that is a part of that land must accommodate what it is holding and shift to a corresponding level of imbalance. That shift will literally deplete the soil of the nutritional makeup that held it in balance and create another nutritional makeup that supports the imbalance.

When you did the Energy Cleansing and/or Battle Energy Release processes, you removed the emotional energy that was causing the imbalance. If left on its own, the land and the form on that land will immediately begin its shift to return to a state of balance that corresponds with the new balance in the house. But this will take time, for the shift is gradual. In the meantime, the land and its form are in the vulnerable state of a healing process and can, during this time, attract to it emotional energy from outside your environment that is similar in makeup to that which you just released. In essence, the land has now become a temporary magnet. Like attracting like. And suddenly, you'll feel the house shift back to that old, odd feeling.

The energy processes you used before will have to be done over. And if something isn't done to demagnetize this land, you will have to continue doing them from time to time until the land has completed its healing process and started attracting balanced energies.

Here's where the Soil Balancing Process comes in. By working with the devas and nature spirits, you can bypass the normal sequential healing time and etherically shift the necessary nutrients into the land in question immediately after doing the energy processes. That places the land in a balance that corresponds to the new balance of the house and closes down the magnetic attraction of energy similar to what you just released. In turn, the balanced land stabilizes the entire energy and environmental balancing process you seek to create.

I first did the Soil Balancing Process for the Perelandra garden several days after I did the Battle Energy Release Process. Now, it would seem that I had easy access to that soil. But the information I got from the Deva of the Garden told me that I would be working with the soil at a five-foot depth—and that's not easily accessible. Let me give you those insights I received when I began working with this process. To some extent it will be a reiteration of what's been said so far by Universal Light, but I think it might help you to understand if you read how the deva (Universal Light is not a deva.) expresses these concepts.

DEVA OF THE PERELANDRA GARDEN

You have found that the energy balancing of an area in most cases must be coupled with the nutritional balance of the area's soil. Without the latter, the weakened soil environment will be susceptible to attract-

ing new but similar traumatic vibrations to it. Form conforms to the makeup of the energy it contains. The land where these traumatic emotions have been held for so long physically reflects that imbalance. Once the energies have been released, the land, if left on its own, will go through an evolutionary process leading to the point where it will reflect the clearer energy state. However, while the land is in this time of transition, it will be vulnerable—not yet removed from the old, not yet stabilized in the new. When important and where necessary, we can eliminate the transition period by using the nature spirit level to balance the land nutritionally.

The intent of this process should be the complete and full stabilization of the five-foot-deep soil base of the garden or any land area you wish to work with. The soil's interaction with man's environment is primarily held within this five-foot-deep layer. This is why the Energy Cleansing Process sheet of light should be formed five feet below the land's surface. Below five feet, the interaction rate is minimal and can safely be left to evolve in "form time." From five feet and above, the evolution can occur at what we may call "energy time," which is why the nature spirit level is utilized. They know how to transcend relative time in an evolutionary process. So, not only are they assisting you by shifting form into energy then, after application, back to form again, they are also changing the relative time aspect of the evolutionary process.

By completing the Soil Balancing Process, you have stopped any influx of traumatic emotional energy from outside Perelandra that was being drawn to the Perelandra environment because of the principle of like attracting like. Another way of saying this is "imbalance attracting similar imbalance." We should say here, however, that because of your extensive work with us on the nature levels, that influx to Perelandra was minimal. This last step has fully closed that door.

To maintain the balance at Perelandra from this point on, we suggest a basic rhythmic energy cleansing which will process through any normal, day-to-day, ungrounded emotional energies that, if left unattended, would themselves be absorbed by nature in a custodian-like relationship. We see that during this period of transition (Piscean to Aquarian) and until man gets a fuller grasp on what it is he must understand and do in order to ground those energies that originate on his emotional level, the energy cleansing should be considered part of man's mundane, rhythmic life—such as brushing his teeth or taking a shower. Although it may not be necessary to do the energy cleansing daily, it would be a safe bet in most cases to assume that the cleansing should be done weekly.

One last thing regarding the multilevel Soil Balancing Process. Although we foresee no major environmental shifts that would be forceful enough to come into Perelandra from outside and throw off its stabilized foundation, we cannot guarantee that it won't happen. Therefore, we suggest that you check the soil balance foundation each year around this time [February]. *We suspect you will find no problems. We recommend this as a precaution.*

At first glance, it would seem that this process involves a little magic. But it is based on solid principles of energy and matter. Remember that the nature spirits are true masters of working with energy and form. At will, they can shift energy out of form, move it to another form, and even make the form itself disappear. It all has to do with the universal principles of energy and matter. And this is what is utilized during the Soil Balancing Process which you will be directly participating in.

Tools for the Process

You will need to make available to the nature spirits small amounts of nutrients which together as a set create a balanced fertilizing unit. For convenience, I made a kit using one-ounce bottles which hold:

Bone Meal	Cottonseed Meal
Rock Phosphate	Dolomite Lime
Nitro-10 (nitrogen)	Kelp
Greensand	Comfrey Flower Essence (I'll explain this one later.)

Except for the Comfrey Flower Essence, these are the nutrients I add to my garden. They represent a full nutritional unit and allow me to respond when doing the Soil Balancing Process no matter what the deficiency is. If you use different organic fertilizers, that's perfectly fine—as long as you make available something for phosphorus, nitrogen, potassium, and the acid/alkaline balance.

If you are planning to do the process at sites away from your garden, you may wish to make a small kit also. Stopper bottles (with the glass stopper removed) are convenient, small envelopes or zip-lock bags can be used as well. You only need to have the equivalent of about two tablespoons of each nutrient. For those of you who use animal manures only: the natural earth additives are preferred for this process because of the depth of the work. One normally does not find cow manure five feet below the surface of the ground. But greensand, rock phosphate and bone meal can be integrated into that level without changing the character of the soil.

Optional nutrients to check:

In addition, I make available the trace minerals found in the earth. I bought small, inexpensive bottles of each at a health food store. They are:

Zinc	Iron
Magnesium	Sulfur
Calcium	Boron
Manganese	Molybdenum
Copper	Chlorine

Also: paper and pencil. Armed with your tools, you are now ready.

The Soil Balancing Process

1. Physically be present at the site you wish to balance. If it is huge, break down the site into manageable sections and proceed through the process with each section.

2. Connect with the Deva of the Soil. (Verify your connection.)

3. State your intent to do the Soil Balancing Process and ask that you be given the information of what nutrients are needed. Then read to the deva the nutrients you offer for use. (This tells the deva exactly what it can work with.)

4. Ask the deva what is needed. If you are balancing more than one section, indicate precisely to the deva which section you wish to presently focus on. At Perelandra, for example, I break down the garden into its three sections and will say:

For the Blueberry section, do I need:

- Bone Meal? (Test)
- Rock Phosphate? (Test)
- Nitro-10? (Test)
- Greensand? (Test)
- Cottonseed Meal? (Test)
- Dolomite Lime? (Test)
- Kelp? (Test)

Then, if you are including minerals, ask which are needed and test each one.

Whatever gets a positive response is what is needed for that section. (This is where the pencil and paper come in handy for recording what your positive responses are.)

5. Now ask that a nature spirit assist you. A nature spirit will be made available to you immediately. *Verify your connection.* If you don't feel or sense its presence, simply proceed forward in faith that it is right there with you. Often, something will happen during the process that will be a verification to you that you are indeed being assisted.

6. Pour a small amount of the first nutrient or place one mineral tablet into your hand and hold it out in front of you. State:

> I ask the nature spirit to receive the energy from this nutrient and shift it in the appropriate amount and to the appropriate depth for the section in question.

You may feel an immediate sensation in your hand or a change in the nutrient you are holding. Hold your hand out for about ten seconds. Once complete, just drop the nutrient on the ground. Don't try to save it because it is now form without energy and is no longer useful.

At this point, the nature spirit is shifting the energy of the substance you are providing from the form in your hand and using it as the base to expand the energy to the amount needed. The nature spirit will re-infuse that expanded energy into the ground in the proper concentration and at the needed depth. Once the energy is in place, the nature spirit you are working with will shift the energy to the form level. In short, by using the expertise of the nature spirits, you can infuse thirty tons of greensand over a one-square-mile area to a depth of five feet and it all starts with a teaspoon of greensand in your hand.

Offer the nature spirit each of the other nutrients needed one by one.

6A. Comfrey Flower Essence: If you have this available, test with the Deva of the Soil for the need for comfrey. This essence is for the healing of higher vibrational soul damage which may be a result of this or another lifetime, or in the case of land, deep soul-energy damage resulting from the present times or the past. In my work with this process, I have found that the Comfrey Essence is frequently called for in the testing. After adding the nutrients, I test for it, and if needed, I put one drop of the essence in my hand and offer it to the nature spirit exactly as I did the nutrients.

7. Repeat steps 4, 5, and 6 for each of the sections you wish to balance. Always be clear in your focus and work what section you are dealing with and what land area is included in that section. You may wish to draw a simple map indicating the sections in order to facilitate clarity.

8. Once complete, spend a moment sensing the land you have just balanced. Note any changes. If you sense nothing, don't be disappointed. Because of the nature of this work, its effects may take a few days or weeks to show or be felt. Over a period of time, gardeners will note a change in the garden balance, the devic information received, how everything in the garden weaves together more easily. They'll see the garden rhythms change. Things that an outsider wouldn't even notice, but the very things one working intimately with the land will pick up immediately.

9. Close out the process by acknowledging the work you, the Deva of the Soil and the nature spirit have just accomplished, and ask that you now be disconnected from them.

When I completed the process the first time, I received the following from the Overlighting Deva of Perelandra, the Deva of the Garden, the Deva of Soil, and Pan. It truly expresses the power one small garden, through co-creation with nature, can have on the whole.

COMBINED NATURE SESSION

The sense of celebration you feel on both the devic and nature spirit levels is most accurate. We now have a spot of land on Earth where human and nature have come together to create deep, inner balance. We keep referring to this balance as deep and inner because what occurred today was not a surface shift in the soil. We would like to refer to it as a "soul shift" within nature. A shift so deep within all the levels of form that one might say its impact is "of the soul." When we refer to the stabilizing effect of today, we mean a stabilization of such depth that again, one could sense it to be of the soul.

From this point on, there will be a strong vibrational rippling effect that will flow from the Perelandra garden complex to every corner of Earth. Now, this may sound a bit dramatic to you, perhaps even overblown or exaggerated, but believe us, we do not exaggerate about this. We are celebrating and joyous, but our exuberance does not lead us to exaggeration. The positive flow that is already radiating from Pere-

landra will affect the entire planet. The higher realms of nature are now alert to today's shift. Your action has served notice that man and nature are coming together in new partnership. That fact alone will do much to begin to heal the battered soul of the planet. The soil work of today will act as a salve to that soul.

Mankind wishes to shift his awareness, his life, his intent from Piscean to Aquarian. Those on Earth cannot do this unless they re-establish their relationship to nature on all levels. Today's success touches into another aspect of this area of relationship. In order for man to be physically, emotionally, mentally and spiritually supported as he evolves into the Aquarian Age, he must, in partnership with nature, work toward full ecological balance. Nature has corresponding levels which relate to the human physical, emotional, mental and spiritual levels. Now, some understand nature supporting human form, his physical. The other support relationships are not understood very well at all. What we wish to get across to you now is that the quality of the work you did today created such deep stability within nature that the quality of support and nurturing from nature to mankind on the levels beyond physical has increased dramatically. Mankind's shift, change, and evolution can now be supported in kind by the nature energy radiating from the Perelandra garden complex.

We thank you for today. As has been suggested, it's been a long time coming. We are overjoyed and we rejoice. You will feel our continuing celebration throughout this night of the full moon. Join us in any way you wish. We are especially close to you tonight.

Suggestions And Help

If you have not incorporated the Energy Cleansing Process into your life and the life of the garden on a regular basis, but wish to do the Soil Balancing Process, I suggest you precede it with the Energy Cleansing Process just to "clear the air."

Also, if you wish to know precisely what is being added to the soil, you may get this information from the Deva of the Soil at the time you are identifying which nutrients are needed. Let's say you need to add bone meal to the area being worked with. Set up to receive the more precise information by asking:

> Per _____ (this section, this acre, this ten acres....) how much bone meal is needed?

Then do a sequential count in increments of 10 pounds—or 50 pounds for a larger area, or tons for a large lot or field. Example: For the blueberry section, 286 pounds of dolomite lime was added to a depth of 5 feet.

Also: I do not use the Soil Balancing Process in place of physically supplying fertilizers to the topsoil of the garden. I have been told that whenever possible, it is preferable to maintain horizontal compatibility. The plants, the soil, and their activity respond best to form consistency, i.e., physical fertilizer being physically mixed in the soil.

MORE HELP FROM THE "GIVE ME A BREAK" DEPARTMENT

For those of you who:

1. live in the city and have no access to organic fertilizers but wish to work with the Soil Balancing Process in conjunction with the other two energy processes in your environment,

2. live anywhere but have no garden and don't plan to have one (What are you doing with this book?) and also don't have easy access to the fertilizers but wish to work with the process,

3. have no direct personal relationship with land (as stated above) but feel moved to work with the balancing of battlefields,

4. have a garden or farm and are firm believers of using animal manures only, but would like to incorporate the Soil Balancing Process which requires the other organic fertilizers and don't wish to purchase bags of it just to make a little kit,

I am offering the Soil Balancing Process kit with the same major ingredients I use (bone meal, rock phosphate, Nitro-10, greensand, cottonseed meal, dolomite lime, kelp, and Comfrey Essence). Ordering information is in the back of the book.

19

EXPANDING CO-CREATIVE ENERGY GARDENING TO FARMING AND GROUP PROCESS

I have presented this co-creative energy gardening process for one individual doing one garden. Primarily, this is my experience. But I am surrounded by farms and I have visited gardeners who function in groups within a community setting. Both situations have raised questions in my mind as to how what I have presented can be expanded to a larger scale, either with land size or people.

FARMING

This, I believe, would be easy to accomplish. Instead of dealing with sections and rows within a garden, the farmer would be focused on a collection of fields. Instead of a garden chart, there would be a farm chart that would lay out the fields. The devic level would still be worked with in much the same manner. Only now, instead of asking what gets planted in each row, when, and with what fertilizer, that same information will be gotten for each field. The devic level would indicate the best field placement for each crop, the best planting time, the fertilizers needed, and the annual rotation of those crops. There would be new information regarding field management and animal herds. In essence, all the questions and considerations that applied to the garden may be expanded to apply to all farm issues. Instead of treating the garden as one environment moving toward a level of balance, the farmer would be balancing the farm as a whole.

The starting point for getting information would be the overlighting deva of the specific farm. That's where the primary, overall blueprint is created. Once individual sections or fields are identified, then one can work with the deva of each field much as was done with the deva of each vegetable in the garden. The Deva of Soil would have the fertilizer and soil management information for all the fields. And kinesiology would still be the tool used for translating the devic information.

Practically speaking, if you are a farmer faced with one hundred acres or a thousand acres, it might be best to choose just one field in the beginning to try out the co-creative processes. See if that field, when managed according to devic information and worked with in cooperation with the nature spirit levels, shows a change from what it had been before and from the condition of the surrounding fields now. Also, working with one field first will make the task of changing and integrating the process more manageable.

GROUP PROCESS

By group process, I mean a number of gardeners seeking to function with group consensus, rather than one head gardener taking the full responsibility of planning the garden and organizing helpers to assist.

In the group process, I can think of three approaches using kinesiology to translate information from the nature intelligences.

1. As a group, ask to be connected with the specific deva or nature spirit. That intelligence will open to everyone there. Pick one person who does kinesiology well as the tester. As everyone asks yes/no questions, that person will test the answer. Because everyone is connected, there will be a great deal of common intuitive verification. A faulty test will clank with someone—or everyone. The thrust of this setup is the special dynamic that can occur as everyone participates in the questions. Option and direction will come through everyone and be verified by the tester. Proceed through the charts and information gathering as presented in the book, but with this group setup.

2. As a group, ask to be connected with the specific nature intelligence. This time, after each question is asked, everyone can test kinesiologically at the same time. Now, this works. I have done it in a group context. Its advantage is that there is instant verification of the answer. Its disadvantage is that everyone must understand each question precisely. A question that is asked aloud by one person is immediately translated in the minds of everyone hearing that question. So you can end up with five people testing positive and one person testing negative. At this point, the question needs to be reviewed so that all six people truly understand exactly what is being asked. Then retest.

3. Do the major garden chart as a group using one of the above methods, then break down the garden into areas with one person being responsible for a specific assignment or area. For example, one person gets all of the pertinent information on the broccoli row. Or one person works only with the Deva of Soil and gets the soil information for the entire garden. Then come back together as a group once the information has been gotten and weave all the threads into place. This exercise will go a long way to verify the accuracy of everyone's work. It has to weave without knotting up into a big ball. Where there are questions, they may be asked using either of the first two setups or having the individual originally responsible for this area of information function again as the tester.

Whatever setup is used, always be sure everyone involved is connected with the nature intelligence and verify that connection. When each session is over, be sure everyone has disconnected with the nature intelligences they were working with.

A NOTE ON GREENHOUSES, NURSERIES AND LANDSCAPING

With all three of these, treat them as if each were a garden and approach them exactly as you would approach a co-creative energy garden. Keep in mind that the goal is to create an energy-balanced environment. Where plants, bushes, and trees are located in each of these environments is of prime importance. The overall health may require that the traditional way of arranging plants will need to be modified or abandoned altogether in order to achieve a level of balanced energy. All the information you will need can be obtained by using the co-creative energy garden setup and applying it to either the greenhouse, nursery or landscaping job.

A special note on landscaping: Landscapers must deal with an additional element: the owner contracting the job. I think it will save a landscaper a lot of aggravation if it is remembered that ultimately the landowner is the one responsible for the evolution and healing of the land. He is, after all, the recognized custodian of that piece of land. This recognition extends to the nature intelligences as well. If you sense or devically receive that a bush should be placed at spot X, but the landowner wants it at spot Y no matter what you say, the bush goes at spot Y. You may suggest and recommend, as is your responsibility as the professional, but you can't override the landowner's position with that land's development. Nature doesn't look to us to come charging in from outside and taking over.

To be honest, I don't think this kind of conflict is going to be a major issue with those landscapers who open to and develop co-creative energy gardening insight and methods. I believe they will find that they will draw to them customers who are open to a different approach to the land and have similar concerns regarding health and balance. Like attracting like. And I wouldn't be at all surprised if the landowner already intuitively knows that a specific bush is to be planted at spot X.

20

OVERLIGHTING DEVA OF PLANET EARTH

I have looked forward to this moment, to the opportunity to add to the effort being made through the vehicle of this book. I am the overlighting consciousness of the planet upon which you live. I have been referred to as "Ghia" by many. I would like to give you insight into the physical evolution of the planet as seen from my perspective.

All that exists in the solar system of which planet Earth is a part and in the countless realms and dimensions beyond is presently moving through a major shift. This you refer to as the movement from the Piscean era to the Aquarian era. Earth is not an out-of-step planet struggling within an in-step universe to reach the level of perfection that surrounds it. It is quite a common thing for the humans on Earth to perceive themselves as lesser, behind in development, and out of step. This very notion is what one may call "Piscean" in its dynamic. It sets up the planet and those souls who are choosing to experience the lessons of form in a parent/child situation—the universe being the parent, the planet and its inhabitants being the child. It was an important dynamic of the Piscean era, this continuous sense of the child striving and moving forward toward the all-knowing parent, and a dynamic which was played out in one way or another on every level of interaction on Earth. The notion of the parent served as the impetus to keep the child moving forward in the hope that one day, after much work and growth, the child would attain the peer position with the parent.

OVERLIGHTING DEVA OF PLANET EARTH

The parent/child notion has not been exclusive to Earth. It is a dynamic that has been a part of reality on all other dimensions and levels. And as already stated, has been an important dynamic of the Piscean era for the souls on all levels to come to grips with in whatever manner needed. I point this out to emphasize that Earth is a part of an ever-evolving whole and not the bastard child of that whole.

The important lesson to be integrated into the picture of reality from the parent/child dynamic was the conscious, personal dedication of the individual to move forward. The parent dynamic stood before the child within all and encouraged those vital steps forward toward the perceived notion of perfection represented by the parent. It served to weave into the individual's fabric of life that continuous sense of constant forward motion and the knowing that its resulting change led to better and greater.

Now, although the parent/child dynamic has been a tangible force that has permeated the levels of reality during the Piscean era, the actual fact of all being the child seeking to move toward a parent has been illusion. It is how a Piscean dynamic was translated into a workable reality. An impulse was released within all levels of reality some two thousand years ago and each individual receiving the impulse translated it into an understandable, tangible concept. The main thrust of the overall translation on planet Earth has been the parent/child dynamic. There has been, in fact, no parent outside and beyond who has enticed and encouraged the children forward. Just as the child is within all, so, too, is the parent. But in order to develop the tools one needs to move forward in confidence, individuals needed to establish that sense of the all-knowing parent standing before them in the unknown, ready to catch, comfort and receive them as they take those shaky steps forward.

I have not forgotten to address the planet Earth. I needed to lay the foundation for you to understand how the principles presented in this book fit into the larger picture—and that includes Earth.

When the impulse of what I have referred to as "the parent/child dynamic" was released throughout reality, it was received not only by individual human souls, but by the planet as a whole. I have stated that the impulse was sounded on all levels of reality. In order for there to be harmonious evolution, there must be a sense of tandem movement within the whole. The impulse was received and seated within planet Earth, which in turn, stabilized the seating of the impulse within individuals. Now, as human souls translated that impulse into the workable parent/child dynamic, that translation itself seated into the planet and its various natural forms, thus modifying the original impulse to conform to the translation. This is natural law. Form conforming to the

OVERLIGHTING DEVA OF PLANET EARTH

energy within. It is a necessary part of the support system between spirit and matter. One cannot have the spirit reflecting one reality seated within a form energized by another reality. It would be as if two horses were hitched to one another but pulling in opposite directions. There would be no chance of forward movement. So, form must conform in order for there to be mutual support and evolution between matter and spirit.

To broaden this picture even more, let me say that the impulse and the translation of the impulse, as with all the Piscean impulses and their translations, placed the individuals and the planet squarely and solidly into the evolutionary picture of its universe as a whole—not out of step from it. The planet has been an active participant in understanding and working with what we might call "contemporary issues," for the issues have been the same throughout reality, only the translations have differed. It has been vital that the specific parent/child translation, for example, be fully explored and understood by those on Earth so that the resulting knowledge could be made accessible to the whole. Likewise, other translations of the very same impulse have been made accessible to the whole and have been received at various times throughout the Piscean era by individuals and the intelligences of nature on Earth.

Now a new set of impulses has been sounded throughout reality, and they are the impulses commonly referred to as "Aquarian." All of reality has moved into a period of transition. The impulses are in the process of being fully seated in and translated everywhere. On Earth, we have full reception of the initial Aquarian impulses. They are seated well within the planet and are now serving the shift of those living on the planet from Piscean to Aquarian.

insight: Bruce + Maggie rearing Julian free of adultism / is an Aquarian pattern/impulse Honor it

If you have followed my train of thought, you will realize that with the planet itself holding the Aquarian impulses, all that exists on the planet and all its individuals are not only receiving the similar impulses but the impetus and support from the planet to change as well. This means that those translations and the resulting systems and procedures from the old simply will not function as smoothly in the present. The soul energy of the planet has shifted and no longer correlates with the old form translations which exist on its surface. And very shortly, you will see a rapid deterioration of all that has worked so well in the past. New translations are required. New systems and procedures. The planet is already holding the new impulses.

The co-creative gardening technique as presented in this book is a translation of the new. It works because it once again aligns spirit and matter with parallel intent and purpose. In this case, one could say we

OVERLIGHTING DEVA OF PLANET EARTH

have a double alignment. We have the spirit of the human translating impulse into new form and action, and we have the reconnection of the spirit of the human with the new impulses contained within the planet around him. As you incorporate these translations into thought and action, you will see evidence of effortless change all around you. As already stated, this is because the intent of spirit and the intent of matter are realigning and once again moving in tandem.

This brings me back to the parent/child notion of the Piscean era. One of the translations of this dynamic from humans has been in the arena of nature. That is, humans have tended to look at nature either as the parent looking at a child in need of discipline, or the child seeking beneficial aid and assistance from the powerful and all-knowing parent. In essence, humans have translated the parent/child dynamic in nature as either manipulation or worship. Both translations were working, viable frameworks for learning, but they are both now no longer workable. For humans to continue attempting to respond and act within these two mindsets is wrecking havoc on the planet itself.

With the Aquarian dynamic, the parent/child is uniting as one balanced, integrated force within the individual. It is the uniting of the universal wisdom contained within all and the absolute knowledge that in order to have full conscious access to that universal wisdom, one must continue to move forward in the learning and changing mode. The parent and child come together in balanced partnership.

The co-creative energy garden translates this fundamental Aquarian dynamic into the arena of nature. Human and nature come together in conscious, equal partnership, both functioning from a position of wisdom and change. Wherever such a garden is initiated, it will immediately sound a note outward into the universe and inward into the core of the planet, the very soul of the planet, that the shift from Piscean to Aquarian dynamics within the nature arena is in the process of change. And immediately, the evolving intent of the garden will be aligned with the prevailing universal flow and the corresponding planetary impulses, one buttressing from above, the other buttressing from below within the planet. The result will be forward motion in tandem—the gardener in tandem with his planet and his universe. With this massive support, it is no wonder the co-creative energy garden works.

Allow me to give you another insight. The Aquarian impulses are already seated within the planet. Visualize, if you will, the planet as a container of these impulses. Energy held beneath the Earth's surface. This energy is seated within the very soul of the planet, seated within its heart. It is there to be released and integrated into all levels of life on the planet. Now, picture one, small co-creative garden on the planet's *surface. See it as a window into the interior of the planet, into its soul. As the gardener works to align this garden to the new dynamics, watch the window open and the energy contained within the core of the planet gently gravitate to and release through the window. Feel the sense of relief and freedom within the Earth's core as the energy moves outward and up. And watch the actions and the form living on the Earth's surface suddenly shift to reflect the impact of the heart energy which has now surfaced. That which exists on the surface has begun to connect to and integrate with the heart and soul of the planet, which, in turn, is fully aligned with the heart and soul force of the universe. As with the experience the human receives when he consciously shifts his perceptions in such a way that the heart energy he holds deep within is suddenly released and allowed to surface, so, too, will Earth as each person opens the window through the framework of the co-creative garden to the heart and soul energy of the planet.*

OVERLIGHTING DEVA OF PLANET EARTH

It is not enough to move about the planet in a state of benevolent love for it. Human state alone will not create the passageways through which the heart energy of the planet is allowed to release. It must be accomplished through the state of the human mind, his consciousness, combined with parallel and appropriate action. Once released, this heart energy from the planet will permeate all living reality upon its surface and support the evolutionary process of the planet and its inhabitants in tandem movement with the universe into the Aquarian era.

I fully understand that I am aligning deep planetary change and universal movement with the actions of one gardener tending one small garden. This is precisely what I mean to do. One need not wait for group consensus in such matters. One need only move forward, sound the note for change, and follow that intonation with parallel action. Each gardener, in the role of the Knower, shall hold the seed to his heart and shall plant this seed in the earth. The fruit of this plant shall be the winged and shafted Sun above his head, and a new kingdom shall be grounded on Earth. This I can promise you. This is what awaits you.

GLOSSARY

ACID SOIL: See pH

ALKALINE SOIL: See pH

ANNUAL: A plant that completes its life cycle in a single growing season.

AQUARIAN (AQUARIAN AGE): The term used to describe the coming phase of evolution facing not only those on planet Earth, but all souls and all life forms within the universe as well. Although it is termed "Aquarian" because of its loose connection to the astronomical alignment of Aquarius, it is more importantly a term that connotes an emphasized pattern and rhythm in life behavior. The Age of Aquarius will see the coming to the fore of the concepts of balance, teamwork and partnership played out on all levels of life.

ARAGONITE: A grainy, sand-like, high-calcium lime mined from the ocean floor near Bermuda.

BONE MEAL: Finely ground, steamed animal bone used for fertilizer. Contains 20 to 25 percent phosphoric acid and 1 to 2 percent nitrogen.

CLAY: Soil composed of fine particles that tend to compact. It is rubbery when wet but hard when dry. It takes water slowly, holds it tightly, drains slowly, and generally inhibits water and air circulation.

CO-CREATIVE ENERGY GARDENING: A method of gardening in partnership with the nature intelligences which emphases balance and teamwork. The balance is a result of concentrating on the laws of the life energy behind form. The teamwork is established between the individual and the intelligent levels inherent in nature.

COLLOIDAL PHOSPHATE: A mixture of fine particles of phosphate suspended in a clay base. Contains 18 percent phosphorus and 15 percent calcium.

COMPANION PLANTS: Plants, that when planted close together, influence each other, either beneficially or detrimentally.

COMPOST: Mixture of manure, loose vegetation, or other once-living wastes that is left to decay through bacterial action. Used for fertilizing and soil conditioning.

CONING: An energy vortex created when an individual "calls together" one or more consciousnesses from the higher realms in reality. For example, the calling together of several devas for the purpose of receiving a more complex and expanded range of input and insight is equal to "opening a coning." An advantage of working with a coning is that it has inherent in it both clarity and protection. At Perelandra, I work in a 4-point coning: the Overlighting Deva of Perelandra, Pan, Hyperithon (from the White Brotherhood) and my own higher self—and if the occasion dictates, I'll include anyone else who needs to be present for the specific task or situation being faced. The 4-point coning has built into it an involutionary/evolutionary balance. Nature (the deva and Pan) infuses the vortex with involutionary energy, and Hyperithon and I introduce evolutionary energy. Thus while moving forward, there is natural grounding.

COTTONSEED MEAL: Ground cottonseeds. Used for fertilizer. Contains 6 to 9 percent nitrogen, 2 to 3 percent phosphorus and 2 percent potassium.

CROP ROTATION: Growing different crops in a plot or field in successive years for the purpose of balancing the drain on soil nutrients and inhibiting the growth of certain plant diseases.

DEVA: An intelligent level of consciousness within nature that functions in an architectural mode within all that is of form and serves as the organizer of all that is a part of each form. Devas are universal in dynamic.

DOLOMITE LIME: A limestone rich in magnesium. Neutralizes soil acidity.

DRIED BLOOD: Dried animal blood used for fertilizer. Contains 9 to 15 percent nitrogen.

EARTH: The planet upon which most of us reading this book reside. The word "Earth" also can refer to a specific level of reality—i.e., form.

ENERGY: The dynamic reality contained within and behind all form.

EPSOM SALTS: A crystallized soluble salt containing up to 20 percent magnesium.

FISH EMULSION: A liquid mixture containing discarded soluble fish parts, used as fertilizer. Contains 5 to 10 percent nitrogen and lesser amounts of phosphorus and potassium.

FLAT: A shallow box in which seeds are planted to produce seedlings, generally indoors.

FORM: That which may be perceived by any or all of the five human senses.

GENESA CRYSTAL: An energy device which looks like a ball formed by four precisely positioned bands and which functions as an antenna. The genesa crystal form draws to it life energy, then cleanses it, shifts it up "a spiral," and shoots it back out into the environment. A two-foot-diameter genesa crystal affects the life form within a three-mile radius. The odd-looking wire ball in the middle of the Perelandra garden and pictured on the cover of this book is a genesa crystal.

GERMINATION: Sprouting of a new plant from seed.

GRANITE MEAL OR DUST: Finely ground granite, used as a fertilizer. Contains about 8 percent potassium and a number of trace elements.

GREEN MANURE: Crops which are commonly cultivated to be later plowed or tilled into the soil, adding soil nutrients. Also, as a cover, they protect topsoil from soil and wind erosion.

GREENSAND: Sea deposit containing silicates of iron, potassium, and other trace elements. Usually mixed with clay or sand. Contains 6 to 8 percent potassium and is used for fertilizer.

GROUNDED ENERGY: Energy that has moved through its complete involutionary process and is thus fully accessible to the form level. When an individual is grounded, the life and movement of that person is "of form" and accessible to others through the five human senses. A distinction of grounded action or energy is clarity.

GYPSUM: Mineral containing the soil nutrients calcium and sulfur and often used as a soil conditioner.

HIGH CALCIUM LIMESTONE: Contains 72 percent calcium carbonate. Especially useful where the magnesium level is already high.

HILLS: Mounded soil containing 2 to 3 plants that generally need room to spread - such as watermelon, cucumber, zucchini, squash.

INTERPLANTING: Planting two vegetables close together, usually in the same row or space. Often one is quick-maturing and the other slow-growing. The quick-maturing vegetable is harvested first, giving more room for the continued growth of the other.

KELP: A loosely defined group of large brown seaweeds. Used as a fertilizer and soil conditioner. Contains 2 to 6 percent potash, 1 to 2 percent nitrogen.

KINESIOLOGY: A method of discerning the strength or weakness of an individual's body electrical system through the use of muscle testing.

LOAM: Soil containing a fertile and well-textured mixture of clay, sand, and humus.

MANURE: Livestock dung used as fertilizer.

MULCH: Protective covering placed over the soil between plants in order to reduce evaporation, maintain even soil temperature, reduce erosion, and inhibit weed sprouting.

MULCH GARDENING: A gardening method originated by Ruth Stout in which 6 to 8 inches of mulch is left on the garden year-round.

NATURE SPIRITS: An intelligent level of consciousness within nature that works in partnership with the devic level and is responsible for the fusing and maintaining of energy to appropriate form. Nature spirits are regional and attached to specific land areas.

NITROGEN: One of the three most important plant nutrients, the others being phosphorus and potassium. Particularly essential in production of leaves and stems. An excess of nitrogen can produce abundant foliage and few flowers and fruit.

NUTRIENT: Any of the sixteen elements that, in usable form are absorbed by plants as nourishment. Plants obtain carbon, hydrogen, and oxygen from water and air, and the other elements from the soil. The main soil elements are nitrogen, phosphorus, and potassium; the trace elements are boron, calcium, chlorine, copper, iron, manganese, magnesium, molybdenum, sulfur, and zinc.

ORGANIC: Deriving from living organisms, either plants or animals.

ORGANIC GARDENING: Grown with fertilizers and mulches consisting only of animal or vegetable matter, with no use of chemical fertilizers or pesticides.

OVERLIGHTING DEVA: A deva who oversees a larger and broader aspect of reality such as a large land area like a battlefield, farm or country. Within this broader scope are individual devas working with the specific components that make up the larger picture. In essence, the over-lighting deva would "oversee the whole operation."

OYSTER SHELLS: Ground oyster shells. Used as an amendment to composts and as a liming material. Contains 31 to 36 percent calcium.

PAN: A specific nature spirit who functions as the organizing force among the nature spirits and that level. Although a nature spirit, Pan has devic qualities in that he is universal and will often represent the nature spirits as "spokesman."

PERELANDRA: Of the heart.

PERENNIAL: A plant that continues living over a number of years.

pH: Index of the acidity or alkalinity of a soil. Technically, it refers to the relative concentration of hydrogen ions in the soil. The index ranges from 0 for extreme acidity to 7 for neutral, to 14 for extreme alkalinity. The extremes are rarely reached. A pH of 4.0 would be considered strongly acid; 9.0, strongly alkaline. Adding peat moss, sawdust, or rotted bark to the soil increases acidity; adding lime increases alkalinity.

PHOSPHORUS: One of the three most important plant nutrients, the others being nitrogen and potassium. Especially associated with the production of seeds and fruits and with the development of good roots.

PISCEAN (PISCEAN AGE): That period of time, roughly 2000 years long, out of which planet Earth and the universe are presently passing, and during which specific universal laws were grounded onto the planet. In a broad and loose nutshell, one may say that the Piscean era explored and worked with the dynamic of the parent/child, higher/lower, and masculine-energy-dominate relationship and expressed this dynamic in both action and structure throughout all levels of form reality.

POTASSIUM: One of the three most important plant nutrients, the others being nitrogen and phosphorus. Promotes the general vigor of a plant and increases its resistance to disease and cold. Also promotes sturdy roots.

POTASH: Any potassium or potassium compound used for fertilizer.

RING-PASS-NOT: The boundary or scope of limitations we each have which separates our working and workable knowledge and reality from the rest of all knowledge and reality. As we evolve, the ring-pass-not shifts appropriately so that we have access to what we need but are not overwhelmed by all that there is.

ROCK PHOSPHATE: Finely ground rock powder containing calcium phosphate. Contains up to 30 percent phosphoric acid.

SAND: Tiny, water-worn particles of silicon and other rocks, each usually less than 2 millimeters in diameter. The granules allow free water and air movement; so free, however, that water readily flows out and leaches out nutrients quickly.

SOIL AERATION: Flow of oxygen and carbon dioxide within the soil, between the ground surface and plant roots and soil microorganisms.

SUBSOIL: Bed of earthy soil immediately beneath the topsoil. The size of the soil particles may be larger than that of topsoil, sometimes approaching gravel size.

SUCCESSION PLANTING: Planting a new crop as soon as the first one is harvested within the same growing season.

SUGAR BEET WASTE: A compost readily available in sugar beet growing regions. Contains 1 to 4 percent nitrogen.

SULFUR: A nonmetallic natural trace element which has a major importance to plant growth.

SUL-PO-MAG: Sulphur (22 percent), potash (22 percent), magnesium (22 percent). A soluble fertilizer derived from the mineral langbeinite.

THINNING: Pulling up young plants from a group so that the ones that are left in the soil have more room to develop.

TOPSOIL: Surface layer of soil, containing fine rock particles and decayed or decaying organic matter. Its thickness varies from 1 to 2 inches to several feet, depending on the geographic region and past treatment of the soil.

UNIVERSAL LIGHT: An overseeing consciousness connected with the White Brotherhood.

UNIVERSE: All existing things, including the Earth, the heavens, the galaxies, and all therein, regarded as a whole.

WHITE BROTHERHOOD: An organization of higher souls who are keenly and deeply involved with the evolution of planet Earth and, to this end, function with us and in us in various capacities.

SUPPLIES AND RESOURCES

Necessary Trading Company
New Castle, VA 24127
tele: 703-864-5103

Faith Mountain
Sperryville, VA 22740
(For herbs: Request "Plant and Herb Catalog": $2)

W. Atlee Burpee Company
300 Park Ave.
Warminster, PA 18974
tele: 215-674-4900

Park Seed
PO Box 46
Greenwood, SC 29648-0046
tele: 803-374-3341

Seed Savers Exchange
203 Rural Ave.
Decorah, Iowa 52101
(Cost for paperback: $12.00.)

The Gruber Almanack Co.
111 W. Washington St.
PO Box 609
Hagerstown, MD 21741-2530
(Current Almanack price: $1.45 + $1.05 handling/shipping.)

Bach Flower Remedies Ltd.
Dr. E. Bach Centre
Mount Vernon
Sotwell
Wallingford
Oxon OX10 0P2
England

Official U.S./Canada Distributor:
The Dr. Edward Bach Healing Society
PO Box 320
Woodmere, NY 11598

Flower Essence Services
PO Box 586
Nevada City, CA 95959
tele: 916-273-6363

Wright, Machaelle Small. *Behaving As If the God In All Life Mattered: A New Age Ecology.*
Perelandra, Ltd.
Box 136
Jeffersonton, VA 22724

Lorusso & Glick. *Healing Stoned: the therapeutic use of gems and minerals.*
Brotherhood of Life
110 Dartmouth, SE
Albuquerque, NM 87106
($7.95, not including postage.)

Maclean Dorothy. *To Hear the Angels Sing.*
Lorian Press 1980
PO Box 1095
Elgin, IL 60120

Stout, Ruth.
The Ruth Stout No-Work Garden Book. (with Richard Clemence). 1971.
How to Have a Green Thumb Without an Aching Back. 1955.
Gardening Without Work. 1961.
I've Always Done It My Way. 1975.

All Ruth Stout's books available from:
Rodale Books
Rodale Press, Inc.
33 East Minor Street
Emmaus, PA 18049

For information on genesa crystals:
Langham, Derald G. *Circle Gardening*. 1978.
Devin-Adair Co.
6 N. Water St.
Greenwich, CT 06830

FERTILIZER CHART

YEAR ______________ SECTION ______________

PLANT	Phosphorus	Potash	Nitrogen	Balancer			

Planting & Fertilizing Rhythms

Year ________

March 1	March 2	March 3	March 4
April 1	April 2	April 3	April 4
May 1	May 2	May 3	May 4
June 1	June 2	June 3	June

July 1	July 2	July 3	July 4
August 1	August 2	August 3	August 4
September 1	September 2	September 3	September 4
October 1	October 2	October 3	October 4

THE PERELANDRA GARDEN WORKBOOK

ORDER FORM

___ THE PERELANDRA GARDEN WORKBOOK: A Complete Guide to Gardening With Nature Intelligences . . . . $19.95.

___ BEHAVING AS IF THE GOD IN ALL LIFE MATTERED: A New Age Ecology $9.95

___ PERELANDRA SOIL BALANCING KIT $14.95

PERELANDRA TAPE SERIES

___ 1. Relaxation Exercise (side 1) $8.95
Energy Movement and Focusing Exercise (side 2)

___ 2. Energy Cleansing Process (side 1) $8.95
Object Meditation (side 2)

PERELANDRA GARDEN ESSENCES

COMPLETE SET: Consists of two boxes containing a total of eighteen one-half ounce dropper bottles, the guide with the long definitions and instructions on how to test for need and dosage, plus two short definition box-sized cards for taping inside each box lid.

___ Complete Set $70.00

SET OF NINE: Includes nine one-half ounce bottles of Perelandra Garden Essences of *your choice*. With each set is included a box, the complete guide and a short definition box-sized card for the inner box lid. Check list below for choice of essences. (Choice does not include the Perelandra Rose Essences.)

___ Set of Nine $37.00

INDIVIDUAL GARDEN ESSENCES: One-half ounce dropper bottles numbering less than nine, plus the complete guide.

___ Individual Bottles (check below) $5.50

___Broccoli
___Cauliflower
___Celery
___Chives
___Comfrey
___Corn
___Cucumber
___Dill
___Nasturtium
___Okra
___Salvia
___Snap Pea
___Summer Squash
___Sw. Bell Pepper
___Tomato
___Yellow Yarrow
___Zinnia
___Zucchini

PERELANDRA ROSE ESSENCES

Short Definitions

GRUSS AN AACHEN: Stability. Balances and stabilizes the body/soul unit on all p.e.m.s. (physical, emotional, mental, spiritual) levels as it moves forward in its evolutionary process.

PEACE: Courage. Opens the individual to the inner dynamic of courage that is aligned to universal courage.

ECLIPSE: Acceptance and insight. Enhances the individual's appreciation of his own inner knowing. Supports the mechanism which allows the body to receive the soul's input and insight.

ORANGE RUFFLES: Receptivity. Stabilizes the individual during the expansion of his sensory system.

AMBASSADOR: Pattern. Aids in seeing the relationship of the part to the whole, in perceiving pattern and purpose.

NYMPHENBURG: Strength. Supports and holds the strength created by the balance of the body/soul fusion, and facilitates the individual's ability to regain that balance.

WHITE LIGHTNIN': Synchronized movement. Stabilizes the inner timing of all p.e.m.s. levels moving in concert, and enhances the body/soul fusion.

ROYAL HIGHNESS: Final Stabilization. The mop-up essence which helps to insulate, protect and stabilize the individual and to stabilize the shift during its final stages while vulnerable.

FULL SET: Eight one-half ounce dropper bottles, the complete guide with definitions and instructions on how to test for need and dosage, and the short definitions box-sized card.

___ Single 1/2 oz. set $32.00

___ Double order: two 1/2 oz sets $60.00

NAME ______________________________

STREET ______________________________

CITY ____________________ STATE ____________ ZIP __________

Send check or money order to:
PERELANDRA, BOX 136,
JEFFERSONTON VA 22724

Subtotal:		
Postage and Handling:		
Va. residents 4-1/2% sales tax:		
Total:		

For Foreign Orders: Please write to us for a foreign order form which will include prices for foreign shipping.

POSTAGE AND HANDLING	
under $6	$1.00
$6.01 to 10.00	1.50
$10.01 to 25.00	2.00
$25.01 to 50.00	3.00
$50.01 to 75.00	4.00
$75.01 to 100.00	5.00
$100.01 to 150.00	6.00
$150.00 and over	7.00

Canadian Shipment: Double Above Postage